CRIMINAL JUSTICE, LAW ENFORCEMENT AND CORRECTIONS

POLICE REFORM IN THE AFTERMATH OF GEORGE FLOYD'S DEATH

ROBERT B. SMITH
EDITOR

New York

CRIMINAL JUSTICE, LAW ENFORCEMENT AND CORRECTIONS

POLICE REFORM IN THE AFTERMATH OF GEORGE FLOYD'S DEATH

Criminal Justice, Law Enforcement and Corrections

Additional books and e-books in this series can be found on Nova's website under the Series tab.

Library of Congress Cataloging-in-Publication Data

ISBN: 978-1-53618-504-1

Published by Nova Science Publishers, Inc. † New York

Contents

(JAG) or Community Oriented Policing Services (COPS) programs; and authorizing new grant programs.

Some examples of conditions H.R. 7120 and S. 3985 would place on existing DOJ grant programs include the following:

- H.R. 7120 would authorize grants to states and tribal governments to assist with implementing statutes that provide for the independent investigation or prosecution of law enforcement officers who allegedly use deadly force. The bill would authorize $750 million each fiscal year from FY2020 to FY2022.
- H.R. 7120 would prohibit federal law enforcement officers from seeking a no-knock warrant in drug cases. State and local governments would not be eligible for COPS funding unless they have a law that similarly prohibits the use of no-knock warrants in drug cases.
- S. 3985 would require state and local governments to submit data to the Federal Bureau of Investigation's (FBI's) Use of Force Data Collection program. State and local governments that do not submit data to the FBI would be subject to a 20% penalty on their JAG allocation for the first year of noncompliance and up to a 25% penalty for each subsequent year of noncompliance.
- S. 3985 would establish incentives for state and local law enforcement agencies to limit the use of chokeholds. State and local governments would be ineligible for JAG or COPS funding unless they have a policy that prohibits the use of chokeholds by state and local law enforcement officers, respectively, except when deadly force is authorized.

Some examples of new grant programs that would be authorized by H.R. 7120 and S. 3985 include the following:

- H.R. 7120 would authorize grants to states and tribal governments to assist with implementing statutes that provide for the independent prosecution of law enforcement officers who use deadly force. The bill would authorize $750 million each fiscal year from FY2020 to FY2022.
- H.R. 7120 would authorize grants to states to conduct pattern and practice investigations. The bill would authorize $100 million each fiscal year from FY2020 to FY2022.
- S. 3985 would authorize DOJ to make grants to assist state and local governments with collecting data on use of force and no-knock warrants. The bill would also appropriate $112 million for these grants, to remain available until expended.

S. 3985 would require DOJ to make grants to states for the purpose of providing training to law enforcement officers on alternatives to use of force, on de-escalation tactics, or on techniques and strategies for responding to a behavioral health crisis. The bill would appropriate $50 million each fiscal year for these grants, to remain available until expended, from FY2021 to FY2025.

Chapter 6 - In the wake of unrest arising from George Floyd's death on May 25, 2020, after a Minneapolis police officer pressed a knee into his neck, broader questions have arisen with regard to how existing law regulates the conduct of local police officers. While these issues are explored more broadly in these separate Sidebars, one particular issue of recent judicial and legislative focus has been the doctrine of qualified immunity. Qualified immunity is a judicially created doctrine shielding public officials who are performing discretionary functions from civil liability. The doctrine plays a particularly prominent role in defense of civil rights lawsuits against federal law enforcement officials under the *Bivens* doctrine and against state and local police under 42 U.S.C. § 1983 (Section 1983). With regard to its role in civil lawsuits concerning violations of constitutional norms regulating the police, defenders of the doctrine have suggested that qualified immunity plays an important role in affording police officers some level of deference when making split-second decisions about whether to, for example, use force to subdue a fleeing or resisting suspect. Critics of the doctrine have questioned its legal origins and have argued that its practice has provided too much deference to the police at the expense of accountability and the erosion of criminal suspects' constitutional rights. With increasing focus on whether Congress should legislate to abrogate or otherwise modify the doctrine, this Sidebar explores the legal basis for qualified immunity, how it has operated in practice, and current debate over the efficacy of the doctrine. The Sidebar concludes by discussing considerations for Congress regarding qualified immunity.

Chapter 7 - A series of high-profile deaths of people of color at the hands of law enforcement personnel have generated interest among policymakers about what steps could be taken to promote police accountability. In the wake of these high- profile deaths, policymakers have shown increased interest in considering legislation that would promote police accountability for the use of excessive force. The 21st Century Policing Task Force (Task Force), established by Executive Order 13684 in 2015 in response to a number of serious incidents between law enforcement and members of the communities they serve, recommended a series of actions that would help law enforcement agencies establish a culture of transparency and accountability in order to build public trust and legitimacy. This In Focus provides an overview of some frequently proposed measures, many of which were recommended by the Task Force, that policymakers could consider if they move forward with legislation to promote accountability in policing.

Chapter 8 - The death of George Floyd in Minneapolis, MN, while he was in the custody of law enforcement, and several other recent high-profile deaths of African Americans at the hands of police, have generated interest in legislation to reform policing practices. Two major pieces of legislation that contain police reform proposals are before Congress: H.R. 7120, the George Floyd Justice in Policing Act of 2020—passed by the House on June 25, 2020—and S. 3985, the Just and Unifying Solutions to Invigorate Communities Everywhere (JUSTICE) Act. Each bill would establish programs to collect data on a variety of policing activities, such as the use of force, racial profiling, the use of no-knock warrants, and in-custody deaths. In

- There are almost 1,100 wandering officers in any given year in Florida, and they constitute about 3% of all officers in the state.
- Fired officers tend to take longer to find new work than officers who separate from their agency voluntarily. Fired officers also tend to move to smaller agencies with fewer resources in communities with slightly higher proportions of residents of color.
- Wandering officers are more likely to be fired from their next job or to receive a complaint for a “moral character violation” than both officers hired as rookies and those hired as veterans who have never been fired.

Chapter 14 - In the early 1990s, bystander video footage of Los Angeles police beating, clubbing, and stomping on black motorist Rodney King sparked national outrage, protests, and rioting. In response, Congress passed the Violent Crime Control and Law Enforcement Act of 1994, which contained a notable provision originally codified as 42 U.S.C. § 14141 and now found at 34 U.S.C. § 12601 (Section 12601). Specifically, Section 12601 serves as the primary federal law aiming to ensure that law enforcement agencies comply with the Constitution. More recently, bystander footage of Minneapolis police pinning George Floyd in a neckhold ignited protests, anger, and violence throughout the nation, prompting renewed interest among lawmakers in the role of the federal government in ensuring constitutional policing. Indeed, Floyd’s death is only one in a series of similar incidents arousing public concern and protest. Some of these events, including the death of Freddie Gray in Baltimore police custody and the fatal shooting of Michael Brown by Ferguson, Missouri, police, spurred not only public outcry but also legal action by the Department of Justice (DOJ) under Section 12601. This Sidebar discusses the Section’s requirements, DOJ’s enforcement actions in recent years, and considerations for Congress.

In: Police Reform …
Editor: Robert B. Smith
ISBN: 978-1-53618-504-1

Chapter 1

GEORGE FLOYD JUSTICE IN POLICING ACT OF 2020*

Committee on the Judiciary

Mr. Nadler, from the Committee on the Judiciary, submitted the following report together with minority views [To accompany H.R. 7120] The Committee on the Judiciary, to whom was referred the bill (H.R. 7120) to hold law enforcement accountable for misconduct in court, improve transparency through data collection, and reform police training and policies, having considered the same, reports favorably thereon with an amendment and recommends that the bill as amended do pass.

The amendment is as follows: Strike all after the enacting clause and insert the following:

SECTION 1. SHORT TITLE; TABLE OF CONTENTS.

SHORT TITLE.—This Act may be cited as the "George Floyd Justice in Policing Act of 2020."

---

* This is an edited, reformatted and augmented version of 116th Congress 2d Session; House of Representatives, Publication No. REPT. 116–434; Part 1, dated JUNE 19, 2020.

(B) the use of a weapon, including a personal body weapon, chemical agent, impact weapon, extended range impact weapon, sonic weapon, sensory weapon, conducted energy device, or firearm, against an individual; or

(C) any intentional pointing of a firearm at an individual.

(12) LESS LETHAL FORCE.—The term "less lethal force" means any degree of force that is not likely to cause death or serious bodily injury.

(13) FACIAL RECOGNITION.—The term "facial recognition" means an automated or semiautomated process that analyzes biometric data of an individual from video footage to identify or assist in identifying an individual.

TITLE I—POLICE ACCOUNTABILITY

Subtitle A—Holding Police Accountable in the Courts

Sec. 101. Deprivation of Rights under Color of Law

Section 242 of title 18, United States Code, is amended—

(1) by striking "willfully" and inserting "knowingly or recklessly";

(2) by striking, "or may be sentenced to death"; and

(3) by adding at the end the following: "For purposes of this section, an act shall be considered to have resulted in death if the act was a substantial factor contributing to the death of the person."

Sec. 102. Qualified Immunity Reform

Section 1979 of the Revised Statutes of the United States (42 U.S.C. 1983) is amended by adding at the end the following: "It shall not be a defense or immunity in any action brought under this section against a local law enforcement officer (as such term is defined in section 2 of the George Floyd Justice in Policing Act of 2020), or in any action under any source of law against a Federal investigative or law enforcement officer (as such term is defined in section 2680(h) of title 28, United States Code), that—

“(1) the defendant was acting in good faith, or that the defendant believed, reasonably or otherwise, that his or her conduct was lawful at the time when the conduct was committed; or

“(2) the rights, privileges, or immunities secured by the Constitution and laws were not clearly established at the time of their deprivation by the defendant, or that at such time, the state of the law was otherwise such that the defendant could not reasonably have been expected to know whether his or her conduct was lawful.”

Sec. 103. Pattern and Practice Investigations

(a) SUBPOENA AUTHORITY.—Section 210401 of the Violent Crime Control and Law Enforcement Act of 1994 (34 U.S.C. 12601) is amended—

(1) in subsection (a), by inserting, “by prosecutors,” after “conduct by law enforcement officers”;

(2) in subsection (b), by striking “paragraph (1)” and inserting “subsection (a)”; and

(3) by adding at the end the following:

“(c) SUBPOENA AUTHORITY.—In carrying out the authority in subsection (b), the Attorney General may require by subpoena the production of all information, documents, reports, answers, records, accounts, papers, and other data in any medium (including electronically stored information), as well as any tangible thing and documentary evidence, and the attendance and testimony of witnesses necessary in the performance of the Attorney General under subsection (b). Such a subpoena, in the case of contumacy or refusal to obey, shall be enforceable by order of any appropriate district court of the United States.

“(d) CIVIL ACTION BY STATE ATTORNEYS GENERAL.—Whenever it shall appear to the attorney general of any State, or such other official as a State may designate, that a violation of subsection (a) has occurred within their State, the State attorney general or official, in the name of the State, may bring a civil action in the appropriate district court of the United States to obtain appropriate equitable and declaratory relief to eliminate the pattern or practice. In carrying out the authority in this subsection, the State attorney general or official shall have the same subpoena authority as is available to the Attorney General under subsection (c).

"(e) RULE OF CONSTRUCTION.—Nothing in this section may be construed to limit the authority of the Attorney General under subsection (b) in any case in which a State attorney general has brought a civil action under subsection (d).

"(f) REPORTING REQUIREMENTS.—On the date that is one year after the enactment of the George Floyd Justice in Policing Act of 2020, and annually thereafter, the Civil Rights Division of the Department of Justice shall make publicly available on an internet website a report on, during the previous year—

"(1) the number of preliminary investigations of violations of subsection (a) that were commenced;

"(2) the number of preliminary investigations of violations of subsection (a) that were resolved; and

"(3) the status of any pending investigations of violations of subsection (a)."

GRANT PROGRAM.—

(1) GRANTS AUTHORIZED.—The Attorney General may award a grant to a State to assist the State in conducting pattern and practice investigations under section 210401(d) of the Violent Crime Control and Law Enforcement Act of 1994 (34 U.S.C. 12601).

(2) APPLICATION.—A State seeking a grant under paragraph (1) shall submit an application in such form, at such time, and containing such information as the Attorney General may require.

(3) FUNDING.—There are authorized to be appropriated $100,000,000 to the Attorney General for each of fiscal years 2021 through 2023 to carry out this subsection.

(c) DATA ON EXCESSIVE USE OF FORCE.—Section 210402 of the Violent Crime Control and Law Enforcement Act of 1994 (34 U.S.C. 12602) is amended—

(NLPOA), the National Organization of Black Law Enforcement Executives (NOBLE), Women in Law Enforcement, the Native American Law Enforcement Association (NALEA), the International Association of Chiefs of Police (IACP), the National Sheriffs' Association (NSA), the Fraternal Order of Police (FOP), or the National Association of School Resource Officers.

PROFESSIONAL CIVILIAN OVERSIGHT ORGANIZATION.—The term "professional civilian oversight organization" means a membership organization formed to address and advance civilian oversight of law enforcement and whose members are from Federal, State, regional, local, or Tribal organizations that review issues or complaints against law enforcement agencies or officers, such as the National Association for Civilian Oversight of Law Enforcement (NACOLE).

Sec. 113. Accreditation of Law Enforcement Agencies

(a) STANDARDS.—

(1) INITIAL ANALYSIS.—The Attorney General shall perform an initial analysis of existing accreditation standards and methodology developed by law enforcement accreditation organizations nationwide, including national, State, regional, and Tribal accreditation organizations. Such an analysis shall include a review of the recommendations of the Final Report of the President's Taskforce on 21st Century Policing, issued by the Department of Justice, in May 2015.

(2) DEVELOPMENT OF UNIFORM STANDARDS.—After completion of the initial review and analysis under paragraph (1), the Attorney General shall—

(A) recommend, in consultation with law enforcement accreditation organizations and community-based organizations, the adoption of additional standards that will result in greater community accountability of law enforcement agencies and an increased focus on policing with a guardian mentality, including standards relating to—

(i) early warning systems and related intervention programs;

(ii) use of force procedures;

(iii) civilian review procedures;

(iv) traffic and pedestrian stop and search procedures;

(v) data collection and transparency;

(vi) administrative due process requirements;

(vii) video monitoring technology;

(viii) youth justice and school safety; and

(ix) recruitment, hiring, and training; and

(B) recommend additional areas for the development of national standards for the accreditation of law enforcement agencies in consultation with existing law enforcement accreditation organizations, professional law enforcement associations, labor organizations, community-based organizations, and professional civilian oversight organizations.

(3) CONTINUING ACCREDITATION PROCESS.—The Attorney General shall adopt policies and procedures to partner with law enforcement accreditation organizations, professional law enforcement associations, labor organizations, community-based organizations, and professional civilian oversight organizations to—

(A) continue the development of further accreditation standards consistent with paragraph (2);

(B) encourage the pursuit of accreditation of Federal, State, local, and Tribal law enforcement agencies by certified law enforcement accreditation organizations; and

(C) develop recommendations for implementation of a national accreditation requirement tied to Federal grant eligibility.

(b) USE OF FUNDS REQUIREMENTS.—Section 502(a) of title I of the Omnibus Crime Control and Safe Streets Act of 1968 (34 U.S.C. 10153(a)) is amended by adding at the end the following:

"(7) An assurance that, for each fiscal year covered by an application, the applicant will use not less than 5 percent of the total amount of the grant award for the fiscal year to assist law enforcement agencies of the applicant, including campus public safety departments, gain or maintain accreditation from certified law enforcement accreditation organizations in accordance with section 113 of the Law Enforcement Trust and Integrity Act of 2020."

Sec. 114. Law Enforcement Grants

(a) USE OF FUNDS REQUIREMENT.—Section 502(a) of title I of the Omnibus Crime Control and Safe Streets Act of 1968 (34 U.S.C. 10153(a)), as amended by section 113, is amended by adding at the end the following:

"(8) An assurance that, for each fiscal year covered by an application, the applicant will use not less than 5 percent of the total amount of the grant award for the fiscal year to study and implement effective management, training, recruiting, hiring, and oversight standards and programs to promote effective community and problem solving strategies for law enforcement agencies in accordance with section 114 of the Law Enforcement Trust and Integrity Act of 2020."

(b) GRANT PROGRAM FOR COMMUNITY ORGANIZATIONS.—The Attorney General may make grants to community-based organizations to study and implement—

(1) effective management, training, recruiting, hiring, and oversight standards and programs to promote effective community and problem solving strategies for law enforcement agencies; or

(2) effective strategies and solutions to public safety, including strategies that do not rely on Federal and local law enforcement agency responses.

USE OF FUNDS.—Grant amounts described in paragraph (8) of section 502(a) of title I of the Omnibus Crime Control and Safe Streets Act of 1968 (34 U.S.C. 10153(a)), as added by subsection (a) of this section, and grant amounts awarded under subsection (b) shall be used to—

(1) study management and operations standards for law enforcement agencies, including standards relating to administrative due process, residency requirements, compensation and benefits, use of force, racial profiling, early warning and intervention systems, youth justice, school safety, civilian review boards or analogous procedures, or research into the effectiveness of existing programs, projects, or other activities designed to address misconduct; and

(2) develop pilot programs and implement effective standards and programs in the areas of training, hiring and recruitment, and oversight that

PREFACE

The death of George Floyd in Minneapolis, MN, while he was in the custody of law enforcement, combined with several other recent high-profile deaths of African Americans at the hands of the police, have generated congressional interest in legislation to reform state and local policing practices, and to require law enforcement agencies to collect more data on law enforcement actions and activities and share these data with the public.

Two major pieces of legislation that contain police reform proposals are before Congress: H.R. 7120, the George Floyd Justice in Policing Act of 2020—passed by the House on June 25, 2020—and S. 3985, the Just and Unifying Solutions to Invigorate Communities Everywhere (JUSTICE) Act. This book discusses the current issues associated with police reform.

Chapter 1 - This is an edited, reformatted and augmented version of 116th Congress 2d Session; House of Representatives, Publication No. REPT. 116–434; Part 1, dated JUNE 19, 2020.

Chapter 2 - On May 25, 2020, George Floyd died in the custody of the Minneapolis police after an officer pressed his knee into Floyd's neck while restraining him. That incident, others like it, and subsequent nationwide protests have sparked heightened interest in the federal government's ability to prevent and remedy police misconduct, especially the use of excessive force against people of color. The events of May and June 2020 have prompted action by the Executive Branch and legislative proposals in both houses of Congress. On June 16, 2020, President Donald Trump issued an Executive Order on Safe Policing for Safe Communities. On June 8, 2020, Members of the House of Representatives, led by the Congressional Black Caucus, introduced the George Floyd Justice in Policing Act of 2020 (Justice in Policing Act), and on June 17, 2020, Senate Republicans unveiled the Just and Unifying Solutions To Invigorate Communities Everywhere Act of 2020 (JUSTICE Act). Aprevious Legal Sidebar briefly summarized the Executive Order and both bills, along with other recent reform proposals. This Legal Sidebar provides a comparison of the Justice in Policing Act and the JUSTICE Act. While this Sidebar does not purport to detail every provision of the two bills exhaustively, it analyzes key similarities and differences that are most relevant when evaluating the two proposals. The Sidebar first outlines subject matters that both bills cover, detailing similarities and differences between each bill on those subjects. It concludes by discussing provisions unique to each bill. This Sidebar was updated on July 6, 2020, and reflects amendments to each bill up to that date.

Chapter 3 - In May and June 2020, protests erupted nationwide after the publication of video footage of a Minneapolis police officer pressing his knee into the neck of George Floyd, leading to his death. That incident and its aftermath have sparked heightened interest in Congress's ability to implement reforms of state and local law enforcement. As a companion to this chapter outlines in greater detail, congressional power to regulate state and local law enforcement is not without limits. The Constitution grants the federal government only certain enumerated authorities, with the Tenth Amendment reserving all other powers for the states. The regulation of state and municipal law enforcement is an area that the Constitution generally entrusts to the states. However, Congress possesses some authority to legislate on that subject, primarily through statutes designed to enforce the protections of the Fourteenth Amendment and legislation requiring states to take specified action in exchange for federal funds disbursed under the Spending Clause. This Sidebar provides an overview of existing federal authorities intended to prevent and redress constitutional violations by state and local public safety officials. It then presents some recent proposals that would change federal regulation of state and local law enforcement. The Sidebar concludes with a list of additional CRS resources related to law enforcement reform.

Chapter 4 - Nationwide protests in response to the publication of video footage of a Minneapolis police officer pressing his knee into the neck of George Floyd leading to his death have generated renewed interest in the issue of reforming the policing practices of state and local officials. As discussed in more detail in this companion sidebar, several *existing* federal laws seek to prevent and redress constitutional violations by state and local law enforcement officials. However, because the Constitution generally grants states the authority to regulate issues of local concern—which includes policing and criminal law—Congress is limited in its ability to legislate on matters related to state and local law enforcement—limits that may inform any *new* laws Congress seeks to enact on this evolving issue. This Sidebar begins with an overview of Congress's authority to enact legislation and the limits on those powers. It then discusses in more detail two of the enumerated powers—congressional powers that are found within the Constitution—that may be most relevant when Congress legislates on matters relating to state and local law enforcement.

Chapter 5 - The death of George Floyd in Minneapolis, MN, while he was in the custody of law enforcement, combined with several other recent high-profile deaths of African Americans at the hands of the police, have generated congressional interest in legislation to reform state and local policing practices, and to require law enforcement agencies to collect more data on law enforcement actions and activities and share these data with the public. Two pieces of legislation—the George Floyd Justice in Policing Act of 2020 (H.R. 7120), and the Just and Unifying Solutions to Invigorate Communities Everywhere Act of 2020 (JUSTICE Act; S. 3985)—were introduced in June 2020. Both bills are omnibus measures that would address a variety of policing reform topics and approaches. These include attempting to reform state and local policing practices through two means: placing conditions on existing Department of Justice (DOJ) grant programs, such as the Edward Byrne Memorial Justice Assistance Grant some cases, state and local law enforcement agencies would report these data directly to the Department of Justice (DOJ). In other instances, states would be required to establish systems for collecting required data and reporting them to DOJ. Both pieces of legislation would provide incentives for state and local governments to report data by attaching conditions to the Edward Byrne Memorial Justice Assistance Grant (JAG) or the Community Oriented Policing Services (COPS) programs. DOJ currently operates programs to collect and report data on the use of force by police officers and in -custody deaths. For instance, the Federal Bureau of Investigation (FBI) collects data on use-of-force incidents that result in the death or serious bodily injury of a person, as well as when a police officer discharges a firearm at or in the direction of a person. DOJ also collects data on deaths of people who are temporarily detained, under arrest, in the process of being arrested, en route to be incarcerated, or incarcerated at a municipal or county jail, a state prison, a state-run boot camp prison, a boot camp prison that is contracted out by the state, any state or local contract facility, or any other local or state correctional facility (including juvenile facilities), per the requirement of the Death in Custody Reporting Act of 2013 (P.L. 113-242). The data collection programs proposed by the House and Senate bills might raise the following questions that policymakers could consider:

- Could these programs require state and local governments to submit duplicative data to DOJ, and might the requirement to submit overlapping data to different components of DOJ decrease the quality of the data due to "reporting fatigue"?
- Is the purpose of collecting data on racial profiling to further knowledge about how the police might use an individual's race or ethnicity in decisions about enforcing the law, or is it to serve as a potential deterrent to racial profiling?
- Could the requirement for states to collect data fromlocal law enforcement agencies and then submit these data to DOJ—while possibly lessening the administrative burden on DOJ—result in less accurate and incomplete data? A local law enforcement agency may be more likely to recognize a reportable excessive

use-of-force incident by one of its officers than a state official. State officials may be faced with the choice of accepting submissions at face value or putting in place a mechanismfor auditing the data submitted to themby local law enforcement (similar to what the FBI uses to audit data submitted to the UniformCrime Reporting Program).

- Could attaching conditions to JAGand COPS funding as a means of incentivizing state and local governments to report data prohibit agencies such as the FBI and the Bureau of Justice Statistics (BJS)— both ofwhich have experience with managing large data collection programs—fromcollecting data for the programs? The entity that collects these data would be responsible for certifying that grant recipients are meeting the reporting requirements, but Office of Budget and Management guidance requires statistical agencies to operate separately frompolicymaking activities.

Does the threat of reducing a local government's JAGfunding provide enough incentive for it to comply with data reporting requirements, especially if the costs of complying would exceed the amount of funding the local government would lose for noncompliance? JAGfunding, thougha large grant programat DOJ, most likely accounts for a relatively small portion of any local government's policing budget.

Chapter 9 - The May 2020 death of George Floyd in police custody and subsequent nationwide protests against the use of force by law enforcement have sparked heightened interest in Congress's ability to prevent and remedy civil rights abuses by public safety officers. Among other existing legal remedies, a provision of the federal criminal code, 18 U.S.C. § 242 (Section 242) makes it a crime for government officials, including law enforcement officers, to subject any person to a deprivation of federally protected rights or impose different punishments based on a person's race. This Sidebar provides an overview of Section 242 before discussing proposals to amend the law, as well as certain legal considerations related to those proposals.

Chapter 10 - In the wake of unrest arising from the May 2020 death of George Floyd, broader questions have arisen regarding Congress's authority to regulate law enforcement officers. While federalism principles limit the extent to which Congress may pass laws directly affecting state and local police officers, Congress has broader authority to regulate *federal* law enforcement officers and agencies such as the Federal Bureau of Investigation (FBI), the Drug Enforcement Administration (DEA), or the Customs and Border Protection (CBP). This Sidebar explores the existing criminal, administrative, and civil remedies that impose liability on federal law enforcement officials for claims of excessive use of force, including those brought under the *Bivens* doctrine and the Federal Tort Claims Act (FTCA). It then concludes by discussing considerations for Congress regarding further regulation of federal law enforcement officials.

Chapter 11 - Over the past few years, several high-profile police-involved shootings and alleged instances of excessive force have generated congressional interest in state and local policing. Congressional interest in policing reformrevolves primarily around the public's confidence in the police and accountability for excessive use of force. What role should Congress play in facilitating efforts to bolster confidence in the police? Should Congress seek to improve law enforcement's accountability regarding the excessive use of force? These questions are bounded by limits of congressional authority.

Chapter 12 - Following the death of George Floyd in police custody in May and the fatal February shooting of Ahmaud Arbery, interest has heightened in legislation that would criminalize lynching—often described as death or bodily injury caused by two or more individuals acting without legal authority. A number of states have enacted anti-lynching laws, as localized crimes like murder tend to be a subject of state, rather than federal law. Although the conduct criminalized under those state laws can implicate various federal laws, there is no federal law expressly governing lynching notwithstanding decades of legislative proposals on that front. In June, Members introduced two police reform bills—the George Floyd Justice in Policing Act of 2020 (Justice in Policing Act) and the Just and Unifying Solutions To Invigorate Communities Everywhere Act of 2020

(JUSTICE Act)—both of which include "substantively identical" sections that are described as anti-lynching provisions. These sections build on earlier legislation from this and other Congresses. Indeed, the anti-lynching provisions contained in the JUSTICE Act and the Justice in Policing Act are largely identical to the proscribed conduct in two bills that had already gained significant traction in the 116th Congress. One, the Justice for Victims of Lynching Act of 2019 (H.R. 3536, S. 488), passed the Senate on February 14, 2019. A nearly identical anti-lynching bill titled the Emmett Till Anti-Lynching Act (H.R. 35) passed the House on February 26, 2020. Similar attempts to enact federal anti-lynching laws did not achieve bicameral approval in the 115th Congress—a fate for approximately 200 anti-lynching proposals in the last century. For example, in 1918 Representative Leonidas Dyer of Missouri introduced an anti-lynching bill to remedy the refusal of states to prosecute "the perpetrators of . . . lynchings" under their own laws.

Chapter 13 - Two major policing reform bills before Congress would attempt to reform law enforcement practices, especially practices that are considered to be biased against people of color. The two bills, H.R. 7120 and S. 3985, would, among other things, require state and local governments to report data on the use of force, promote the use of body-worn cameras, expand de-escalation training, and reduce racial profiling. Both pieces of legislation would also attempt to curb so-called "wandering officers" (i.e., law enforcement officers who are fired or resign under threat of termination but are later hired by another law enforcement agency, often in another state).

There are a litany of stories about law enforcement officers who are alleged or found to have engaged in misconduct, including the use of excessive force, being hired at law other enforcement agencies, and it is only discovered later that the officers had similar records at previous agencies. There is disagreement over how common the wandering officer phenomenon is and to what extent these officers may be a threat to the public. A 2020 study of law enforcement officers in Florida found the following:

TABLE OF CONTENTS.—The table of contents for this Act is as follows:

SEC. 2. DEFINITIONS.

In this Act:

(1) BYRNE GRANT PROGRAM.—The term "Byrne grant program" means any grant program under subpart 1 of part E of title I of the Omnibus Crime Control and Safe Streets Act of 1968 (34 U.S.C. 10151 et seq.), without regard to whether the funds are characterized as being made available under the Edward Byrne Memorial State and Local Law Enforcement Assistance Programs, the Local Government Law Enforcement Block Grants Program, the Edward Byrne Memorial Justice Assistance Grant Program, or otherwise.

(2) COPS GRANT PROGRAM.—The term "COPS grant program" means the grant program authorized under section 1701 of title I of the Omnibus Crime Control and Safe Streets Act of 1968 (34 U.S.C. 10381).

(3) FEDERAL LAW ENFORCEMENT AGENCY.—The term "Federal law enforcement agency" means any agency of the United States authorized to engage in or supervise the prevention, detection, investigation, or prosecution of any violation of Federal criminal law.

(4) FEDERAL LAW ENFORCEMENT OFFICER.—The term "Federal law enforcement officer" has the meaning given the term in section 115 of title 18, United States Code.

(5) INDIAN TRIBE.—The term "Indian Tribe" has the meaning given the term "Indian tribe" in section 901 of title I of the Omnibus Crime Control and Safe Streets Act of 1968 (34 U.S.C. 10251).

(6) LOCAL LAW ENFORCEMENT OFFICER.—The term "local law enforcement officer" means any officer, agent, or employee of a State or unit of local government authorized by law or by a government agency to engage in or supervise the prevention, detection, or investigation of any violation of criminal law.

(7) STATE.—The term "State" has the meaning given the term in section 901 of title I of the Omnibus Crime Control and Safe Streets Act of 1968 (34 U.S.C. 10251).

(8) TRIBAL LAW ENFORCEMENT OFFICER.—The term "tribal law enforcement officer" means any officer, agent, or employee of an Indian tribe, or the Bureau of Indian Affairs, authorized by law or by a government agency to engage in or supervise the prevention, detection, or investigation of any violation of criminal law.

(9) UNIT OF LOCAL GOVERNMENT.—The term "unit of local government" has the meaning given the term in section 901 of title I of the Omnibus Crime Control and Safe Streets Act of 1968 (34 U.S.C. 10251).

(10) DEADLY FORCE.—The term "deadly force" means that force which a reasonable person would consider likely to cause death or serious bodily harm, including—

(A) the discharge of a firearm;

(B) a maneuver that restricts blood or oxygen flow to the brain, including chokeholds, strangleholds, neck restraints, neckholds, and carotid artery restraints; and

(C) multiple discharges of an electronic control weapon.

USE OF FORCE.—The term "use of force" includes—

(A) the use of a firearm, Taser, explosive device, chemical agent (such as pepper spray), baton, impact projectile, blunt instrument, hand, fist, foot, canine, or vehicle against an individual;

(1) in subsection (a)—

(A) by striking "The Attorney General" and inserting the following: "(1) FEDERAL COLLECTION OF DATA.—The Attorney General"; and

(B) by adding at the end the following:

"(2) STATE COLLECTION OF DATA.—The attorney general of a State may, through appropriate means, acquire data about the use of excessive force by law enforcement officers and such data may be used by the attorney general in conducting investigations under section 210401. This data may not contain any information that may reveal the identity of the victim or any law enforcement officer." and

(2) by amending subsection (b) to read as follows:

"(b) LIMITATION ON USE OF DATA ACQUIRED BY THE ATTORNEY GENERAL.—Data acquired under subsection (a)(1) shall be used only for research or statistical purposes and may not contain any information that may reveal the identity of the victim or any law enforcement officer."

Sec. 104. Independent Investigations

(a) IN GENERAL.—

(1) DEFINITIONS.—In this subsection:

(A) INDEPENDENT INVESTIGATION.—The term "independent investigation" means a criminal investigation or prosecution of a law enforcement officer's use of deadly force, including one or more of the following:

(i) Using an agency or civilian review board that investigates and independently reviews all allegations of use of deadly force made against law enforcement officers in the jurisdiction.

(ii) Assigning of the attorney general of the State in which the alleged use of deadly force was committed to conduct the criminal investigation and prosecution.

(iii) Adopting a procedure under which an independent prosecutor is assigned to investigate and prosecute the casc, including a procedure under which an automatic referral is made to an independent prosecutor appointed and overseen by the attorney general of the State in which the alleged use of deadly force was committed.

(iv) Adopting a procedure under which an independent prosecutor is assigned to investigate and prosecute the case.

(v) Having law enforcement agencies agree to and implement memoranda of understanding with other law enforcement agencies under which the other law enforcement agencies—

(I) shall conduct the criminal investigation into the alleged use of deadly force; and

(II) upon conclusion of the criminal investigation, shall file a report with the attorney general of the State containing a determination regarding whether—

(aa) the use of deadly force was appropriate; and

(bb) any action should be taken by the attorney general of the State.

(vi) Any substantially similar procedure to ensure impartiality in the investigation or prosecution.

(B) INDEPENDENT INVESTIGATION OF LAW ENFORCEMENT STATUTE.—The term "independent investigation of law enforcement statute" means a statute requiring an independent investigation in a criminal matter in which—

(i) one or more of the possible defendants is a law enforcement officer;

(ii) one or more of the alleged offenses involves the law enforcement officer's use of deadly force in the course of carrying out that officer's duty; and

(iii) the non-Federal law enforcement officer's use of deadly force resulted in a death or injury.

INDEPENDENT PROSECUTOR.—The term "independent prosecutor" means, with respect to a criminal investigation or prosecution of a law enforcement officer's use of deadly force, a prosecutor who—

(i) does not oversee or regularly rely on the law enforcement agency by which the law enforcement officer under investigation is employed; and

(ii) would not be involved in the prosecution in the ordinary course of that prosecutor's duties.

(2) GRANT PROGRAM.—The Attorney General may award grants to eligible States and Indian Tribes to assist in implementing an independent investigation of law enforcement statute.

(3) ELIGIBILITY.—To be eligible for a grant under this subsection, a State or Indian Tribe shall have in effect an independent investigation of law enforcement statute.

(4) AUTHORIZATION OF APPROPRIATIONS.—There are authorized to be appropriated to the Attorney General $750,000,000 for fiscal years 2021 through 2023 to carry out this subsection.

(b) COPS GRANT PROGRAM USED FOR CIVILIAN REVIEW BOARDS.—Part Q of title I of the of the Omnibus Crime Control and Safe Streets Act of 1968 (34 U.S.C. 10381 et seq.) is amended—

(1) in section 1701(b) (34 U.S.C. 10381(b))—

(A) by redesignating paragraphs (22) and (23) as paragraphs (23) and (24), respectively;

(B) in paragraph (23), as so redesignated, by striking "(21)" and inserting "(22)"; and

(C) by inserting after paragraph (21) the following:

"(22) to develop best practices for and to create civilian review boards;" and

(2) in section 1709 (34 U.S.C. 10389), by adding at the end the following:

"(8) 'civilian review board' means an administrative entity that investigates civilian complaints against law enforcement officers and—

"(A) is independent and adequately funded;

"(B) has investigatory authority and subpoena power; "(C) has representative community diversity;

"(D) has policy making authority;

"(E) provides advocates for civilian complainants; "(F) may conduct hearings; and

"(G) conducts statistical studies on prevailing complaint trends."

Subtitle B—Law Enforcement Trust and Integrity Act

Sec. 111. Short Title

This subtitle may be cited as the "Law Enforcement Trust and Integrity Act of 2020."

Sec. 112. Definitions

In this subtitle:

(1) COMMUNITY-BASED ORGANIZATION.—The term "community-based organization" means a grassroots organization that monitors the issue of police misconduct and that has a local or national presence and membership, such as the National Association for the Advancement of Colored People (NAACP), the American Civil Liberties Union (ACLU), Unidos US, the National Urban League, the National Congress of American Indians, or the National Asian Pacific American Legal Consortium (NAPALC).

(2) LAW ENFORCEMENT ACCREDITATION ORGANIZATION.—The term "law enforcement accreditation organization" means a professional law enforcement organization involved in the development of standards of accreditation for law enforcement agencies at the national, State, regional, or Tribal level, such as the Commission on Accreditation for Law Enforcement Agencies (CALEA).

(3) LAW ENFORCEMENT AGENCY.—The term "law enforcement agency" means a State, local, Indian tribal, or campus public agency engaged in the prevention, detection, investigation, prosecution, or adjudication of violations of criminal laws.

(4) PROFESSIONAL LAW ENFORCEMENT ASSOCIATION.—The term "professional law enforcement association" means a law enforcement membership association that works for the needs of Federal, State, local, or Indian tribal law enforcement agencies and with the civilian community on matters of common interest, such as the Hispanic American Police Command Officers Association (HAPCOA), the National Asian Pacific Officers Association (NAPOA), the National Black Police Association (NBPA), the National Latino Peace Officers Association

are designed to improve management and address misconduct by law enforcement officers.

(d) COMPONENTS OF PILOT PROGRAM.—A pilot program developed under subsection (c)(2) shall include implementation of the following:

(1) TRAINING.—The implementation of policies, practices, and procedures addressing training and instruction to comply with accreditation standards in the areas of—

(A) the use of deadly force, less lethal force, and de-escalation tactics and techniques;

(B) investigation of officer misconduct and practices and procedures for referring to prosecuting authorities allegations of officer use of excessive force or racial profiling;

(C) disproportionate contact by law enforcement with minority communities;

(D) tactical and defensive strategy;

(E) arrests, searches, and restraint;

(F) professional verbal communications with civilians;

(G) interactions with—

(i) youth;

(ii) individuals with disabilities;

(iii) individuals with limited English proficiency; and

(iv) multi-cultural communities;

(H) proper traffic, pedestrian, and other enforcement stops; and

(1) community relations and bias awareness.

(2) RECRUITMENT, HIRING, RETENTION, AND PROMOTION OF DIVERSE LAW ENFORCEMENT OFFICERS.—Policies, procedures, and practices for—

(A) the hiring and recruitment of diverse law enforcement officers who are representative of the communities they serve;

(B) the development of selection, promotion, educational, background, and psychological standards that comport with title VII of the Civil Rights Act of 1964 (42 U.S.C. 2000e et seq.); and

(C) initiatives to encourage residency in the jurisdiction served by the law enforcement agency and continuing education.

(3) OVERSIGHT.—Complaint procedures, including the establishment of civilian review boards or analogous procedures for jurisdictions across a range of sizes and agency configurations, complaint procedures by community-based organizations, early warning systems and related intervention programs, video monitoring technology, data collection and transparency, and administrative due process requirements inherent to complaint procedures for members of the public and law enforcement.

(4) YOUTH JUSTICE AND SCHOOL SAFETY.—Uniform standards on youth justice and school safety that include best practices for law enforcement interaction and communication with children and youth, taking into consideration adolescent development and any disability, including—

(A) the right to effective and timely notification of a parent or legal guardian of any law enforcement interaction, regardless of the immigration status of the individuals involved; and

(B) the creation of positive school climates by improving school conditions for learning by—

(i) eliminating school-based arrests and referrals to law enforcement;

(ii) using evidence-based preventative measures and alternatives to school-based arrests and referrals to law enforcement, such as restorative justice and healing practices; and

(iii) using school-wide positive behavioral interventions and supports.

(5) VICTIM SERVICES.—Counseling services, including psychological counseling, for individuals and communities impacted by law enforcement misconduct.

(e) TECHNICAL ASSISTANCE.—

(1) IN GENERAL.—The Attorney General may provide technical assistance to States and community-based organizations in furtherance of the purposes of this section.

(2) MODELS FOR REDUCTION OF LAW ENFORCEMENT MISCONDUCT.—The technical assistance provided by the Attorney

General may include the development of models for States and community-based organizations to reduce law enforcement officer misconduct. Any development of such models shall be in consultation with community-based organizations.

(f) USE OF COMPONENTS.—The Attorney General may use any component or components of the Department of Justice in carrying out this section.

(g) APPLICATIONS.—An application for a grant under subsection (b) shall be submitted in such form, and contain such information, as the Attorney General may prescribe by rule.

(h) PERFORMANCE EVALUATION.—

(1) MONITORING COMPONENTS.—

(A) IN GENERAL.—Each program, project, or activity funded under this section shall contain a monitoring component, which shall be developed pursuant to rules made by the Attorney General.

(B) REQUIREMENT.—Each monitoring component required under subparagraph (A) shall include systematic identification and collection of data about activities, accomplishments, and programs throughout the duration of the program, project, or activity and presentation of such data in a usable form.

(2) EVALUATION COMPONENTS.—

(A) IN GENERAL.—Selected grant recipients shall be evaluated on the local level or as part of a national evaluation, pursuant to rules made by the Attorney General.

(B) REQUIREMENTS.—An evaluation conducted under subparagraph (A) may include independent audits of police behavior and other assessments of individual program implementations. For community-based organizations in selected jurisdictions that are able to support outcome evaluations, the effectiveness of funded programs, projects, and activities may be required.

(3) PERIODIC REVIEW AND REPORTS.—The Attorney General may require a grant recipient to submit biannually to the Attorney General the results of the monitoring and evaluations required under paragraphs (1)

and (2) and such other data and information as the Attorney General determines to be necessary.

(i) REVOCATION OR SUSPENSION OF FUNDING.—If the Attorney General determines, as a result of monitoring under subsection (h) or otherwise, that a grant recipient under the Byrne grant program or under subsection (b) is not in substantial compliance with the requirements of this section, the Attorney General may revoke or suspend funding of that grant, in whole or in part.

(j) CIVILIAN REVIEW BOARD DEFINED.—In this section, the term "civilian review board" means an administrative entity that investigates civilian complaints against law enforcement officers and—

(1) is independent and adequately funded;

(2) has investigatory authority and subpoena power;

(3) has representative community diversity;

(4) has policy making authority;

(5) provides advocates for civilian complainants;

(6) may conduct hearings; and

(7) conducts statistical studies on prevailing complaint trends.

(k) AUTHORIZATION OF APPROPRIATIONS.—There are authorized to be appropriated to the Attorney General $25,000,000 for fiscal year 2021 to carry out the grant program authorized under subsection (b).

Sec. 115. Attorney General to Conduct Study

(a) STUDY.—

(1) IN GENERAL.—The Attorney General shall conduct a nationwide study of the prevalence and effect of any law, rule, or procedure that allows a law enforcement officer to delay the response to questions posed by a local internal affairs officer, or review board on the investigative integrity and prosecution of law enforcement misconduct, including pre-interview warnings and termination policies.

(2) INITIAL ANALYSIS.—The Attorney General shall perform an initial analysis of existing State laws, rules, and procedures to determine whether, at a threshold level, the effect of the type of law, rule, or

(2) REALLOCATION.—Amounts not allocated by reason of this subsection shall be reallocated to States not disqualified by failure to comply with this section.

(f) REGULATIONS.—The Attorney General shall prescribe regulations to carry out this section.

TITLE II—POLICING TRANSPARENCY THROUGH DATA

Subtitle A—National Police Misconduct Registry

Sec. 201. Establishment of National Police Misconduct Registry

(a) IN GENERAL.—Not later than 180 days after the date of enactment of this Act, the Attorney General shall establish a National Police Misconduct Registry to be compiled and maintained by the Department of Justice.

(b) CONTENTS OF REGISTRY.—The Registry required to be established under subsection (a) shall contain the following data with respect to all Federal and local law enforcement officers:

(1) Each complaint filed against a law enforcement officer, aggregated by—

(A) complaints that were found to be credible or that resulted in disciplinary action against the law enforcement officer, disaggregated by whether the complaint involved a use of force or racial profiling (as such term is defined in section 302);

(B) complaints that are pending review, disaggregated by whether the complaint involved a use of force or racial profiling; and

(C) complaints for which the law enforcement officer was exonerated or that were determined to be unfounded or not sustained, disaggregated by whether the complaint involved a use of force or racial profiling.

(2) Discipline records, disaggregated by whether the complaint involved a use of force or racial profiling.

(3) Termination records, the reason for each termination, disaggregated by whether the complaint involved a use of force or racial profiling.

(4) Records of certification in accordance with section 202.

(5) Records of lawsuits against law enforcement officers and settlements of such lawsuits.

(c) FEDERAL AGENCY REPORTING REQUIREMENTS.—Not later than 1 year after the date of enactment of this Act, and every 6 months thereafter, the head of each Federal law enforcement agency shall submit to the Attorney General the information described in subsection (b).

(d) STATE AND LOCAL LAW ENFORCEMENT AGENCY REPORTING REQUIREMENTS.— Beginning in the first fiscal year that begins after the date that is one year after the date of enactment of this Act and each fiscal year thereafter in which a State receives funds under the Byrne grant program, the State shall, once every 180 days, submit to the Attorney General the information described in subsection (b) for the State and each local law enforcement agency within the State.

(e) PUBLIC AVAILABILITY OF REGISTRY.—

(1) IN GENERAL.—In establishing the Registry required under subsection (a), the Attorney General shall make the Registry available to the public on an internet website of the Attorney General in a manner that allows members of the public to search for an individual law enforcement officer's records of misconduct, as described in subsection (b), involving a use of force or racial profiling.

(2) PRIVACY PROTECTIONS.—Nothing in this subsection shall be construed to supersede the requirements or limitations under section 552a of title 5, United States Code (commonly known as the "Privacy Act of 1974").

Sec. 202. Certification Requirements for Hiring of Law Enforcement Officers

(a) IN GENERAL.— Beginning in the first fiscal year that begins after the date that is one year after the date of the enactment of this Act, a State or unit of local government, other than an Indian Tribe, may not receive funds under the Byrne grant program for that fiscal year if, on the day before the first day of the fiscal year, the State or unit of local government has not—

(1) submitted to the Attorney General evidence that the State or unit of local government has a certification and decertification program for purposes of employment as a law enforcement officer in that State or unit of local government that is consistent with the rules made under subsection (c); and

(2) submitted to the National Police Misconduct Registry established under section 201 records demonstrating that all law enforcement officers of the State or unit of local government have completed all State certification requirements during the 1-year period preceding the fiscal year.

(b) AVAILABILITY OF INFORMATION.—The Attorney General shall make available to law enforcement agencies all information in the registry under section 201 for purposes of compliance with the certification and decertification programs described in subsection (a)(1) and considering applications for employment.

(c) RULES.—The Attorney General shall make rules to carry out this section and section 201, including uniform reporting standards.

Subtitle B—PRIDE Act

Sec. 221. Short Title

This subtitle may be cited as the "Police Reporting Information, Data, and Evidence Act of 2020" or the "PRIDE Act of 2020."

Sec. 222. Definitions

In this subtitle:

(1) LOCAL EDUCATIONAL AGENCY.—The term "local educational agency" has the meaning given the term in section 8101 of the Elementary and Secondary Education Act of 1965 (20 U.S.C. 7801).

(2) LOCAL LAW ENFORCEMENT OFFICER.—The term "local law enforcement officer" has the meaning given the term in section 2, and includes a school resource officer.

(3) SCHOOL.—The term "school" means an elementary school or secondary school (as those terms are defined in section 8101 of the Elementary and Secondary Education Act of 1965 (20 U.S.C. 7801)).

(4) SCHOOL RESOURCE OFFICER.—The term "school resource officer" means a sworn law enforcement officer who is—

(A) assigned by the employing law enforcement agency to a local educational agency or school;

(B) contracting with a local educational agency or school; or

(C) employed by a local educational agency or school.

Sec. 223. Use of Force Reporting

(a) REPORTING REQUIREMENTS.—

(1) IN GENERAL.—Beginning in the first fiscal year that begins after the date that is one year after the date of enactment of this Act and each fiscal year thereafter in which a State or Indian Tribe receives funds under a Byrne grant program, the State or Indian Tribe shall—

(A) report to the Attorney General, on a quarterly basis and pursuant to guidelines established by the Attorney General, information regarding—

(i) any incident involving the use of deadly force against a civilian by—

(I) a local law enforcement officer who is employed by the State or by a unit of local government in the State; or

(II) a tribal law enforcement officer who is employed by the Indian Tribe;

(ii) any incident involving the shooting of a local law enforcement officer or tribal law enforcement officer described in clause (i) by a civilian;

(iii) any incident involving the death or arrest of a local law enforcement officer or tribal law enforcement officer;

(v) any incident during which use of force by or against a local law enforcement officer or tribal law enforcement officer described in clause

(i) occurs, which is not reported under clause (i), (ii), or (iii);

(v) deaths in custody; and

(vi) uses of force in arrests and booking;

procedure that raises material investigatory issues that could impair or hinder a prompt and thorough investigation of possible misconduct, including criminal conduct.

(3) DATA COLLECTION.—After completion of the initial analysis under paragraph (2), and considering material investigatory issues, the Attorney General shall gather additional data nationwide on similar laws, rules, and procedures from a representative and statistically significant sample of jurisdictions, to determine whether such laws, rules, and procedures raise such material investigatory issues.

(b) REPORTING.—

(1) INITIAL ANALYSIS.—Not later than 120 days after the date of the enactment of this Act, the Attorney General shall—

(A) submit to Congress a report containing the results of the initial analysis conducted under subsection (a)(2);

(B) make the report submitted under subparagraph (A) available to the public; and

(C) identify the jurisdictions for which the study described in subsection (a)(3) is to be conducted.

(2) DATA COLLECTED.—Not later than 2 years after the date of the enactment of this Act, the Attorney General shall submit to Congress a report containing the results of the data collected under this section and publish the report in the Federal Register.

Sec. 116. Authorization of Appropriations

There are authorized to be appropriated for fiscal year 2021, in addition to any other sums authorized to be appropriated—

(1) $25,000,000 for additional expenses relating to the enforcement of section 210401 of the Violent Crime Control and Law Enforcement Act of 1994 (34 U.S.C. 12601), criminal enforcement under sections 241 and 242 of title 18, United States Code, and administrative enforcement by the Department of Justice of such sections, including compliance with consent decrees or judgments entered into under such section 210401; and

(2) $3,300,000 for additional expenses related to conflict resolution by the Department of Justice's Community Relations Service.

Sec. 117. National Task Force on Law Enforcement Oversight

(a) ESTABLISHMENT.—There is established within the Department of Justice a task force to be known as the Task Force on Law Enforcement Oversight (hereinafter in this section referred to as the "Task Force").

(b) COMPOSITION.—The Task Force shall be composed of individuals appointed by the Attorney General, who shall appoint not less than 1 individual from each of the following:

(1) The Special Litigation Section of the Civil Rights Division.

(2) The Criminal Section of the Civil Rights Division.

(3) The Federal Coordination and Compliance Section of the Civil Rights Division.

(4) The Employment Litigation Section of the Civil Rights Division.

(5) The Disability Rights Section of the Civil Rights Division.

(6) The Office of Justice Programs.

(7) The Office of Community Oriented Policing Services (COPS).

(8) The Corruption/Civil Rights Section of the Federal Bureau of Investigation.

(9) The Community Relations Service.

(10) The Office of Tribal Justice.

(11) The unit within the Department of Justice assigned as a liaison for civilian review boards.

(c) POWERS AND DUTIES.—The Task Force shall consult with professional law enforcement associations, labor organizations, and community-based organizations to coordinate the process of the detection and referral of complaints regarding incidents of alleged law enforcement misconduct.

(d) AUTHORIZATION OF APPROPRIATIONS.—There are authorized to be appropriated $5,000,000 for each fiscal year to carry out this section.

Sec. 118. Federal Data Collection on Law Enforcement Practices

(a) AGENCIES TO REPORT.—Each Federal, State, Tribal, and local law enforcement agency shall report data of the practices enumerated in subsection (c) of that agency to the Attorney General.

(b) BREAKDOWN OF INFORMATION BY RACE, ETHNICITY, AND GENDER.—For each practice enumerated in subsection (c), the reporting law enforcement agency shall provide a breakdown of the numbers of incidents of that practice by race, ethnicity, age, and gender of the officers of the agency and of members of the public involved in the practice.

(c) PRACTICES TO BE REPORTED ON.—The practices to be reported on are the following:

(1) Traffic violation stops.

(2) Pedestrian stops.

(3) Frisk and body searches.

(4) Instances where law enforcement officers used deadly force, including—

(A) a description of when and where deadly force was used, and whether it resulted in death;

(B) a description of deadly force directed against an officer and whether it resulted in injury or death; and

(C) the law enforcement agency's justification for use of deadly force, if the agency determines it was justified.

(d) RETENTION OF DATA.—Each law enforcement agency required to report data under this section shall maintain records relating to any matter reported for not less than 4 years after those records are created.

(e) PENALTY FOR STATES FAILING TO REPORT AS REQUIRED.—

(1) IN GENERAL.—For any fiscal year, a State shall not receive any amount that would otherwise be allocated to that State under section 505(a) of title I of the Omnibus Crime Control and Safe Streets Act of 1968 (34 U.S.C. 10156(a)), or any amount from any other law enforcement assistance program of the Department of Justice, unless the State has ensured, to the satisfaction of the Attorney General, that the State and each local law enforcement agency of the State is in substantial compliance with the requirements of this section.

(B) establish a system and a set of policies to ensure that all use of force incidents are reported by local law enforcement officers or tribal law enforcement officers; and

(C) submit to the Attorney General a plan for the collection of data required to be reported under this section, including any modifications to a previously submitted data collection plan.

(2) REPORT INFORMATION REQUIRED.—

(A) IN GENERAL.—The report required under paragraph (1)(A) shall contain information that includes, at a minimum—

(i) the national origin, sex, race, ethnicity, age, disability, English language proficiency, and housing status of each civilian against whom a local law enforcement officer or tribal law enforcement officer used force;

(ii) the date, time, and location, including whether it was on school grounds, and the zip code, of the incident and whether the jurisdiction in which the incident occurred allows for the open-carry or concealed-carry of a firearm;

(ii) whether the civilian was armed, and, if so, the type of weapon the civilian had;

(iv) the type of force used against the officer, the civilian, or both, including the types of weapons used;

(v) the reason force was used;

(vi) a description of any injuries sustained as a result of the incident;

(vii) the number of officers involved in the incident;

(viii) the number of civilians involved in the incident; and

(ix) a brief description regarding the circumstances surrounding the incident, which shall include information on—

(I) the type of force used by all involved persons;

(II) the legitimate police objective necessitating the use of force;

(III) the resistance encountered by each local law enforcement officer or tribal law enforcement officer involved in the incident;

(IV) the efforts by local law enforcement officers or tribal law enforcement officers to—

(aa) de-escalate the situation in order to avoid the use of force; or

(bb) minimize the level of force used; and

(V) if applicable, the reason why efforts described in subclause (IV) were not attempted.

(B) INCIDENTS REPORTED UNDER DEATH IN CUSTODY REPORTING ACT.—A State or Indian Tribe is not required to include in a report under subsection (a)(1) an incident reported by the State or Indian Tribe in accordance with section 20104(a)(2) of the Violent Crime Control and Law Enforcement Act of 1994 (34 U.S.C. 12104(a)(2)).

(C) RETENTION OF DATA.—Each law enforcement agency required to report data under this section shall maintain records relating to any matter so reportable for not less than 4 years after those records are created.

(3) AUDIT OF USE-OF-FORCE REPORTING.—Not later than 1 year after the date of enactment of this Act, and each year thereafter, each State or Indian Tribe described in paragraph (1) shall—

(A) conduct an audit of the use of force incident reporting system required to be established under paragraph (1)(B); and

(B) submit a report to the Attorney General on the audit conducted under subparagraph (A).

(4) COMPLIANCE PROCEDURE.—Prior to submitting a report under paragraph (1)(A), the State or Indian Tribe submitting such report shall compare the information compiled to be reported pursuant to clause (i) of paragraph (1)(A) to publicly available sources, and shall revise such report to include any incident determined to be missing from the report based on such comparison. Failure to comply with the procedures described in the previous sentence shall be considered a failure to comply with the requirements of this section.

(b) INELIGIBILITY FOR FUNDS.—

(1) IN GENERAL.—For any fiscal year in which a State or Indian Tribe fails to comply with this section, the State or Indian Tribe, at the discretion of the Attorney General, shall be subject to not more than a 10-percent reduction of the funds that would otherwise be allocated for that fiscal year to the State or Indian Tribe under a Byrne grant program.

(2) REALLOCATION.—Amounts not allocated under a Byrne grant program in accordance with paragraph (1) to a State for failure to comply

with this section shall be reallocated under the Byrne grant program to States that have not failed to comply with this section.

(3) INFORMATION REGARDING SCHOOL RESOURCE OFFICERS.—The State or Indian Tribe shall ensure that all schools and local educational agencies within the jurisdiction of the State or Indian Tribe provide the State or Indian Tribe with the information needed regarding school resource officers to comply with this section.

(c) PUBLIC AVAILABILITY OF DATA.—

(1) IN GENERAL.—Not later than 1 year after the date of enactment of this Act, and each year thereafter, the Attorney General shall publish, and make available to the public, a report containing the data reported to the Attorney General under this section.

(2) PRIVACY PROTECTIONS.—Nothing in this subsection shall be construed to supersede the requirements or limitations under section 552a of title 5, United States Code (commonly known as the "Privacy Act of 1974").

(d) GUIDANCE.—Not later than 180 days after the date of enactment of this Act, the Attorney General, in coordination with the Director of the Federal Bureau of Investigation, shall issue guidance on best practices relating to establishing standard data collection systems that capture the information required to be reported under subsection (a)(2), which shall include standard and consistent definitions for terms.

Sec. 224. Use of Force Data Reporting

(a) TECHNICAL ASSISTANCE GRANTS AUTHORIZED.—The Attorney General may make grants to eligible law enforcement agencies to be used for the activities described in subsection (c).

(b) ELIGIBILITY.—In order to be eligible to receive a grant under this section a law enforcement agency shall—

(1) be a tribal law enforcement agency or be located in a State that receives funds under a Byrne grant program;

(2) employ not more that 100 local or tribal law enforcement officers;

(3) demonstrate that the use of force policy for local law enforcement officers or tribal law enforcement officers employed by the law enforcement agency is publicly available; and

(4) establish and maintain a complaint system that—

(A) may be used by members of the public to report incidents of use of force to the law enforcement agency;

(B) makes all information collected publicly searchable and available; and

(C) provides information on the status of an investigation related to a use of force complaint.

(c) ACTIVITIES DESCRIBED.—A grant made under this section may be used by a law enforcement agency for—

(1) the cost of assisting the State or Indian Tribe in which the law enforcement agency is located in complying with the reporting requirements described in section 223;

(2) the cost of establishing necessary systems required to investigate and report incidents as required under subsection (b)(4);

(3) public awareness campaigns designed to gain information from the public on use of force by or against local and tribal law enforcement officers, including shootings, which may include tip lines, hotlines, and public service announcements; and

(4) use of force training for law enforcement agencies and personnel, including training on de-escalation, implicit bias, crisis intervention techniques, and adolescent development.

Sec. 225. Compliance with Reporting Requirements

(a) IN GENERAL.—Not later than 1 year after the date of enactment of this Act, and each year thereafter, the Attorney General shall conduct an audit and review of the information provided under this subtitle to determine whether each State or Indian Tribe described in section 223(a)(1) is in compliance with the requirements of this subtitle.

(b) CONSISTENCY IN DATA REPORTING.—

(1) IN GENERAL.—Any data reported under this subtitle shall be collected and reported—

(A) in a manner consistent with existing programs of the Department of Justice that collect data on local law enforcement officer encounters with civilians; and

(B) in a manner consistent with civil rights laws for distribution of information to the public.

(2) GUIDELINES.—Not later than 1 year after the date of enactment of this Act, the Attorney General shall—

(A) issue guidelines on the reporting requirement under section 223; and

(B) seek public comment before finalizing the guidelines required under subparagraph (A).

Sec. 226. Federal Law Enforcement Reporting

The head of each Federal law enforcement agency shall submit to the Attorney General, on a quarterly basis and pursuant to guidelines established by the Attorney General, the information required to be reported by a State or Indian Tribe under section 223.

Sec. 227. Authorization of Appropriations

There are authorized to be appropriated to the Attorney General such sums as are necessary to carry out this subtitle.

TITLE III—IMPROVING POLICE TRAINING AND POLICIES

Subtitle A—End Racial and Religious Profiling Act

Sec. 301. Short Title

This subtitle may be cited as the "End Racial and Religious Profiling Act of 2020" or "ERRPA."

Sec. 302. Definitions

In this subtitle:

(1) COVERED PROGRAM.—The term "covered program" means any program or activity funded in whole or in part with funds made available under—

(A) a Byrne grant program; and

(B) the COPS grant program, except that no program, project, or other activity specified in section 1701(b)(13) of part Q of title I of the Omnibus Crime Control and Safe Streets Act of 1968 (34 U.S.C. 10381 et seq.) shall be a covered program under this paragraph.

(2) GOVERNMENTAL BODY.—The term "governmental body" means any department, agency, special purpose district, or other instrumentality of Federal, State, local, or Indian Tribal government.

(3) HIT RATE.—The term "hit rate" means the percentage of stops and searches in which a law enforcement agent finds drugs, a gun, or something else that leads to an arrest. The hit rate is calculated by dividing the total number of searches by the number of searches that yield contraband. The hit rate is complementary to the rate of false stops.

(4) LAW ENFORCEMENT AGENCY.—The term "law enforcement agency" means any Federal, State, or local public agency engaged in the prevention, detection, or investigation of violations of criminal, immigration, or customs laws.

(5) LAW ENFORCEMENT AGENT.—The term "law enforcement agent" means any Federal, State, or local official responsible for enforcing criminal, immigration, or customs laws, including police officers and other agents of a law enforcement agency.

(6) RACIAL PROFILING.—

(A) IN GENERAL.—The term "racial profiling" means the practice of a law enforcement agent or agency relying, to any degree, on actual or perceived race, ethnicity, national origin, religion, gender, gender identity, or sexual orientation in selecting which individual to subject to routine or spontaneous investigatory activities or in deciding upon the scope and substance of law enforcement activity following the initial investigatory procedure, except when there is trustworthy information, relevant to the locality and timeframe, that links a person with a particular characteristic described in this paragraph to an identified criminal incident or scheme.

(B) EXCEPTION.—For purposes of subparagraph (A), a tribal law enforcement officer exercising law enforcement authority within Indian country, as that term is defined in section 1151 of title 18, United States Code, is not considered to be racial profiling with respect to making key jurisdictional determinations that are necessarily tied to reliance on actual or perceived race, ethnicity, or tribal affiliation.

(7) ROUTINE OR SPONTANEOUS INVESTIGATORY ACTIVITIES.—The term "routine or spontaneous investigatory activities" means the following activities by a law enforcement agent:

(A) Interviews.

(B) Traffic stops.

(C) Pedestrian stops.

(D) Frisks and other types of body searches.

(E) Consensual or nonconsensual searches of the persons, property, or possessions (including vehicles) of individuals using any form of public or private transportation, including motorists and pedestrians.

(F) Data collection and analysis, assessments, and predicated investigations.

(G) Inspections and interviews of entrants into the United States that are more extensive than those customarily carried out.

(H) Immigration-related workplace investigations.

(I) Such other types of law enforcement encounters compiled for or by the Federal Bureau of Investigation or the Department of Justice Bureau of Justice Statistics.

(8) REASONABLE REQUEST.—The term "reasonable request" means all requests for information, except for those that—

(A) are immaterial to the investigation;

(B) would result in the unnecessary disclosure of personal information; or

(C) would place a severe burden on the resources of the law enforcement agency given its size.

Part I—Prohibition of Racial Profiling

Sec. 311. Prohibition

No law enforcement agent or law enforcement agency shall engage in racial profiling.

Sec. 312. Enforcement

(a) REMEDY.—The United States, or an individual injured by racial profiling, may enforce this part in a civil action for declaratory or injunctive relief, filed either in a State court of general jurisdiction or in a district court of the United States.

(b) PARTIES.—In any action brought under this part, relief may be obtained against—

(1) any governmental body that employed any law enforcement agent who engaged in racial profiling;

(2) any agent of such body who engaged in racial profiling; and

(3) any person with supervisory authority over such agent.

(c) NATURE OF PROOF.—Proof that the routine or spontaneous investigatory activities of law enforcement agents in a jurisdiction have had a disparate impact on individuals with a particular characteristic described in section 302(6) shall constitute prima facie evidence of a violation of this part.

(d) ATTORNEY'S FEES.—In any action or proceeding to enforce this part against any governmental body, the court may allow a prevailing plaintiff, other than the United States, reasonable attorney's fees as part of the costs, and may include expert fees as part of the attorney's fee. The term "prevailing plaintiff" means a plaintiff that substantially prevails pursuant to a judicial or administrative judgment or order, or an enforceable written agreement.

Part II—Programs to Eliminate Racial Profiling by Federal Law Enforcement Agencies

Sec. 321. Policies to Eliminate Racial Profiling

(a) IN GENERAL.—Federal law enforcement agencies shall—

(1) maintain adequate policies and procedures designed to eliminate racial profiling; and

(2) cease existing practices that permit racial profiling.

POLICIES.—The policies and procedures described in subsection (a)(1) shall include—

(1) a prohibition on racial profiling;

(2) training on racial profiling issues as part of Federal law enforcement training;

(3) the collection of data in accordance with the regulations issued by the Attorney General under section 341;

(4) procedures for receiving, investigating, and responding meaningfully to complaints alleging racial profiling by law enforcement agents; and

(5) any other policies and procedures the Attorney General determines to be necessary to eliminate racial profiling by Federal law enforcement agencies.

Part III—Programs to Eliminate Racial Profiling by State and Local Law Enforcement Agencies

Sec. 331. Policies Required for Grants

(a) IN GENERAL.—An application by a State or a unit of local government for funding under a covered program shall include a certification that such State, unit of local government, and any law enforcement agency to which it will distribute funds—

(1) maintains adequate policies and procedures designed to eliminate racial profiling; and

(2) has eliminated any existing practices that permit or encourage racial profiling.

POLICIES.—The policies and procedures described in subsection (a)(1) shall include—

(1) a prohibition on racial profiling;

(2) training on racial profiling issues as part of law enforcement training;

(3) the collection of data in accordance with the regulations issued by the Attorney General under section 341; and

(4) participation in an administrative complaint procedure or independent audit program that meets the requirements of section 332.

(c) EFFECTIVE DATE.—This section shall take effect 12 months after the date of enactment of this Act.

Sec. 332. Involvement of Attorney General

(a) REGULATIONS.—

(1) IN GENERAL.—Not later than 6 months after the date of enactment of this Act and in consultation with stakeholders, including Federal, State, and local law enforcement agencies and community, professional, research, and civil rights organizations, the Attorney General shall issue regulations for the operation of administrative complaint procedures and independent audit programs to ensure that such procedures and programs provide an appropriate response to allegations of racial profiling by law enforcement agents or agencies.

(2) GUIDELINES.—The regulations issued under paragraph (1) shall contain guidelines that ensure the fairness, effectiveness, and independence of the administrative complaint procedures and independent auditor programs.

(b) NONCOMPLIANCE.—If the Attorney General determines that the recipient of a grant from any covered program is not in compliance with the requirements of section 331 or the regulations issued under subsection (a), the Attorney General shall withhold, in whole or in part (at the discretion of the Attorney General), funds for one or more grants to the recipient under the covered program, until the recipient establishes compliance.

(c) PRIVATE PARTIES.—The Attorney General shall provide notice and an opportunity for private parties to present evidence to the Attorney General that a recipient of a grant from any covered program is not in compliance with the requirements of this part.

Sec. 333. Data Collection Demonstration Project

(a) TECHNICAL ASSISTANCE GRANTS FOR DATA COLLECTION.—

(1) IN GENERAL.—The Attorney General may, through competitive grants or contracts, carry out a 2-year demonstration project for the purpose of developing and implementing data collection programs on the hit rates for stops and searches by law enforcement agencies. The data collected shall be disaggregated by race, ethnicity, national origin, gender, and religion.

(2) NUMBER OF GRANTS.—The Attorney General shall provide not more than 5 grants or contracts under this section.

(3) ELIGIBLE GRANTEES.—Grants or contracts under this section shall be awarded to law enforcement agencies that serve communities where there is a significant concentration of racial or ethnic minorities and that are not already collecting data voluntarily.

(b) REQUIRED ACTIVITIES.—Activities carried out with a grant under this section shall include—

(1) developing a data collection tool and reporting the compiled data to the Attorney General; and

(2) training of law enforcement personnel on data collection, particularly for data collection on hit rates for stops and searches.

(c) EVALUATION.—Not later than 3 years after the date of enactment of this Act, the Attorney General shall enter into a contract with an institution of higher education (as defined in section 101 of the Higher Education Act of 1965 (20 U.S.C. 1001)) to analyze the data collected by each of the grantees funded under this section.

(d) AUTHORIZATION OF APPROPRIATIONS.—There are authorized to be appropriated to carry out activities under this section—

(1) $5,000,000, over a 2-year period, to carry out the demonstration program under subsection (a); and

(2) $500,000 to carry out the evaluation under subsection (c).

Sec. 334. Development of Best Practices

(a) USE OF FUNDS REQUIREMENT.—Section 502(a) of title I of the Omnibus Crime Control and Safe Streets Act of 1968 (34 U.S.C. 10153(a)), as amended by sections 113 and 114, is amended by adding at the end the following:

"(9) An assurance that, for each fiscal year covered by an application, the applicant will use not less than 10 percent of the total amount of the grant award for the fiscal year to develop and implement best practice devices and systems to eliminate racial profiling in accordance with section 334 of the End Racial and Religious Profiling Act of 2020."

(b) DEVELOPMENT OF BEST PRACTICES.—Grant amounts described in paragraph

(9) of section 502(a) of title I of the Omnibus Crime Control and Safe Streets Act of 1968 (34 U.S.C. 10153(a)), as added by subsection (a) of this section, shall be for programs that include the following:

(1) The development and implementation of training to prevent racial profiling and to encourage more respectful interaction with the public.

(2) The acquisition and use of technology to facilitate the accurate collection and analysis of data.

(3) The development and acquisition of feedback systems and technologies that identify law enforcement agents or units of agents engaged in, or at risk of engaging in, racial profiling or other misconduct.

(4) The establishment and maintenance of an administrative complaint procedure or independent auditor program.

Sec. 335. Authorization of Appropriations

There are authorized to be appropriated to the Attorney General such sums as are necessary to carry out this part.

Part IV—Data Collection

Sec. 341. Attorney General to Issue Regulations

(1) REGULATIONS.—Not later than 6 months after the date of enactment of this Act, the Attorney General, in consultation with stakeholders, including Federal, State, and local law enforcement agencies and community, professional, research, and civil rights organizations, shall issue regulations for the collection and compilation of data under sections 321 and 331.

(b) REQUIREMENTS.—The regulations issued under subsection (a) shall—

(1) provide for the collection of data on all routine and spontaneous investigatory activities;

(2) provide that the data collected shall—

(A) be disaggregated by race, ethnicity, national origin, gender, disability, and religion;

(B) include the date, time, and location of such investigatory activities;

(C) include detail sufficient to permit an analysis of whether a law enforcement agency is engaging in racial profiling; and

(D) not include personally identifiable information;

(3) provide that a standardized form shall be made available to law enforcement agencies for the submission of collected data to the Department of Justice;

(4) provide that law enforcement agencies shall compile data on the standardized form made available under paragraph (3), and submit the form to the Civil Rights Division and the Department of Justice Bureau of Justice Statistics;

(5) provide that law enforcement agencies shall maintain all data collected under this subtitle for not less than 4 years;

(6) include guidelines for setting comparative benchmarks, consistent with best practices, against which collected data shall be measured;

(7) provide that the Department of Justice Bureau of Justice Statistics shall—

(A) analyze the data for any statistically significant disparities, including—

(i) disparities in the percentage of drivers or pedestrians stopped relative to the proportion of the population passing through the neighborhood;

(ii) disparities in the hit rate; and

(iii) disparities in the frequency of searches performed on racial or ethnic minority drivers and the frequency of searches performed on nonminority drivers; and

(B) not later than 3 years after the date of enactment of this Act, and annually thereafter—

(i) prepare a report regarding the findings of the analysis conducted under subparagraph (A);

(ii) provide such report to Congress; and

(iii) make such report available to the public, including on a website of the Department of Justice, and in accordance with accessibility standards under the Americans with Disabilities Act of 1990 (42 U.S.C. 12101 et seq.); and

(8) protect the privacy of individuals whose data is collected by—

(A) limiting the use of the data collected under this subtitle to the purposes set forth in this subtitle;

(B) except as otherwise provided in this subtitle, limiting access to the data collected under this subtitle to those Federal, State, or local employees or agents who require such access in order to fulfill the purposes for the data set forth in this subtitle;

(C) requiring contractors or other nongovernmental agents who are permitted access to the data collected under this subtitle to sign use agreements incorporating the use and disclosure restrictions set forth in subparagraph (A); and

(D) requiring the maintenance of adequate security measures to prevent unauthorized access to the data collected under this subtitle.

Sec. 342. Publication of Data

The Director of the Bureau of Justice Statistics of the Department of Justice shall provide to Congress and make available to the public, together with each annual report described in section 341, the data collected pursuant to this subtitle, excluding any personally identifiable information described in section 343.

Sec. 343. Limitations on Publication of Data

The name or identifying information of a law enforcement agent, complainant, or any other individual involved in any activity for which data is collected and compiled under this subtitle shall not be—

(1) released to the public;

(2) disclosed to any person, except for—

(A) such disclosures as are necessary to comply with this subtitle;

(B) disclosures of information regarding a particular person to that person; or

(C) disclosures pursuant to litigation; or

(3) subject to disclosure under section 552 of title 5, United States Code (commonly known as the Freedom of Information Act), except for disclosures of information regarding a particular person to that person.

Part V—Department of Justice Regulations and Reports on Racial Profiling in the United States

Sec. 351. Attorney General to Issue Regulations and Reports

(a) REGULATIONS.—In addition to the regulations required under sections 333 and 341, the Attorney General shall issue such other regulations as the Attorney General determines are necessary to implement this subtitle.

(b) REPORTS.—

(1) IN GENERAL.—Not later than 2 years after the date of enactment of this Act, and annually thereafter, the Attorney General shall submit to Congress a report on racial profiling by law enforcement agencies.

(2) SCOPE.—Each report submitted under paragraph (1) shall include—

(A) a summary of data collected under sections 321(b)(3) and 331(b)(3) and from any other reliable source of information regarding racial profiling in the United States;

(B) a discussion of the findings in the most recent report prepared by the Department of Justice Bureau of Justice Statistics under section 341(b)(7);

(C) the status of the adoption and implementation of policies and procedures by Federal law enforcement agencies under section 321 and by the State and local law enforcement agencies under sections 331 and 332; and

(D) a description of any other policies and procedures that the Attorney General believes would facilitate the elimination of racial profiling.

Subtitle B—Additional Reforms

Sec. 361. Training on Racial Bias and Duty to Intervene

(a) IN GENERAL.—The Attorney General shall establish—

(1) a training program for law enforcement officers to cover racial profiling, implicit bias, and procedural justice; and

(2) a clear duty for Federal law enforcement officers to intervene in cases where another law enforcement officer is using excessive force against a civilian, and establish a training program that covers the duty to intervene.

(b) MANDATORY TRAINING FOR FEDERAL LAW ENFORCEMENT OFFICERS.—The head of each Federal law enforcement agency shall require each Federal law enforcement officer employed by the agency to complete the training programs established under subsection (a).

(c) LIMITATION ON ELIGIBILITY FOR FUNDS.—Beginning in the first fiscal year that begins after the date that is one year after the date of enactment of this Act, a State or unit of local government may not receive funds under the Byrne grant program for a fiscal year if, on the day before the first day of the fiscal year, the State or unit of local government does not require each law enforcement officer in the State or unit of local government to complete the training programs established under subsection (a).

(d) GRANTS TO TRAIN LAW ENFORCEMENT OFFICERS ON USE OF FORCE.—Section 501(a)(1) of title I of the Omnibus Crime Control and Safe Streets Act of 1968 (34 U.S.C. 10152(a)(1)) is amended by adding at the end the following:

"(I) Training programs for law enforcement officers, including training programs on use of force and a duty to intervene."

Sec. 362. Ban on No-Knock Warrants in Drug Cases

(a) BAN ON FEDERAL WARRANTS IN DRUG CASES.—Section 509 of the Controlled Substances Act (21 U.S.C. 879) is amended by adding at the end the following: "A search warrant authorized under this section shall require that a law enforcement officer execute the search warrant only after providing notice of his or her authority and purpose."

(b) LIMITATION ON ELIGIBILITY FOR FUNDS.—Beginning in the first fiscal year that begins after the date that is one year after the date of enactment of this Act, a State or unit of local government may not receive funds under the COPS grant program for a fiscal year if, on the day before the first day of the fiscal year, the State or unit of local government does not have in effect a law that prohibits the issuance of a no-knock warrant in a drug case.

(c) DEFINITION.—In this section, the term "no-knock warrant" means a warrant that allows a law enforcement officer to enter a property without requiring the law enforcement officer to announce the presence of the law enforcement officer or the intention of the law enforcement officer to enter the property.

Sec. 363. Incentivizing Banning of Chokeholds and Carotid Holds

(a) DEFINITION.—In this section, the term "chokehold or carotid hold" means the application of any pressure to the throat or windpipe, the use of maneuvers that restrict blood or oxygen flow to the brain, or carotid artery restraints that prevent or hinder breathing or reduce intake of air of an individual.

(b) LIMITATION ON ELIGIBILITY FOR FUNDS.—Beginning in the first fiscal year that begins after the date that is one year after the date of enactment of this Act, a State or unit of local government may not receive funds under the Byrne grant program or the COPS grant program for a fiscal year if, on the day before the first day of the fiscal year, the State or unit of local government does not have in effect a law that prohibits law enforcement officers in the State or unit of local government from using a chokehold or carotid hold.

(c) CHOKEHOLDS AS CIVIL RIGHTS VIOLATIONS.—

(1) SHORT TITLE.—This subsection may be cited as the "Eric Garner Excessive Use of Force Prevention Act."

(2) CHOKEHOLDS AS CIVIL RIGHTS VIOLATIONS.—Section 242 of title 18, United States Code, as amended by section 101, is amended by adding at the end the following: "For the purposes of this section, the application of any pressure to the throat or windpipe, use of maneuvers that restrict blood or oxygen flow to the brain, or carotid artery restraints which prevent or hinder breathing or reduce intake of air is a punishment, pain, or penalty."

Sec. 364. Peace Act

(a) SHORT TITLE.—This section may be cited as the "Police Exercising Absolute Care With Everyone Act of 2020" or the "PEACE Act of 2020."

(b) USE OF FORCE BY FEDERAL LAW ENFORCEMENT OFFICERS.—

(1) DEFINITIONS.—In this subsection:

(A) DEESCALATION TACTICS AND TECHNIQUES.—The term "deescalation tactics and techniques" means proactive actions and approaches used by a Federal law enforcement officer to stabilize the situation so that more time, options, and resources are available to gain a person's voluntary compliance and reduce or eliminate the need to use force, including verbal persuasion, warnings, tactical techniques, slowing down the pace of an incident, waiting out a subject, creating distance between the officer and the threat, and requesting additional resources to resolve the incident.

(B) NECESSARY.—The term "necessary" means that another reasonable Federal law enforcement officer would objectively conclude, under the totality of the circumstances, that there was no reasonable alternative to the use of force.

(C) REASONABLE ALTERNATIVES.—

(i) IN GENERAL.—The term "reasonable alternatives" means tactics and methods used by a Federal law enforcement officer to effectuate an arrest that do not unreasonably increase the risk posed to the law enforcement officer or another person, including verbal communication, distance, warnings, deescalation tactics and techniques, tactical repositioning, and other tactics and techniques intended to stabilize the situation and reduce the immediacy of the risk so that more time, options, and resources can be called upon to resolve the situation without the use of force.

(ii) DEADLY FORCE.—With respect to the use of deadly force, the term "reasonable alternatives" includes the use of less lethal force.

(D) TOTALITY OF THE CIRCUMSTANCES.—The term "totality of the circumstances" means all credible facts known to the Federal law enforcement officer leading up to and at the time of the use of force, including the actions of the person against whom the Federal law enforcement officer uses such force and the actions of the Federal law enforcement officer.

(2) PROHIBITION ON LESS LETHAL FORCE.—A Federal law enforcement officer may not use any less lethal force unless—

(A) the form of less lethal force used is necessary and proportional in order to effectuate an arrest of a person who the officer has probable cause to believe has committed a criminal offense; and

(B) reasonable alternatives to the use of the form of less lethal force have been exhausted.

(3) PROHIBITION ON DEADLY USE OF FORCE.—A Federal law enforcement officer may not use deadly force against a person unless—

(A) the form of deadly force used is necessary, as a last resort, to prevent imminent and serious bodily injury or death to the officer or another person;

(B) the use of the form of deadly force creates no substantial risk of injury to a third person; and

(C) reasonable alternatives to the use of the form of deadly force have been exhausted.

(4) REQUIREMENT TO GIVE VERBAL WARNING.—When feasible, prior to using force against a person, a Federal law enforcement officer shall identify himself or herself as a Federal law enforcement officer, and issue a verbal warning to the person that the Federal law enforcement officer seeks to apprehend, which shall—

(A) include a request that the person surrender to the law enforcement officer; and

(B) notify the person that the law enforcement officer will use force against the person if the person resists arrest or flees.

(5) GUIDANCE ON USE OF FORCE.—Not later than 120 days after the date of enactment of this Act, the Attorney General, in consultation with impacted persons, communities, and organizations, including representatives of civil and human rights organizations, victims of police use of force, and representatives of law enforcement associations, shall provide guidance to Federal law enforcement agencies on—

(A) the types of less lethal force and deadly force that are prohibited under paragraphs (2) and (3); and

(B) how a Federal law enforcement officer can—

(i) assess whether the use of force is appropriate and necessary; and

(ii) use the least amount of force when interacting with—

(I) pregnant individuals;

(II) children and youth under 21 years of age;

(III) elderly persons;

(IV) persons with mental, behavioral, or physical disabilities or impairments;

(V) persons experiencing perceptual or cognitive impairments due to use of alcohol, narcotics, hallucinogens, or other drugs;

(VI) persons suffering from a serious medical condition; and

(VII) persons with limited English proficiency.

(6) TRAINING.—The Attorney General shall provide training to Federal law enforcement officers on interacting people described in subclauses (I) through

(VII) of paragraph (5)(B)(ii).

(7) LIMITATION ON JUSTIFICATION DEFENSE.—

(A) IN GENERAL.—Chapter 51 of title 18, United States Code, is amended by adding at the end the following:

"§ 1123. Limitation on Justification Defense for Federal Law Enforcement Officers

"(a) IN GENERAL.—It is not a defense to an offense under section 1111 or 1112 that the use of less lethal force or deadly force by a Federal law enforcement officer was justified if—

"(1) that officer's use of use of such force was inconsistent with section 364(b) of the George Floyd Justice in Policing Act of 2020; or

"(2) that officer's gross negligence, leading up to and at the time of the use of force, contributed to the necessity of the use of such force.

"(b) DEFINITIONS.—In this section—

"(1) the terms 'deadly force' and 'less lethal force' have the meanings given such terms in section 2 and section 364 of the George Floyd Justice in Policing Act of 2020; and

"(2) the term 'Federal law enforcement officer' has the meaning given such term in section 115."

CLERICAL AMENDMENT.—The table of sections for chapter 51 of title 18, United States Code, is amended by inserting after the item relating to section 1122 the following:

"1123. Limitation on justification defense for Federal law enforcement officers."

(c) LIMITATION ON THE RECEIPT OF FUNDS UNDER THE EDWARD BYRNE MEMORIAL JUSTICE ASSISTANCE GRANT PROGRAM.—

(1) LIMITATION.—A State or unit of local government, other than an Indian Tribe, may not receive funds that the State or unit of local government would otherwise receive under a Byrne grant program for a fiscal year if, on the day before the first day of the fiscal year, the State or unit of local government does not have in effect a law that is consistent with subsection (b) of this section and section 1123 of title 18, United States Code, as determined by the Attorney General.

(2) SUBSEQUENT ENACTMENT.—

(A) IN GENERAL.—If funds described in paragraph (1) are withheld from a State or unit of local government pursuant to paragraph (1) for 1 or more fiscal years, and the State or unit of local government enacts or puts in place a law described in paragraph (1), and demonstrates substantial efforts to enforce such law, subject to subparagraph (B), the State or unit of local government shall be eligible, in the fiscal year after the fiscal year during which the State or unit of local government demonstrates such substantial efforts, to receive the total amount that the State or unit of local government would have received during each fiscal year for which funds were withheld.

(B) LIMIT ON AMOUNT OF PRIOR YEAR FUNDS.—A State or unit of local government may not receive funds under subparagraph (A) in an amount that is more than the amount withheld from the State or unit of local government during the 5-fiscal-year period before the fiscal year during which funds are received under subparagraph (A).

(3) GUIDANCE.—Not later than 120 days after the date of enactment of this Act, the Attorney General, in consultation with impacted persons, communities, and organizations, including representatives of civil and human rights organizations, individuals against whom a law enforcement officer used force, and representatives of law enforcement associations, shall make guidance available to States and units of local government on the criteria that the Attorney General will use in determining whether the

State or unit of local government has in place a law described in paragraph (1).

(4) APPLICATION.—This subsection shall apply to the first fiscal year that begins after the date that is 1 year after the date of the enactment of this Act, and each fiscal year thereafter.

Sec. 365. Stop Militarizing Law Enforcement Act

(a) FINDINGS.—Congress makes the following findings:

(1) Under section 2576a of title 10, United States Code, the Department of Defense is authorized to provide excess property to local law enforcement agencies. The Defense Logistics Agency, administers such section by operating the Law Enforcement Support Office program.

(2) New and used material, including mine-resistant ambush-protected vehicles and weapons determined by the Department of Defense to be "military grade" are transferred to Federal, Tribal, State, and local law enforcement agencies through the program.

(3) As a result local law enforcement agencies, including police and sheriff's departments, are acquiring this material for use in their normal operations.

(4) As a result of the wars in Iraq and Afghanistan, military equipment purchased for, and used in, those wars has become excess property and has been made available for transfer to local and Federal law enforcement agencies.

(5) In Fiscal Year 2017, $504,000,000 worth of property was transferred to law enforcement agencies.

(6) More than $6,800,000,000 worth of weapons and equipment have been transferred to police organizations in all 50 States and four territories through the program.

(7) In May 2012, the Defense Logistics Agency instituted a moratorium on weapons transfers through the program after reports of missing equipment and inappropriate weapons transfers.

(8) Though the moratorium was widely publicized, it was lifted in October 2013 without adequate safeguards.

(9) On January 16, 2015, President Barack Obama issued Executive Order 13688 to better coordinate and regulate the federal transfer of military weapons and equipment to State, local, and Tribal law enforcement agencies.

(10) In July, 2017, the Government Accountability Office reported that the program's internal controls were inadequate to prevent fraudulent applicants' access to the program.

(11) On August, 28, 2017, President Donald Trump rescinded Executive Order 13688 despite a July 2017 Government Accountability Office report finding deficiencies with the administration of the 1033 program.

(12) As a result, Federal, State, and local law enforcement departments across the country are eligible again to acquire free "military-grade" weapons and equipment that could be used inappropriately during policing efforts in which people and taxpayers could be harmed.

(13) The Department of Defense categorizes equipment eligible for transfer under the 1033 program as "controlled" and "un-controlled" equipment. "Controlled equipment" includes weapons, explosives such as flash-bang grenades, mine-resistant ambush-protected vehicles, long-range acoustic devices, aircraft capable of being modified to carry armament that are combat coded, and silencers, among other military grade items.

(b) LIMITATION ON DEPARTMENT OF DEFENSE TRANSFER OF PERSONAL PROPERTY TO LOCAL LAW ENFORCEMENT AGENCIES.—

(1) IN GENERAL.—Section 2576a of title 10, United States Code, is amended—

(A) in subsection (a)—

(i) in paragraph (1)(A), by striking "counterdrug, counterterrorism, and border security activities" and inserting "counterterrorism"; and

(ii) in paragraph (2), by striking, "the Director of National Drug Control Policy,"

() in subsection (b)—

(i) in paragraph (5), by striking "and" at the end;

(ii) in paragraph (6), by striking the period and inserting a semicolon; and

(iii) by adding at the end the following new paragraphs:

"(7) the recipient submits to the Department of Defense a description of how the recipient expects to use the property;

"(8) the recipient certifies to the Department of Defense that if the recipient determines that the property is surplus to the needs of the recipient, the recipient will return the property to the Department of Defense;

"(9) with respect to a recipient that is not a Federal agency, the recipient certifies to the Department of Defense that the recipient notified the local community of the request for personal property under this section by—

"(A) publishing a notice of such request on a publicly accessible Internet website;

"(B) posting such notice at several prominent locations in the jurisdiction of the recipient; and

"(C) ensuring that such notices were available to the local community for a period of not less than 30 days; and

"(10) the recipient has received the approval of the city council or other local governing body to acquire the personal property sought under this section.";

(C) by striking subsection (d);

(D) by redesignating subsections (e) and (f) as subsections (o) and (p), respectively; and

(E) by inserting after subsection (c) the following new subsections:

"(d) ANNUAL CERTIFICATION ACCOUNTING FOR TRANSFERRED PROPERTY.—(1) For each fiscal year, the Secretary shall submit to Congress certification in writing that each Federal or State agency to which the Secretary has transferred property under this section—

"(A) has provided to the Secretary documentation accounting for all controlled property, including arms and ammunition, that the Secretary has transferred to the agency, including any item described in subsection (f) so transferred before the date of the enactment of the George Floyd Justice in Policing Act of 2020; and

"(B) with respect to a non-Federal agency, carried out each of paragraphs (5) through (8) of subsection (b).

"(2) If the Secretary does not provide a certification under paragraph (1) for a Federal or State agency, the Secretary may not transfer additional property to that agency under this section.

"(e) ANNUAL REPORT ON EXCESS PROPERTY.—Before making any property available for transfer under this section, the Secretary shall annually submit to Congress a description of the property to be transferred together with a certification that the transfer of the property would not violate this section or any other provision of law. "(f) LIMITATIONS ON TRANSFERS.—(1) The Secretary may not transfer to Federal, Tribal, State, or local law enforcement agencies the following under this section:

"(A) Controlled firearms, ammunition, bayonets, grenade launchers, grenades (including stun and flash-bang),and explosives.

"(B) Controlled vehicles, highly mobile multi-wheeled vehicles, mine-resistant ambush-protected vehicles, trucks, truck dump, truck utility, and truck carryall.

"(C) Drones that are armored, weaponized, or both. "(D) Controlled aircraft that—

"(i) are combat configured or combat coded; or

"(ii) have no established commercial flight application. "(E) Silencers.

"(F) Long-range acoustic devices.

"(G) Items in the Federal Supply Class of banned items.

"(2) The Secretary may not require, as a condition of a transfer under this section, that a Federal or State agency demonstrate the use of any small arms or ammunition.

"(3) The limitations under this subsection shall also apply with respect to the transfer of previously transferred property of the Department of Defense from one Federal or State agency to another such agency.

"(4)(A) The Secretary may waive the applicability of paragraph (1) to a vehicle described in subparagraph (B) of such paragraph (other than a mine-resistant ambush-protected vehicle), if the Secretary determines that such a waiver is necessary for disaster or rescue purposes or for another purpose where life and public safety are at risk, as demonstrated by the proposed recipient of the vehicle.

"(B) If the Secretary issues a waiver under subparagraph (A), the Secretary shall—

"(i) submit to Congress notice of the waiver, and post such notice on a public Internet website of the Department, by not later than 30 days after the date on which the waiver is issued; and

"(ii) require, as a condition of the waiver, that the recipient of the vehicle for which the waiver is issued provides public notice of the waiver and the transfer, including the type of vehicle and the purpose for which it is transferred, in the jurisdiction where the recipient is located by not later than 30 days after the date on which the waiver is issued.

"(5) The Secretary may provide for an exemption to the limitation under subparagraph (D) of paragraph (1) in the case of parts for aircraft described in such subparagraph that are transferred as part of regular maintenance of aircraft in an existing fleet.

"(6) The Secretary shall require, as a condition of any transfer of property under this section, that the Federal or State agency that receives the property shall return the property to the Secretary if the agency—

"(A) is investigated by the Department of Justice for any violation of civil liberties; or

"(B) is otherwise found to have engaged in widespread abuses of civil liberties. "(g) CONDITIONS FOR EXTENSION OF PROGRAM.—Notwithstanding any other provision of law, amounts authorized to be appropriated or otherwise made available for any fiscal year may not be obligated or expended to carry out this section unless the Secretary submits to Congress certification that for the preceding fiscal year that—

"(1) each Federal or State agency that has received controlled property transferred under this section has—

"(A) demonstrated 100 percent accountability for all such property, in accordance with paragraph (2) or (3), as applicable; or

"(B) been suspended from the program pursuant to paragraph (4);

"(2) with respect to each non-Federal agency that has received controlled property under this section, the State coordinator responsible for each such agency has verified that the coordinator or an agent of the coordinator has conducted an in-person inventory of the property transferred to the agency and that 100 percent of such property was accounted for during the inventory or that the agency has been suspended from the program pursuant to paragraph (4);

"(3) with respect to each Federal agency that has received controlled property under this section, the Secretary of Defense or an agent of the Secretary has conducted an in-person inventory of the property transferred to the agency and that 100 percent of such property was accounted for during the inventory or that the agency has been suspended from the program pursuant to paragraph (4);

"(4) the eligibility of any agency that has received controlled property under this section for which 100 percent of the property was not accounted for during an inventory described in paragraph (1) or (2), as applicable, to receive any property transferred under this section has been suspended; and

"(5) each State coordinator has certified, for each non-Federal agency located in the State for which the State coordinator is responsible that—

"(A) the agency has complied with all requirements under this section; or "(B) the eligibility of the agency to receive property transferred under this section has been suspended; and

"(6) the Secretary of Defense has certified, for each Federal agency that has received property under this section that—

"(A) the agency has complied with all requirements under this section; or "(B) the eligibility of the agency to receive property transferred under this section has been suspended.

"(h) PROHIBITION ON OWNERSHIP OF CONTROLLED PROPERTY.—A Federal or State agency that receives controlled property under this section may not take ownership of the property.

"(i) NOTICE TO CONGRESS OF PROPERTY DOWNGRADES.—Not later than 30 days before downgrading the classification of any item of personal property from controlled or Federal Supply Class, the Secretary shall submit to Congress notice of the proposed downgrade.

"(j) NOTICE TO CONGRESS OF PROPERTY CANNIBALIZATION.—Before the Defense Logistics Agency authorizes the recipient of property transferred under this section to cannibalize the property, the Secretary shall submit to Congress notice of such authorization, including the name of the recipient requesting the authorization, the purpose of the proposed cannibalization, and the type of property proposed to be cannibalized.

"(k) QUARTERLY REPORTS ON USE OF CONTROLLED EQUIPMENT.—Not later than 30 days after the last day of a fiscal quarter, the Secretary shall submit to Congress a report on any uses of controlled property transferred under this section during that fiscal quarter.

"(l) REPORTS TO CONGRESS.—Not later than 30 days after the last day of a fiscal year, the Secretary shall submit to Congress a report on the following for the preceding fiscal year:

"(1) The percentage of equipment lost by recipients of property transferred under this section, including specific information about the type of property lost, the monetary value of such property, and the recipient that lost the property. "(2) The transfer of any new (condition code A) property transferred under this section, including specific information about the type of property, the recipient of the property, the monetary value of each item of the property, and the total monetary value of all such property transferred during the fiscal year."

(2) EFFECTIVE DATE.—The amendments made by paragraph (1) shall apply with respect to any transfer of property made after the date of the enactment of this Act.

Sec. 366. Public Safety Innovation Grants

(a) BYRNE GRANTS USED FOR LOCAL TASK FORCES ON PUBLIC SAFETY INNOVATION.—Section 501(a) of the Omnibus Crime Control and Safe Streets Act of 1968 (34 U.S.C. 10151(a)), as amended by this Act, is further amended by adding at the end the following:

"(3) LOCAL TASK FORCES ON PUBLIC SAFETY INNOVATION.—

"(A) IN GENERAL.—A law enforcement program under paragraph (1)(A) may include the development of best practices for and the creation of local task forces on public safety innovation, charged with exploring and developing new strategies for public safety, including non-law enforcement strategies.

"(B) DEFINITION.—The term 'local task force on public safety innovation' means an administrative entity, created from partnerships between community-based organizations and other local stakeholders, that may develop innovative law enforcement and non-law enforcement strategies to enhance just and equitable public safety, repair breaches of trust between law enforcement agencies and the community they pledge to serve, and enhance accountability of law enforcement officers."

(b) CRISIS INTERVENTION TEAMS.—Section 501(c) of title I of the Omnibus Crime Control and Safe Streets Act of 1968 (34 U.S.C. 10152(c)) is amended by adding at the end the following:

"(3) In the case of crisis intervention teams funded under subsection (a)(1)(H), a program assessment under this subsection shall contain a report on best practices for crisis intervention."

(c) USE OF COPS GRANT PROGRAM TO HIRE LAW ENFORCEMENT OFFICERS WHO ARE RESIDENTS OF THE COMMUNITIES THEY SERVE.—Section 1701(b) of title I of the Omnibus Crime Control and Safe Streets Act of 1968 (34 U.S.C. 10381(b)), as amended by this Act, is further amended—

(1) by redesignating paragraphs (23) and (24) as paragraphs (26) and (27), respectively;

(2) in paragraph (26), as so redesignated, by striking "(22)" and inserting "(25)"; and

(3) by inserting after paragraph (22) the following:

"(23) to recruit, hire, incentivize, retain, develop, and train new, additional career law enforcement officers or current law enforcement officers who are willing to relocate to communities—

"(A) where there are poor or fragmented relationships between police and residents of the community, or where there are high incidents of crime; and "(B) that are the communities that the law enforcement officers serve, or that are in close proximity to the communities that the law enforcement officers serve;

"(24) to collect data on the number of law enforcement officers who are willing to relocate to the communities where they serve, and whether such law enforcement officer relocations have impacted crime in such communities;

"(25) to develop and publicly report strategies and timelines to recruit, hire, promote, retain, develop, and train a diverse and inclusive law enforcement workforce, consistent with merit system principles and applicable law."

Subtitle C—Law Enforcement Body Cameras

Part 1—Federal Police Camera and Accountability Act

Sec. 371. Short Title

This part may be cited as the "Federal Police Camera and Accountability Act."

Sec. 372. Requirements for Federal Law Enforcement Officers Regarding the Use of Body Cameras

(a) DEFINITIONS.—In this section:

(1) MINOR.—The term "minor" means any individual under 18 years of age.

(2) SUBJECT OF THE VIDEO FOOTAGE.—The term "subject of the video footage"—

(A) means any identifiable Federal law enforcement officer or any identifiable suspect, victim, detainee, conversant, injured party, or other similarly situated person who appears on the body camera recording; and

(B) does not include people who only incidentally appear on the recording.

(3) VIDEO FOOTAGE.—The term "video footage" means any images or audio recorded by a body camera.

REQUIREMENT TO WEAR BODY CAMERA.—

(1) IN GENERAL.—Federal law enforcement officers shall wear a body camera.

(2) REQUIREMENT FOR BODY CAMERA.—A body camera required under paragraph (1) shall—

(A) have a field of view at least as broad as the officer's vision; and

(B) be worn in a manner that maximizes the camera's ability to capture video footage of the officer's activities.

(c) REQUIREMENT TO ACTIVATE.—

(1) IN GENERAL.—Both the video and audio recording functions of the body camera shall be activated whenever a Federal law enforcement officer is responding to a call for service or at the initiation of any other law enforcement or investigative stop (as such term is defined in section 373) between a Federal law enforcement officer and a member of the public, except that when an immediate threat to the officer's life or safety makes activating the camera impossible or dangerous, the officer shall activate the camera at the first reasonable opportunity to do so.

(2) ALLOWABLE DEACTIVATION.—The body camera shall not be deactivated until the stop has fully concluded and the Federal law enforcement officer leaves the scene.

(d) NOTIFICATION OF SUBJECT OF RECORDING.—A Federal law enforcement officer who is wearing a body camera shall notify any subject of the recording that he or she is being recorded by a body camera as close to the inception of the stop as is reasonably possible.

(e) REQUIREMENTS.—Notwithstanding subsection (c), the following shall apply to the use of a body camera:

(1) Prior to entering a private residence without a warrant or in non-exigent circumstances, a Federal law enforcement officer shall ask the occupant if the occupant wants the officer to discontinue use of the officer's body camera. If the occupant responds affirmatively, the Federal law enforcement officer shall immediately discontinue use of the body camera.

(2) When interacting with an apparent crime victim, a Federal law enforcement officer shall, as soon as practicable, ask the apparent crime

victim if the apparent crime victim wants the officer to discontinue use of the officer's body camera. If the apparent crime victim responds affirmatively, the Federal law enforcement officer shall immediately discontinue use of the body camera.

(3) When interacting with a person seeking to anonymously report a crime or assist in an ongoing law enforcement investigation, a Federal law enforcement officer shall, as soon as practicable, ask the person seeking to remain anonymous, if the person seeking to remain anonymous wants the officer to discontinue use of the officer's body camera. If the person seeking to remain anonymous responds affirmatively, the Federal law enforcement officer shall immediately discontinue use of the body camera.

(f) RECORDING OF OFFERS TO DISCONTINUE USE OF BODY CAMERA.—Each offer of a Federal law enforcement officer to discontinue the use of a body camera made pursuant to subsection (e), and the responses thereto, shall be recorded by the body camera prior to discontinuing use of the body camera.

(g) LIMITATIONS ON USE OF BODY CAMERA.—Body cameras shall not be used to gather intelligence information based on First Amendment protected speech, associations, or religion, or to record activity that is unrelated to a response to a call for service or a law enforcement or investigative stop between a law enforcement officer and a member of the public, and shall not be equipped with or employ any real time facial recognition technologies.

(h) EXCEPTIONS.—Federal law enforcement officers—

(1) shall not be required to use body cameras during investigative or enforcement stops with the public in the case that—

(A) recording would risk the safety of a confidential informant, citizen informant, or undercover officer;

(B) recording would pose a serious risk to national security; or

(C) the officer is a military police officer, a member of the United States Army Criminal Investigation Command, or a protective detail assigned to a Federal or foreign official while performing his or her duties; and

(2) shall not activate a body camera while on the grounds of any public, private or parochial elementary or secondary school, except when responding to an imminent threat to life or health.

(i) RETENTION OF FOOTAGE.—

(1) IN GENERAL.—Body camera video footage shall be retained by the law enforcement agency that employs the officer whose camera captured the footage, or an authorized agent thereof, for 6 months after the date it was recorded, after which time such footage shall be permanently deleted.

(2) RIGHT TO INSPECT.—During the 6-month retention period described in paragraph (1), the following persons shall have the right to inspect the body camera footage:

(A) Any person who is a subject of body camera video footage, and their designated legal counsel.

(B) A parent or legal guardian of a minor subject of body camera video footage, and their designated legal counsel.

(C) The spouse, next of kin, or legally authorized designee of a deceased subject of body camera video footage, and their designated legal counsel.

(D) A Federal law enforcement officer whose body camera recorded the video footage, and their designated legal counsel, subject to the limitations and restrictions in this part.

(E) The superior officer of a Federal law enforcement officer whose body camera recorded the video footage, subject to the limitations and restrictions in this part.

(F) Any defense counsel who claims, pursuant to a written affidavit, to have a reasonable basis for believing a video may contain evidence that exculpates a client.

(3) LIMITATION.—The right to inspect subject to subsection (j)(1) shall not include the right to possess a copy of the body camera video footage, unless the release of the body camera footage is otherwise authorized by this part or by another applicable law. When a body camera fails to capture some or all of the audio or video of an incident due to malfunction, displacement of camera, or any other cause, any audio or

video footage that is captured shall be treated the same as any other body camera audio or video footage under this part.

(j) ADDITIONAL RETENTION REQUIREMENTS.—Notwithstanding the retention and deletion requirements in subsection (i), the following shall apply to body camera video footage under this part:

(1) Body camera video footage shall be automatically retained for not less than 3 years if the video footage captures an interaction or event involving—

(A) any use of force; or

(B) an stop about which a complaint has been registered by a subject of the video footage.

(2) Body camera video footage shall be retained for not less than 3 years if a longer retention period is voluntarily requested by—

(A) the Federal law enforcement officer whose body camera recorded the video footage, if that officer reasonably asserts the video footage has evidentiary or exculpatory value in an ongoing investigation;

(B) any Federal law enforcement officer who is a subject of the video footage, if that officer reasonably asserts the video footage has evidentiary or exculpatory value;

(C) any superior officer of a Federal law enforcement officer whose body camera recorded the video footage or who is a subject of the video footage, if that superior officer reasonably asserts the video footage has evidentiary or exculpatory value;

(D) any Federal law enforcement officer, if the video footage is being retained solely and exclusively for police training purposes;

(E) any member of the public who is a subject of the video footage;

(F) any parent or legal guardian of a minor who is a subject of the video footage; or

(G) a deceased subject's spouse, next of kin, or legally authorized designee.

(k) PUBLIC REVIEW.—For purposes of subparagraphs (E), (F), and (G) of subsection (j)(2), any member of the public who is a subject of video footage, the parent or legal guardian of a minor who is a subject of the video footage, or a deceased subject's next of kin or legally authorized designee, shall be permitted to review the specific video footage in question in order to make a determination as to whether they will voluntarily request it be subjected to a minimum 3-year retention period.

(I) DISCLOSURE.—

(1) IN GENERAL.—Except as provided in paragraph (2), all video footage of an interaction or event captured by a body camera, if that interaction or event is identified with reasonable specificity and requested by a member of the public, shall be provided to the person or entity making the request in accordance with the procedures for requesting and providing government records set forth in the section 552a of title 5, United States Code.

(2) EXCEPTIONS.—The following categories of video footage shall not be released to the public in the absence of express written permission from the nonlaw enforcement subjects of the video footage:

(A) Video footage not subject to a minimum 3-year retention period pursuant to subsection (j).

(B) Video footage that is subject to a minimum 3-year retention period solely and exclusively pursuant to paragraph (1)(B) or (2) of subsection (j).

(3) PRIORITY OF REQUESTS.—Notwithstanding any time periods established for acknowledging and responding to records requests in section 552a of title 5, United States Code, responses to requests for video footage that is subject to a minimum 3-year retention period pursuant to subsection (j)(1)(A), where a subject of the video footage is recorded being killed, shot by a firearm, or grievously injured, shall be prioritized and, if approved, the requested video footage shall be provided as expeditiously as possible, but in no circumstances later than 5 days following receipt of the request.

(4) USE OF REDACTION TECHNOLOGY.—

(A) IN GENERAL.—Whenever doing so is necessary to protect personal privacy, the right to a fair trial, the identity of a confidential source or crime victim, or the life or physical safety of any person appearing in video footage, redaction technology may be used to obscure the face and other personally identifying characteristics of that person, including the tone of the person's voice, provided the redaction does not interfere with a viewer's ability to fully, completely, and accurately comprehend the events captured on the video footage.

(B) REQUIREMENTS.—The following requirements shall apply to redactions under subparagraph (A):

(i) When redaction is performed on video footage pursuant to this paragraph, an unedited, original version of the video footage shall be retained pursuant to the requirements of subsections (i) and (j).

(ii) Except pursuant to the rules for the redaction of video footage set forth in this subsection or where it is otherwise expressly authorized by this Act, no other editing or alteration of video footage, including a reduction of the video footage's resolution, shall be permitted.

(m) PROHIBITED WITHHOLDING OF FOOTAGE.—Body camera video footage may not be withheld from the public on the basis that it is an investigatory record or was compiled for law enforcement purposes where any person under investigation or whose conduct is under review is a police officer or other law enforcement employee and the video footage relates to that person's conduct in their official capacity.

(n) ADMISSIBILITY.—Any video footage retained beyond 6 months solely and exclusively pursuant to subsection (j)(2)(D) shall not be admissible as evidence in any criminal or civil legal or administrative proceeding.

(o) CONFIDENTIALITY.—No government agency or official, or law enforcement agency, officer, or official may publicly disclose, release, or share body camera video footage unless—

(1) doing so is expressly authorized pursuant to this part or another applicable law; or

(2) the video footage is subject to public release pursuant to subsection (l), and not exempted from public release pursuant to subsection (l)(1).

(p) LIMITATION ON FEDERAL LAW ENFORCEMENT OFFICER VIEWING OF BODY CAMERA FOOTAGE.—No Federal law enforcement officer shall review or receive an accounting of any body camera video footage that is subject to a minimum 3-year retention period pursuant to subsection (j)(1) prior to completing any required initial reports, statements, and interviews regarding the recorded event, unless doing so is necessary, while in the field, to address an immediate threat to life or safety.

(q) ADDITIONAL LIMITATIONS.—Video footage may not be—

(1) in the case of footage that is not subject to a minimum 3-year retention period, viewed by any superior officer of a Federal law enforcement officer whose body camera recorded the footage absent a specific allegation of misconduct; or

(2) divulged or used by any law enforcement agency for any commercial or other non-law enforcement purpose.

(r) THIRD PARTY MAINTENANCE OF FOOTAGE.—Where a law enforcement agency authorizes a third party to act as its agent in maintaining body camera footage, the agent shall not be permitted to independently access, view, or alter any video footage, except to delete videos as required by law or agency retention policies.

(s) ENFORCEMENT.—

(1) IN GENERAL.—If any Federal law enforcement officer, or any employee or agent of a Federal law enforcement agency fails to adhere to the recording or retention requirements contained in this part, intentionally interferes with a body camera's ability to accurately capture video footage, or otherwise manipulates the video footage captured by a body camera during or after its operation—

(A) appropriate disciplinary action shall be taken against the individual officer, employee, or agent;

(B) a rebuttable evidentiary presumption shall be adopted in favor of a criminal defendant who reasonably asserts that exculpatory evidence was destroyed or not captured; and

(C) a rebuttable evidentiary presumption shall be adopted on behalf of a civil plaintiff suing the Government, a Federal law enforcement agency, or a Federal law enforcement officer for damages based on misconduct who reasonably asserts that evidence supporting their claim was destroyed or not captured.

(2) PROOF COMPLIANCE WAS IMPOSSIBLE.—The disciplinary action requirement and rebuttable presumptions described in paragraph (1)

may be overcome by contrary evidence or proof of exigent circumstances that made compliance impossible.

(t) USE OF FORCE INVESTIGATIONS.—In the case that a Federal law enforcement officer equipped with a body camera is involved in, a witness to, or within viewable sight range of either the use of force by another law enforcement officer that results in a death, the use of force by another law enforcement officer, during which the discharge of a firearm results in an injury, or the conduct of another law enforcement officer that becomes the subject of a criminal investigation—

(1) the law enforcement agency that employs the law enforcement officer, or the agency or department conducting the related criminal investigation, as appropriate, shall promptly take possession of the body camera, and shall maintain such camera, and any data on such camera, in accordance with the applicable rules governing the preservation of evidence;

(2) a copy of the data on such body camera shall be made in accordance with prevailing forensic standards for data collection and reproduction; and

(3) such copied data shall be made available to the public in accordance with subsection (l).

(u) LIMITATION ON USE OF FOOTAGE AS EVIDENCE.—Any body camera video footage recorded by a Federal law enforcement officer that violates this part or any other applicable law may not be offered as evidence by any government entity, agency, department, prosecutorial office, or any other subdivision thereof in any criminal or civil action or proceeding against any member of the public.

(v) PUBLICATION OF AGENCY POLICIES.—Any Federal law enforcement agency policy or other guidance regarding body cameras, their use, or the video footage therefrom that is adopted by a Federal agency or department, shall be made publicly available on that agency's website.

(w) RULE OF CONSTRUCTION.—Nothing in this part shall be construed to preempt any laws governing the maintenance, production, and destruction of evidence in criminal investigations and prosecutions.

Sec. 373. Patrol Vehicles with in-Car Video Recording Cameras

(a) DEFINITIONS.—In this section:

(1) AUDIO RECORDING.—The term "audio recording" means the recorded conversation between a Federal law enforcement officer and a second party.

(2) EMERGENCY LIGHTS.—The term "emergency lights" means oscillating, rotating, or flashing lights on patrol vehicles.

(3) ENFORCEMENT OR INVESTIGATIVE STOP.—The term "enforcement or investigative stop" means an action by a Federal law enforcement officer in relation to enforcement and investigation duties, including traffic stops, pedestrian stops, abandoned vehicle contacts, motorist assists, commercial motor vehicle stops, roadside safety checks, requests for identification, or responses to requests for emergency assistance.

(4) IN-CAR VIDEO CAMERA.—The term "in-car video camera" means a video camera located in a patrol vehicle.

(5) IN-CAR VIDEO CAMERA RECORDING EQUIPMENT.—The term "in-car video camera recording equipment" means a video camera recording system located in a patrol vehicle consisting of a camera assembly, recording mechanism, and an in-car video recording medium.

(6) RECORDING.—The term "recording" means the process of capturing data or information stored on a recording medium as required under this section.

(7) RECORDING MEDIUM.—The term "recording medium" means any recording medium for the retention and playback of recorded audio and video including VHS, DVD, hard drive, solid state, digital, or flash memory technology.

(8) WIRELESS MICROPHONE.—The term "wireless microphone" means a device worn by a Federal law enforcement officer or any other equipment used to record conversations between the officer and a second party and transmitted to the recording equipment.

(b) REQUIREMENTS.—

(1) IN GENERAL.—Each Federal law enforcement agency shall install in-car video camera recording equipment in all patrol vehicles with

a recording medium capable of recording for a period of 10 hours or more and capable of making audio recordings with the assistance of a wireless microphone.

(2) RECORDING EQUIPMENT REQUIREMENTS.—In-car video camera recording equipment with a recording medium capable of recording for a period of 10 hours or more shall record activities—

(A) whenever a patrol vehicle is assigned to patrol duty;

(B) outside a patrol vehicle whenever—

(i) a Federal law enforcement officer assigned that patrol vehicle is conducting an enforcement or investigative stop;

(ii) patrol vehicle emergency lights are activated or would otherwise be activated if not for the need to conceal the presence of law enforcement; or

(iii) an officer reasonably believes recording may assist with prosecution, enhance safety, or for any other lawful purpose; and

(C) inside the vehicle when transporting an arrestee or when an officer reasonably believes recording may assist with prosecution, enhance safety, or for any other lawful purpose.

(3) REQUIREMENTS FOR RECORDING.—

(A) IN GENERAL.—A Federal law enforcement officer shall begin recording for an enforcement or investigative stop when the officer determines an enforcement stop is necessary and shall continue until the enforcement action has been completed and the subject of the enforcement or investigative stop or the officer has left the scene.

(B) ACTIVATION WITH LIGHTS.—A Federal law enforcement officer shall begin recording when patrol vehicle emergency lights are activated or when they would otherwise be activated if not for the need to conceal the presence of law enforcement, and shall continue until the reason for the activation ceases to exist, regardless of whether the emergency lights are no longer activated.

(C) PERMISSIBLE RECORDING.—A Federal law enforcement officer may begin recording if the officer reasonably believes recording may assist with prosecution, enhance safety, or for any other lawful purpose; and shall continue until the reason for recording ceases to exist.

(4) ENFORCEMENT OR INVESTIGATIVE STOPS.—A Federal law enforcement officer shall record any enforcement or investigative stop. Audio recording shall terminate upon release of the violator and prior to initiating a separate criminal investigation.

(c) RETENTION OF RECORDINGS.—Recordings made on in-car video camera recording medium shall be retained for a storage period of at least 90 days. Under no circumstances shall any recording made on in-car video camera recording medium be altered or erased prior to the expiration of the designated storage period. Upon completion of the storage period, the recording medium may be erased and reissued for operational use unless otherwise ordered or if designated for evidentiary or training purposes.

(d) ACCESSIBILITY OF RECORDINGS.—Audio or video recordings made pursuant to this section shall be available under the applicable provisions of section 552a of title 5, United States Code. Only recorded portions of the audio recording or video recording medium applicable to the request will be available for inspection or copying.

(e) MAINTENANCE REQUIRED.—The agency shall ensure proper care and maintenance of in-car video camera recording equipment and recording medium. An officer operating a patrol vehicle must immediately document and notify the appropriate person of any technical difficulties, failures, or problems with the in-car video camera recording equipment or recording medium. Upon receiving notice, every reasonable effort shall be made to correct and repair any of the in-car video camera recording equipment or recording medium and determine if it is in the public interest to permit the use of the patrol vehicle.

Sec. 374. Facial Recognition Technology

No camera or recording device authorized or required to be used under this part may be equipped with or employ real time facial recognition technology, and footage from such a camera or recording device may not be subjected to facial recognition technology.

Sec. 375. GAO Study

Not later than 1 year after the date of enactment of this Act, the Comptroller General of the United States shall conduct a study on Federal law enforcement officer training, vehicle pursuits, use of force, and interaction with citizens, and submit a report on such study to—

(1) the Committees on the Judiciary of the House of Representatives and of the Senate;

(2) the Committee on Oversight and Reform of the House of Representatives; and

(3) the Committee on Homeland Security and Governmental Affairs of the Senate.

Sec. 376. Regulations

Not later than 6 months after the date of the enactment of this Act, the Attorney General shall issue such final regulations as are necessary to carry out this part.

Sec. 377. Rule of Construction

Nothing in this part shall be construed to impose any requirement on a Federal law enforcement officer outside of the course of carrying out that officer's duty.

Part 2—Police Camera Act

Sec. 381. Short Title

This part may be cited as the "Police Creating Accountability by Making Effective Recording Available Act of 2020" or the "Police CAMERA Act of 2020."

Sec. 382. Law Enforcement Body-Worn Camera Requirements

(a) USE OF FUNDS REQUIREMENT.—Section 502(a) of title I of the Omnibus Crime Control and Safe Streets Act of 1968 (34 U.S.C. 10153(a)), as amended by section 334, is amended by adding at the end the following:

"(10) An assurance that, for each fiscal year covered by an application, the applicant will use not less than 5 percent of the total amount of the grant award for the fiscal year to develop policies and protocols in compliance with part OO."

(b) REQUIREMENTS.—Title I of the Omnibus Crime Control and Safe Streets Act of 1968 (34 U.S.C. 10101 et seq.) is amended by adding at the end the following:

"Part OO—Law Enforcement Body-Worn Cameras and Recorded Data

"Sec. 3051. Use of Grant Funds

"(a) IN GENERAL.—Grant amounts described in paragraph (10) of section 502(a) of this title—

"(1) shall be used—

"(A) to purchase or lease body-worn cameras for use by State, local, and tribal law enforcement officers (as defined in section 2503);

"(B) for expenses related to the implementation of a body-worn camera program in order to deter excessive force, improve accountability and transparency of use of force by law enforcement officers, assist in responding to complaints against law enforcement officers, and improve evidence collection; and

"(C) to implement policies or procedures to comply with the requirements described in subsection (b); and

"(2) may not be used for expenses related to facial recognition technology.

"(b) REQUIREMENTS.—A recipient of a grant under subpart 1 of part E of this title shall—

"(1) establish policies and procedures in accordance with the requirements described in subsection (c) before law enforcement officers use of body-worn cameras;

"(2) adopt recorded data collection and retention protocols as described in subsection (d) before law enforcement officers use of body-worn cameras;

"(3) make the policies and protocols described in paragraphs (1) and (2) available to the public; and

"(4) comply with the requirements for use of recorded data under subsection (f).

"(c) REQUIRED POLICIES AND PROCEDURES.—A recipient of a grant under subpart 1 of part E of this title shall—

"(1) develop with community input and publish for public view policies and protocols for—

"(A) the safe and effective use of body-worn cameras;

"(B) the secure storage, handling, and destruction of recorded data collected by body-worn cameras;

"(C) protecting the privacy rights of any individual who may be recorded by a body-worn camera;

"(D) the release of any recorded data collected by a body-worn camera in accordance with the open records laws, if any, of the State; and

"(E) making recorded data available to prosecutors, defense attorneys, and other officers of the court in accordance with subparagraph (E); and

"(2) conduct periodic evaluations of the security of the storage and handling of the body-worn camera data.

"(d) RECORDED DATA COLLECTION AND RETENTION PROTOCOL.—The recorded data collection and retention protocol described in this paragraph is a protocol that— "(1) requires—

"(A) a law enforcement officer who is wearing a body-worn camera to provide an explanation if an activity that is required to be recorded by the body-worn camera is not recorded;

"(B) a law enforcement officer who is wearing a body-worn camera to obtain consent to be recorded from a crime victim or witness before interviewing the victim or witness;

"(C) the collection of recorded data unrelated to a legitimate law enforcement purpose be minimized to the greatest extent practicable;

"(D) the system used to store recorded data collected by body-worn cameras to log all viewing, modification, or deletion of stored recorded data and to prevent, to the greatest extent practicable, the unauthorized access or disclosure of stored recorded data;

"(E) any law enforcement officer be prohibited from accessing the stored data without an authorized purpose; and

"(F) the law enforcement agency to collect and report statistical data on— "(i) incidences of use of force, disaggregated by race, ethnicity, gender, and age of the victim;

"(ii) the number of complaints filed against law enforcement officers; "(iii) the disposition of complaints filed against law enforcement officers;

"(iv) the number of times camera footage is used for evidence collection in investigations of crimes; and

"(v) any other additional statistical data that the Director determines should be collected and reported;

"(2) allows an individual to file a complaint with a law enforcement agency relating to the improper use of body-worn cameras; and

"(3) complies with any other requirements established by the Director.

"(e) REPORTING.—Statistical data required to be collected under subsection (d)(1)(D) shall be reported to the Director, who shall—

"(1) establish a standardized reporting system for statistical data collected under this program; and

"(2) establish a national database of statistical data recorded under this program.

"(f) USE OR TRANSFER OF RECORDED DATA.—

"(1) IN GENERAL.—Recorded data collected by an entity receiving a grant under a grant under subpart 1 of part E of this title from a body-worn camera shall be used only in internal and external investigations of misconduct by a law enforcement agency or officer, if there is reasonable suspicion that a recording contains evidence of a crime, or for limited training purposes. The Director shall establish rules to ensure that the recorded data is used only for the purposes described in this paragraph.

"(2) PROHIBITION ON TRANSFER.—Except as provided in paragraph (3), an entity receiving a grant under subpart 1 of part E of this title may not transfer any recorded data collected by the entity from a body-worn camera to another law enforcement or intelligence agency.

"(3) EXCEPTIONS.—

"(A) CRIMINAL INVESTIGATION.—An entity receiving a grant under subpart 1 of part E of this title may transfer recorded data collected by the entity from a body-worn camera to another law enforcement agency or intelligence agency for use in a criminal investigation if the requesting law enforcement or intelligence agency has reasonable suspicion that the requested data contains evidence relating to the crime being investigated.

"(B) CIVIL RIGHTS CLAIMS.—An entity receiving a grant under subpart 1 of part E of this title may transfer recorded data collected by the law enforcement agency from a body-worn camera to another law enforcement agency for use in an investigation of the violation of any right, privilege, or immunity secured or protected by the Constitution or laws of the United States.

"(g) AUDIT AND ASSESSMENT.—

"(1) IN GENERAL.—Not later than 2 years after the date of enactment of this part, the Director of the Office of Audit, Assessment, and Management shall perform an assessment of the use of funds under this section and the policies and protocols of the grantees.

"(2) REPORTS.—Not later than September 1 of each year, beginning 2 years after the date of enactment of this part, each recipient of a grant under subpart 1 of part E of this title shall submit to the Director of the Office of Audit, Assessment, and Management a report that—

"(A) describes the progress of the body-worn camera program; and

"(B) contains recommendations on ways in which the Federal Government, States, and units of local government can further support the implementation of the program.

"(3) REVIEW.—The Director of the Office of Audit, Assessment, and Management shall evaluate the policies and protocols of the grantees and take such steps as the Director of the Office of Audit, Assessment, and Management determines necessary to ensure compliance with the program.

"Sec. 3052. Body-Worn Camera Training Toolkit

"(a) IN GENERAL.—The Director shall establish and maintain a body-worn camera training toolkit for law enforcement agencies, academia, and other relevant entities to provide training and technical assistance, including best practices for implementation, model policies and procedures, and research materials.

"(b) MECHANISM.—In establishing the toolkit required to under subsection (a), the Director may consolidate research, practices, templates, and tools that been developed by expert and law enforcement agencies across the country.

"Sec. 3053. Study

"(a) IN GENERAL.—Not later than 2 years after the date of enactment of the Police CAMERA Act of 2020, the Director shall conduct a study on—

"(1) the efficacy of body-worn cameras in deterring excessive force by law enforcement officers;

"(2) the impact of body-worn cameras on the accountability and transparency of the use of force by law enforcement officers;

"(3) the impact of body-worn cameras on responses to and adjudications of complaints of excessive force;

"(4) the effect of the use of body-worn cameras on the safety of law enforcement officers on patrol;

"(5) the effect of the use of body-worn cameras on public safety;

"(6) the impact of body-worn cameras on evidence collection for criminal investigations;

"(7) issues relating to the secure storage and handling of recorded data from the body-worn cameras;

"(8) issues relating to the privacy of individuals and officers recorded on body-worn cameras;

"(9) issues relating to the constitutional rights of individuals on whom facial recognition technology is used;

"(10) issues relating to limitations on the use of facial recognition technology;

"(11) issues relating to the public's access to body-worn camera footage;

"(12) the need for proper training of law enforcement officers that use body-worn cameras;

"(13) best practices in the development of protocols for the safe and effective use of body-worn cameras;

"(14) a review of law enforcement agencies that found body-worn cameras to be unhelpful in the operations of the agencies; and

"(15) any other factors that the Director determines are relevant in evaluating the efficacy of body-worn cameras.

"(b) REPORT.—Not later than 180 days after the date on which the study required under subsection (a) is completed, the Director shall submit to Congress a report on the study, which shall include any policy recommendations that the Director considers appropriate."

TITLE IV—JUSTICE FOR VICTIMS OF LYNCHING ACT

Sec. 401. Short Title

This title may be cited as the "Emmett Till Anti-Lynching Act."

Sec. 402. Findings

Congress finds the following:

(1) The crime of lynching succeeded slavery as the ultimate expression of racism in the United States following Reconstruction.

(2) Lynching was a widely acknowledged practice in the United States until the middle of the 20th century.

(3) Lynching was a crime that occurred throughout the United States, with documented incidents in all but 4 States.

(4) At least 4,742 people, predominantly African Americans, were reported lynched in the United States between 1882 and 1968.

(5) Ninety-nine percent of all perpetrators of lynching escaped from punishment by State or local officials.

(6) Lynching prompted African Americans to form the National Association for the Advancement of Colored People (referred to in this section as the "NAACP") and prompted members of B'nai B'rith to found the Anti-Defamation League.

(7) Mr. Walter White, as a member of the NAACP and later as the executive secretary of the NAACP from 1931 to 1955, meticulously investigated lynchings in the United States and worked tirelessly to end segregation and racialized terror.

(8) Nearly 200 anti-lynching bills were introduced in Congress during the first half of the 20th century.

(9) Between 1890 and 1952, 7 Presidents petitioned Congress to end lynching.

(10) Between 1920 and 1940, the House of Representatives passed 3 strong anti-lynching measures.

(11) Protection against lynching was the minimum and most basic of Federal responsibilities, and the Senate considered but failed to enact anti-lynching legislation despite repeated requests by civil rights groups, Presidents, and the House of Representatives to do so.

(12) The publication of "Without Sanctuary: Lynching Photography in America" helped bring greater awareness and proper recognition of the victims of lynching.

(13) Only by coming to terms with history can the United States effectively champion human rights abroad.

(14) An apology offered in the spirit of true repentance moves the United States toward reconciliation and may become central to a new understanding, on which improved racial relations can be forged.

(15) Having concluded that a reckoning with our own history is the only way the country can effectively champion human rights abroad, 90 Members of the United States Senate agreed to Senate Resolution 39, 109th Congress, on June 13, 2005, to apologize to the victims of lynching and the descendants of those victims for the failure of the Senate to enact anti-lynching legislation.

(16) The National Memorial for Peace and Justice, which opened to the public in Montgomery, Alabama, on April 26, 2018, is the Nation's

first memorial dedicated to the legacy of enslaved Black people, people terrorized by lynching, African Americans humiliated by racial segregation and Jim Crow, and people of color burdened with contemporary presumptions of guilt and police violence.

(17) Notwithstanding the Senate's apology and the heightened awareness and education about the Nation's legacy with lynching, it is wholly necessary and appropriate for the Congress to enact legislation, after 100 years of unsuccessful legislative efforts, finally to make lynching a Federal crime.

(18) Further, it is the sense of Congress that criminal action by a group increases the likelihood that the criminal object of that group will be successfully attained and decreases the probability that the individuals involved will depart from their path of criminality. Therefore, it is appropriate to specify criminal penalties for the crime of lynching, or any attempt or conspiracy to commit lynching.

(19) The United States Senate agreed to unanimously Senate Resolution 118, 115th Congress, on April 5, 2017, "[c]ondemning hate crime and any other form of racism, religious or ethnic bias, discrimination, incitement to violence, or animus targeting a minority in the United States" and taking notice specifically of Federal Bureau of Investigation statistics demonstrating that "among single-bias hate crime incidents in the United States, 59.2 percent of victims were targeted due to racial, ethnic, or ancestral bias, and among those victims, 52.2 percent were victims of crimes motivated by the offenders' anti-Black or anti-African American bias."

(20) On September 14, 2017, President Donald J. Trump signed into law Senate Joint Resolution 49 (Public Law 115–58; 131 Stat. 1149), wherein Congress "condemn[ed] the racist violence and domestic terrorist attack that took place between August 11 and August 12, 2017, in Charlottesville, Virginia" and "urg[ed] the President and his administration to speak out against hate groups that espouse racism, extremism, xenophobia, anti-Semitism, and White supremacy; and use all resources available to the President and the President's Cabinet to address the growing prevalence of those hate groups in the United States."

(21) Senate Joint Resolution 49 (Public Law 115–58; 131 Stat. 1149) specifically took notice of “hundreds of torch-bearing White nationalists, White supremacists, Klansmen, and neo-Nazis [who] chanted racist, anti-Semitic, and anti-immigrant slogans and violently engaged with counter-demonstrators on and around the grounds of the University of Virginia in Charlottesville” and that these groups “reportedly are organizing similar events in other cities in the United States and communities everywhere are concerned about the growing and open display of hate and violence being perpetrated by those groups.”

(22) Lynching was a pernicious and pervasive tool that was used to interfere with multiple aspects of life—including the exercise of federally protected rights, as enumerated in section 245 of title 18, United States Code, housing rights, as enumerated in section 901 of the Civil Rights Act of 1968 (42 U.S.C. 3631), and the free exercise of religion, as enumerated in section 247 of title 18, United States Code. Interference with these rights was often effectuated by multiple offenders and groups, rather than isolated individuals. Therefore, prohibiting conspiracies to violate each of these rights recognizes the history of lynching in the United States and serves to prohibit its use in the future.

Sec. 403. Lynching

(a) OFFENSE.—Chapter 13 of title 18, United States Code, is amended by adding at the end the following:

“§ 250. Lynching

“Whoever conspires with another person to violate section 245, 247, or 249 of this title or section 901 of the Civil Rights Act of 1968 (42 U.S.C. 3631) shall be punished in the same manner as a completed violation of such section, except that if the maximum term of imprisonment for such completed violation is less than 10 years, the person may be imprisoned for not more than 10 years.”

(b) TABLE OF SECTIONS AMENDMENT.—The table of sections for chapter 13 of title 18, United States Code, is amended by inserting after the item relating to section 249 the following:

"250. Lynching."

Title V—Miscellaneous Provisions

Sec. 501. Severability

If any provision of this Act, or the application of such a provision to any person or circumstance, is held to be unconstitutional, the remainder of this Act and the application of the remaining provisions of this Act to any person or circumstance shall not be affected thereby.

Sec. 502. Savings Clause

Nothing in this Act shall be construed—

(1) to limit legal or administrative remedies under section 1979 of the Revised Statutes of the United States (42 U.S.C. 1983), section 210401 of the Violent Crime Control and Law Enforcement Act of 1994 (34 U.S.C. 12601), title I of the Omnibus Crime Control and Safe Streets Act of 1968 (34 U.S.C. 10101 et seq.), or title VI of the Civil Rights Act of 1964 (42 U.S.C. 2000d et seq.);

(2) to affect any Federal, State, or Tribal law that applies to an Indian Tribe because of the political status of the Tribe; or

(3) to waive the sovereign immunity of an Indian Tribe without the consent of the Tribe.

PURPOSE AND SUMMARY

On June 10, 2020, George Floyd's brother, Philonise, told the Committee of the pain he felt watching the video of his brother being killed by a Minneapolis police officer. He gave voice to the pain that much of the Nation has felt over the last few weeks. He also spoke to the anger of knowing that George Floyd was only the latest in a much-too-long list of victims of police brutality—disproportionately people of color. He spoke to the frustration that, time and again, in the face of overwhelming evidence that dramatic reform is urgently needed, Congress has done very little. Mr. Floyd charged Congress with making sure that his brother's death would not be in vain, and he pleaded with Members of the Committee to turn this pain and anger into meaningful change. His words echoed the voices of millions of Americans who have taken to the streets in the last few weeks to demand justice—and to demand action. In advancing H.R. 7120, the "George Floyd Justice in Policing Act of 2020," the most significant policing reform legislation in our Nation's history, the Committee now answers their call.

In response to the American people's demand that Congress pass meaningful policing reform legislation, H.R. 7120 contains numerous policing reform measures that, if enacted, will enhance public safety, ensure police accountability, and repair frayed police-com munity relations. Among other things, the bill includes provisions that:

- revise the *mens rea* requirement in 18 U.S.C. § 242 so that a defendant can be held criminally liable for acting knowingly or recklessly to deprive a person of his or her federal rights;
- eliminate qualified immunity for federal, state, and local law enforcement officers in civil actions for violations of federal rights;
- enhance the Department of Justice's authority to pursue investigations of law enforcement officers and agencies for engaging in a "pattern or practice" of violations of federal rights by granting it subpoena authority and further strengthen the statute by

creating a cause of action for state attorneys general to pursue such "pattern or practice" actions;

- incentivize independent investigations of police uses of deadly force;
- create a national law enforcement misconduct registry;
- establish use of force data reporting requirements;
- prohibit racial and religious profiling by law enforcement officers and mandate training on racial, religious, and discriminatory profiling;
- ban no-knock warrants in drug cases;
- ban the use of chokeholds and carotid holds;
- limit the transfer of military-grade equipment to state and local law enforcement;
- require law enforcement officers to wear body cameras, prohibit the use of facial recognition technology by federal officers and the use of federal funds by states for such technology;
- establish a use-of-force standard for federal law enforcement officers and condition grants for state and local law enforcement agencies on following the same standards, and;
- create public safety innovation grants to foster non-policing innovations that enhance public safety.

In contrast to President Donald Trump's recent "Safe Policing for Safe Communities"' Executive Order, and the Justice Act introduced by Senator Tim Scott, the George Floyd Justice in Policing Act of 2020 offers real and transformational change, rather than a validation of an unacceptable status quo. As we have repeatedly stated, we remain ready, willing, and able to work with our Republican colleagues or the Administration as this bill moves forward in the legislative process. Unfortunately, at present, neither of those measures offers us a path to bipartisan compromise that serve the interests of the American people.[1]

---

[1] As Chairman Nadler explained during the markup of H.R. 7120, the bill was introduced on June 8, 2020 and, at the time, it was explained to the Minority that the Majority had initiated the

An array of leading civil rights organizations, 15 big-city mayors,[2] members of the business community, and many others, has indicated support for H.R. 7120, including the Leadership Conference on Civil and Human Rights, National Association for the Advancement of Colored People (NAACP), NAACP Legal Defense and Educational Fund, the Lawyers' Committee for Civil Rights Under Law, National Action Network, National Urban League, Congressional Asian Pacific American Caucus, the Congressional Progressive Caucus, the Center for American Progress, Demand Progress, Everytown for Gun Safety, New Democrat Coalition, and the United Negro College Fund.[3]

---

process by developing comprehensive legislation with House and Senate colleagues because of the importance of moving quickly given the urgency of the moment the Nation was in. Since that time, the Minority was told that if it wished to help develop the legislation, it needed to make clear to the Majority what changes it wanted and whether those changes would lead to the Minority's support for the bill. Chair Bass has reached out to the Minority Leader and Senator Tim Scott and Majority staff reached out to the Minority in the ten days prior to the markup. Moreover, the Minority was permitted to invite three witnesses for the Committee's hearing on this issue on June 10, 2020.

Rather than engage constructively with the Majority, the Minority did not share a single amendment with the Majority before the markup or otherwise accept the Majority's offers to discuss the bill's substance. During the markup, Members of the Minority refused the Majority's offer to review and work with them on specific amendments that the Majority indicated it could support if there was the opportunity to review and discuss before the bill's consideration on the House floor.

[2] Sylvester Turner (Houston, TX); Eric Garcetti (Los Angeles, CA); Jacob Frey (Minneapolis, MN); Jenny A. Durkan (Seattle, WA); Ron Nirenberg (San Antonio, TX); London Breed (San Francisco, CA); Michael B. Hancock (Denver, CO); Steve Adler (Austin, TX); Libby Schaff (Oakland, CA); Ted Wheeler (Portland, OR); Victoria Woodards (Tacoma, WA); Satya Rhodes-Conway (Madison, WI); Regina Romero (Tucson, AZ); John Cooper (Nashville, TN); and Rusty Bailey (Riverside, CA).

[3] The other organizations expressing support for H.R. 7120 are Adobe, American Association for Justice, American Association of Independent Music, Artists Rights Alliance, BBVA USA, Black Millennial Convention, Black Music Action Coalition, Fund for Leadership, Equity, Access and Diversity, Future of Music Coalition, International Black Women's Public Policy Institute, ITI, Little Listeners of the Carolinas, Music Artists' Coalition, National Advocacy Center of the Sisters of the Good Shepherd, National African American Clergy Network, National Alliance for Public Charter Schools, National Association of Blacks in Criminal Justice, National Organization of Black County Officials, Inc., National Association of Black County Officials, Recording Industry Association of America, Save a Girl, Save a World, Songwriters of North America, The National Coalition on Black Civic Participation, Third Way, Tougaloo College, Voice of the Experienced, and the YWCA.

BACKGROUND AND NEED FOR THE LEGISLATION

Background

The Link between Race and Concerns About Use of Excessive Force by Police

In the face of assertions that the Committee is moving too quickly to advance H.R. 7120, it is well worth remembering the fact that American society has already known for decades of the strong connection between race and the use of excessive, often lethal force by police and yet has failed to act sufficiently in response despite official recommendations. Indeed, in a hearing before the Committee just last week, many witnesses—including those from the law enforcement community—reminded the Committee in their testimony that law enforcement in the United States has a long, ugly history of institutional racism, discrimination, and brutality against African Americans and other marginalized groups, a history that continues to shape policing in America today.[4]

---

[4] *See Policing Practices and Law Enforcement Accountability: Hearing Before the H. Comm. on the Judiciary*, 116th Cong. (2020) [hereinafter "Policing Practices Hearing"] (written testimony of Art Acevedo, Chief of the Houston Police Department and President, Major City Chiefs Association, at 3) [hereinafter "Acevedo Testimony"] (stating "law enforcement's past contains institutional racism, injustices, and brutality" and that "we must recognize that policing has had a disparate impact on disenfranchised communities, especially communities of color and poor communities), (written testimony of Paul Butler, Albert Brick Professor in Law, Georgetown University Law Center, at 2) [hereinafter "Butler Testimony"] ("there has never, not for one minute in American history, been peace between black people and the police"), (written testimony of Ronald L. Davis, Chair, Legislative Committee, National Organization of Black Law Enforcement Executives, at 4) [hereinafter "Davis Testimony"] (stating "most of the systems that determine why we police, how we police, and where we police were constructed in the 1940's, '50s, and '60s to enforce Jim Crow and other discriminatory laws" and that policing systems "still suffer from structural racism and institutional deficiencies . . . [and] even good cops have bad outcomes, and bad and racist cops operate with impunity), (written testimony of Phillip Atiba Goff, Co-Founder and Chief Executive Officer, Center for Policing Equity, at 2, 3) [hereinafter "Goff Testimony"] (noting the "festering wounds of racial violence woven into our history of policing" and stating that what limited data is available shows that "there is no doubt that Black, Native, and Latinx people have more contact with law enforcement than do White people" and that "neither crime nor poverty are sufficient to explain racial disparities in use of force, and in some limited geographic areas, it is not sufficient to explain racial disparities in [police] stops").

More than a half-century ago, in its report on the causes of racial unrest in American cities during the 1960's, the National Advisory Commission on Civil Disorders, also known as the Kerner Commission, wrote (in the language of the time) in assessing the causes of the unrest:

The police are not merely a "spark" factor. To some Negroes police have come to symbolize white power, white racism and white repression. And the fact is that many police do reflect and express these white attitudes. The atmosphere of hostility and cynicism is reinforced by a widespread belief among Negroes in the existence of police brutality and in a "double standard" of justice and protection—one for Negroes and one for whites.

The abrasive relationship between the police and the minority communities has been a major—and explosive—source of grievance, tension and disorder. The blame must be shared by the total society.

The police are faced with demands for increased protection and service in the ghetto. Yet the aggressive patrol practices thought necessary to meet these demands themselves create tension and hostility.

The resulting grievances have been further aggravated by the lack of effective mechanisms for handling complaints against the police. Special programs for bettering police-community relations have been instituted, but these alone are not enough. Police administrators, with the guidance of public officials, and the support of the entire community, must take vigorous action to improve law enforcement and to decrease the potential for disorder.[5]

In 1947, a generation before the Kerner Commission issued its report, a similar commission appointed by President Harry Truman to study the state of civil rights in the United States issued similar findings about the link between societal racism against African Americans and police brutality in its report. The report noted that "There is evidence of lawless police action against whites and Negroes alike, but the dominant pattern is that of race prejudice . . . Negroes have been shot, supposedly in self-

---

[5] Report of the Nat'l Advisory Comm'n on Civil Disorders, at 10, 14–15 (1968) [hereinafter "Kerner Commission Report"], available at http://www.eisenhowerfoundation.org/docs/kerner.pdf.

defense, under circumstances indicating, at best, unsatisfactory police work in the handling of criminals, and, at worst, a callous willingness to kill."[6] Sadly, continued killings of unarmed African Americans by police in recent years appear to have highlighted how little progress has been made to address the problem of police violence against racial minorities, and, more generally, of tensions between police and minority communities, despite decades of official findings identifying the problem. The United States is currently in the sixth year of its most recent national conversation around policing practices that was sparked by several high-profile, fatal applications of force against unarmed African Americans, a national discourse that has been given renewed momentum by a series of such killings in recent months.

On December 18, 2014, then-President Barack Obama issued Executive Order 13684 authorizing a task force to study law enforcement practices. The mission of the President's Task Force on 21st Century Policing (the President's Task Force) was to examine ways of fostering strong, collaborative relationships between local law enforcement and the communities they protect and to make recommendations so that policing practices can promote effective crime reduction while building public trust.[7] The President's Task Force conducted seven listening sessions in three cities, solicited oral and written testimony from over 250 different witnesses and experts, and issued its final report in May 2015 (The President's Task Force Report). In the years that followed, a growing, bipartisan consensus emerged on several policing and criminal justice reforms.

In 2018, the United States Commission on Civil Rights (USCCR) examined the use of force within the context of modern policing practices

---

[6] *To Secure These Rights: The Report of the President's Commission on Civil Rights*, at 26 (1947) [hereinafter "1947 Report"], available at https://www.trumanlibrary.gov/library/to-secure-these-rights; *see also* Adam Harris, *Racism Won't Be Solved By Yet Another Blue-Ribbon Commission*, The Atlantic, June 4, 2020, available at https://www.theatlantic.com/politics/archive/2020/06/george-floyd-racism-police-brutality/612565/ (quoting the 1947 commission report).

[7] OFF. OF CMTY. ORIENTED POLICING SERV., DEP'T OF JUST., THE PRESIDENT'S TASK FORCE ON 21ST CENTURY POLICING, FINAL REPORT 5 (2015) [hereinafter "The President's Task Force"], available at https://cops.usdoj.gov/pdf/taskforce/taskforce/finalreport.pdf.

in light of the series of fatal encounters between unarmed African Americans and police beginning in 2014. It found that:

- Accurate and comprehensive data regarding police uses of force is generally not available to police departments or the American public.
- No comprehensive national database exists that captures rates of police use of force.
- The lack of data on use of force is exacerbated by the absence of mandatory federal reporting and standardized reporting guidelines.
- The best available evidence reflects high rates of use of force nationally, and increased likelihood of police use of force against people of color, people with disabilities, LGBTQ people, people with mental health concerns, people with low incomes, and those at the intersections of those groups.
- Law enforcement officers lack training on critical areas such as de-escalation techniques, anti-bias mechanisms, and strategies for encounters with individuals with physical and mental disabilities.
- Law enforcement agencies lack: (a) transparency about policies and practices in place governing use of force and (b) accountability for noncompliance with any existing use of force policies and procedures.
- Communities perceive that police use of force is unchecked and unlawful based on: (a) repeated and highly publicized fatal applications of force against unarmed civilians, (b) the lack of accurate data on use of force, and (c) the lack of transparency and accountability regarding policies and practices governing use of force.[8]

All the foregoing entities made a series of recommendations for policymakers, many of which are, in some form, reflected in H.R. 7120.

[8] U.S. COMM'N ON CIV. RTS., POLICE USE OF FORCE: AN EXAMINATION OF MODERN POLICING PRACTICES 4 (2018) [hereinafter "USCCR Report"], available at https://www.usccr.gov/pubs/2018/ 11-15-Police-Force.pdf.

For example, among The President's Task Force's recommendations were: (1) clear use of force policies that include deescalation training; (2) policies to prohibit racial profiling; (3) independent investigations of officer-involved shootings, uses of force, and in-custody deaths; (4) collection and public availability of demographic data regarding police interactions; and (5) the incentivization of the establishment of public safety innovation programs to help improve police relations with minority communities.[9] The 2018 USCCR report also outlined a number of recommendations, including: (1) a return by the Department of Justice (DOJ) to vigorous pursuit of cases against local police departments for engaging in a "pattern or practice" of unconstitutional conduct and use consent decrees in such cases as necessary; (2) the creation of federal guidance supporting development of effective training, policies, and internal accountability measures that promote expanded strategies and tactics that safeguard the lives of officers and citizens; (3) training for officers regarding de-escalation techniques and alternatives to use of force; (4) independent investigation and prosecution of police use-of-force cases; and (5) aggregation and public dissemination of data by police departments regarding use of force, disaggregated by race, gender, and disability status.[10] Going further back, the Kerner Commission had recommended, among other things, that cities "review police operations in the ghetto to ensure proper conduct by police officers, and eliminate abrasive practices"; "establish fair and effective mechanisms for the redress of grievances against the police"; "develop and adopt policy guidelines to assist officers in making critical decisions in areas where police conduct can create tension"; "develop and use innovative programs to ensure widespread community support for law enforcement;" and "recruit more Negroes into the regular police force."[11] The 1947 Truman-appointed civil rights commission's report recommended that "police training programs . . . should be instituted. They should be oriented so as to indoctrinate officers with an awareness of civil rights problems. Proper treatment by the police

---

[9] The President's Task Force at 16.
[10] USCCR Report at 4–5.
[11] Kerner Commission Report at 15.

of those who are arrested and incarcerated in local jails should be stressed."[12]

While there has been some progress, police-community relations remain fraught, particularly in light of more recent incidents of police killings of unarmed African Americans. On October 28, 2019, President Donald Trump signed Executive Order 13896, establishing a Commission on Law Enforcement and the Administration of Justice, authorizing Attorney General William Barr to select a commission of experts to study crime, its causal factors, and current law enforcement practices.[13] President Trump authorized the Commission to study criminal justice issues, such as refusals by state and local prosecutors to enforce laws or prosecute categories of crimes, as well as a perceived disrespect for law enforcement. In remarks about the Commission, Attorney General Barr pointedly lamented "a disturbing pattern of cynicism and disrespect shown toward law enforcement."[14]

Since 2014, the annual rate of fatal police-involved shootings nationwide has remained steady—averaging nearly 1000 per year.[15] Meanwhile, in 2020, four more high profile killings of unarmed African Americans under color of law have reignited the public outrage that had been steadily building for years. Protests in Minneapolis, MN and in cities nationwide morphed for a time into physical expressions of rage and despair, and many peaceful protests against police abuses continue nationwide.

---

[12] 1947 Report at 157.

[13] The Barr Commission has been accused of lacking transparency. The NAACP Legal Defense and Educational Fund filed suit to challenge the legality of the Commission and alleged that the Commission has failed to comply with the requirements of the Federal Advisory Committee Act. *See* NAACP Legal Defense and Educational Fund, Inc., *LDF Files Lawsuit Challenging the President's Law Enforcement Commission, Arguing that it Fails to Comply with Federal Advisory Committee Act Requirements*, April 30, 2020, available at https://www.naacpldf.org/wp-content/ uploads/FACA-Suit-Statement-FINAL.pdf.

[14] Dep't of Justice, *Attorney General William P. Barr Delivers Remarks at the Presidential Commission on Law Enforcement and the Administration of Justice Opening Ceremony*, Jan. 22, 2020, available at https://www.justice.gov/opa/speech/attorney-general-william-p-barr-delivers-remarks-presidential-commission-law-enforcement.

[15] Julie Tate, Jennifer Jenkins & Steven Rich, *Fatal Force*, WASH. POST, May 26, 2020, available at https://www.washingtonpost.com/graphics/investigations/police-shootings-database/.

Killings since 2014 of African-Americans in Police Custody and Movement for Police Accountability and Transparency

A series of deaths of unarmed African-American men while in police custody accompanied by public unrest in Ferguson, MO and Baltimore, MD, sparked a movement in the United States to demand transparency and accountability when police use force against civilians:

- July 17, 2014: Eric Garner was choked to death by police in New York, NY.
- August 9, 2014: Michael Brown was shot to death by police in Ferguson, MO.
- August 9–25, 2014: Residents of Ferguson, MO publicly protested the shooting of Michael Brown and the protests escalated into a series of riots.
- October 20, 2014: LaQuan McDonald was shot to death by police in Chicago, IL.
- November 22, 2014: Tamir Rice, aged 12, was shot to death by police in Cleveland, OH.
- April 5, 2015, Walter Scott was shot to death by police in North Charleston, SC.
- April 18, 2015 Freddie Gray died of a spinal cord injury suffered while he was in police custody in Baltimore, MD.
- April 18–April 29, 2015: Baltimore residents began nonviolent protests; however the protests escalated into violence.
- July 5, 2016: Alton Sterling was shot by Baton Rouge, LA, police and, while no officer was criminally charged, one officer was fired.
- July 7, 2016: Philando Castile was shot in his car by a police officer outside St. Paul, MN; the officer involved was tried and acquitted of second-degree manslaughter.
- September 16, 2016: Terence Crutcher was shot by police outside his car in Tulsa, OK; the officer involved was tried and acquitted of manslaughter.

- April 29, 2017: Jordan Edwards was shot by police while sitting in the passenger seat of a car in Balch Springs, TX; the officer involved was convicted of murder.

The public outrage over these incidents, most of which were captured on video, once again catapulted decades of mistrust between police and marginalized communities into the national political discourse. Initially inspired by the Black Lives Matter movement, which was formed in response to the Stand Your Ground laws utilized to justify the 2012 murders of two unarmed African-American teenagers, Trayvon Martin and Jordan Davis, the public outcry over the extrajudicial killings of unarmed civilians continued to grow as protests by professional athletes in the National Football League and the National Basketball Association, as well as comments from President Obama supplemented grassroots calls for reform.

Amid the ongoing debate around policing practices since the protests stemming from the killings of Michael Brown, Eric Garner, Freddie Gray, and others, violent confrontations between police and civilians continued. On March 18, 2018, Sacramento Police fired 20 shots killing Stephon Clark, a 22-year-old African American who had fled into his own backyard, mistaking the cellphone he was holding for a gun. The shooting was captured on video. The officers were not charged with any criminal offenses, and a federal civil rights investigation remains ongoing.

On June 19, 2018, unarmed African American teenager Antwon Rose II, 17, was shot three times in the back, face, and elbow while fleeing from East Pittsburgh Police Officer Michael Rosefeld after a traffic stop.[16] The shooting was captured on video. On March 22, 2019, Rosefeld was acquitted of criminal homicide for Rose's death.[17]

On November 26, 2019, a Baltimore County police officer fatally shot Eric Sopp during a traffic stop after Sopp refused to obey their commands

---

[16] Adeel Hassan, *Antwon Rose Shooting: White Police Officer Acquitted in Death of Black Teenager*, N.Y. TIMES, Mar. 22, 2019, available at https://www.nytimes.com/2019/03/22/us/antwon-rose-shooting.html.

[17] *Id.*

to remain inside his vehicle. Baltimore County prosecutors determined that the shooting was justified because Sopp's erratic behavior placed the officer in a highly dangerous situation.[18] On January 27, 2020, Prince George's County Police Corporal Michael Owen fired seven shots, killing William Green while Green was handcuffed and seated in his car. Owen was charged with voluntary and involuntary manslaughter, first-degree assault and use of a firearm in the commission of a crime of violence and awaits trial.[19]

On February 23, 2020, Travis and Gregory McMichael killed Ahmaud Arbery while he was jogging, purportedly because they suspected him of committing a burglary. The killing of Mr. Arbery and its subsequent investigation are reminiscent of early 20th century lynchings in the Jim Crow South. Gregory McMichael was a former police officer and investigator with the Glynn County Police Department and Brunswick Judicial Circuit, the entities responsible for investigating the killing. The killing was captured on video, yet law enforcement refused to arrest the McMichaels for 74 days—until the video was leaked to the public on May 7, 2020. Gregory McMichael's status as a former law enforcement officer, in addition to his relationship with prosecutors responsible for investigating Mr. Arbery's killing, raise questions as to whether some combination of racial bias, conflicts of interest, or gross negligence led to Mr. Arbery's death and compromised the integrity of the subsequent investigation.

In the early morning hours of March 13, 2020, Breonna Taylor was shot eight times and killed by Louisville Metro Police Department (LMPD) Criminal Interdiction Division officers executing a "no-knock" search warrant on her apartment during the early morning hours of March 13, 2020. Apparently, the subject of the warrant was already in police custody prior to LMPD officers arriving at Ms. Taylor's apartment. Upon arrival,

---

[18] Tom Jackman, *Baltimore County police officer cleared in killing of unarmed, suicidal man*, WASH. POST, Mar. 2, 2020, available at https://www.washingtonpost.com/crime-law/2020/03/02/ baltimore-county-police-officer-cleared-killing-unarmed-suicidal-man/.

[19] Neil Vigdor, Mariel Padilla and Sandra E. Garcia, *Police Officer Charged With Murder in Killing of Handcuffed Suspect in Maryland*, N.Y. TIMES, Jan. 28, 2020, available at https:// www.nytimes.com/2020/01/28/us/prince-georges-maryland-police-shooting.html.

the officers, who were in plain clothes, did not knock and did not identify themselves as police.[20] Ms. Taylor's boyfriend, Kenneth Walker, a licensed gun owner, used his firearm to defend the home against what he believed to be an attempted burglary.[21] The officers fired a hail of bullets into the apartment, over twenty rounds, striking Ms. Taylor eight times and killing her.[22] The officers were not wearing body cameras.[23]

On May 25, 2020, George Floyd was killed when Minneapolis Police Department (MPD) officers applied an illegal chokehold to his neck while he was handcuffed and pinned to the ground. The killing, captured on video, is the latest in a string of high profile and outrageous extrajudicial killings of African Americans suspected of committing minor criminal violations and is eerily reminiscent of the NYPD killing of Eric Garner. The nine-minute video appears to show an officer kneeling on Mr. Floyd's neck as he begs for help, stating repeatedly that he could not breathe.[24]

MPD officers claim that Mr. Floyd was resisting their attempts to arrest him for forgery—a non-violent offense.[25] Newly released video appears to contradict that claim.[26] As the officer applied the force of his full body weight on top of Mr. Floyd with a knee to the neck, bystanders called for officers to reduce the amount of force being applied.[27] "He's not even resisting arrest right now, bro," one bystander tells the officer and his partner.[28] One bystander observed that the officer was cutting off Mr. Floyd's air supply: "You're . . . stopping his breathing right now, you think that's cool?"[29] After about five minutes into the video, Mr. Floyd appears

---

[20] Complaint at 7, *Palmer* v. *Hankison*, No. 20–CI–002694 (Jefferson Cnty. Cir. Ct. Apr. 27, 2020).

[21] *Id.* at 3, 10.

[22] *Id.* at 9.

[23] Nick Picht, *LMPD officers serving warrant at Breonna Taylor's home were not wearing body cameras*, WAVE 3 NEWS, May 16, 2020.

[24] *FBI investigating after man dies in Minneapolis Police custody; video shows him saying "I can't breathe,"* KARE11, May 26, 2020.

[25] *"Being Black in America Should Not Be A Death Sentence": Officials Respond to George Floyd's Death*, WCCO CBS MINNESOTA, May 26, 2020.

[26] Dakin Andone, *Surveillance video does not support police claims that George Floyd resisted arrest*, CNN, May 28, 2020.

[27] *Id.*

[28] *Id.*

[29] *Id.*

to go unconscious.[30] Police then called an ambulance which took Mr. Floyd to the Hennepin County Medical Center, where he was pronounced dead.[31]

The Burden on Law Enforcement

As the spotlight on high-profile applications of fatal force by police has intensified, some members of the law enforcement profession have felt abused, disrespected, and underappreciated given the personal sacrifices they make to perform a dangerous job that often involves split-second life or death decisions. The job of a patrol officer can be deadly. In 2014, New York Police Department (NYPD) officers Wenjian Liu and Raphael Ramos were shot and killed execution-style while sitting in their patrol car. In 2016, 20 law enforcement officers died in planned assaults carried out by gunmen—the highest number in a least a decade— including in high-profile attacks against police in Dallas and Baton Rouge that occurred ten days apart.[32] And on February 9, 2020, NYPD Officer Paul Stroffolino was ambushed while sitting in his marked unit and shot in the head. Officer Stroffolino was expected to survive. Hours later, Officer Stroffolino's assailant entered the 41st Precinct in the Bronx and emptied the entire clip of a 9mm handgun, striking a lieutenant in the upper left arm. The assailant has been charged with several counts of attempted murder and awaits trial. While planned attacks on officers are relatively rare, officers must face the most dangerous encounters as a matter of routine: traffic stops, serving warrants, and responding to domestic violence calls. The public scrutiny and violent attacks have led some to believe that there is a "war on cops" and that in response, police have begun to pull back in their enforcement duties—a phenomenon labelled as "the Ferguson effect."[33] Fewer people are seeking careers in policing, as a majority of police chiefs surveyed said

---

[30] WCCO CBS MINNESOTA.

[31] KARE11.

[32] Ann Givens, *Ambush Shootings of Police Officers Reach Highest Total in Decades*, THE TRACE, Dec. 6, 2016, available at https://www.thetrace.org/2016/12/ambush-shootings-police-officers-reaches-highest-total-decades/.

[33] *See* Mitch Smith, *Policing: What Changed (and Didn't) Since Michael Brown Died*, N.Y. TIMES, Aug. 7, 2019, available at https://www.nytimes.com/2019/08/07/us/racism-ferguson.html.

hiring had become more difficult, with two-thirds reporting difficulty finding nonwhite officers.[34]

Need for Legislation

Post-Incident Accountability Measures

"Pattern or Practice" Enforcement Actions under 34 U.S.C. § 12601

H.R. 7120 makes it easier in several ways to more effectively enforce 34 U.S.C. § 12601, which authorizes the DOJ to pursue civil suits for equitable and declaratory relief against individual officers or police departments to stop them from engaging in a pattern or practice of depriving persons of their constitutional or other federal rights.[35] To prevail, DOJ must prove that a law enforcement agency engaged in such conduct by a preponderance of evidence. The pattern or practice of excessive use of force has been found in the past to have been one type of conduct prohibited by the statute.[36] The DOJ is currently the *only* government agency authorized to eliminate unconstitutional patterns and practices under the statute.

Using its Section 12601 authority, the DOJ had in years past investigated a substantial number of police departments around the country engaged in a variety of constitutional violations. The Obama Administration, for example, launched 25 such investigations.[37] Three factors typically triggered federal investigations: (1) the development of a significant body of complaints by stakeholder groups that create an inference of a pattern of constitutional violations; (2) voluntary requests by elected officials or agency management for a review of agency practices

---

[34] *Id.*

[35] 34 U.S.C.§ 12601 was previously codified as 42 U.S.C. § 14141.

[36] *See,* e.g., DEP'T OF JUST., INVESTIGATION OF THE NEW ORLEANS POLICE DEPARTMENT, Mar. 16, 2011.

[37] Policing Practices Hearing (written testimony of Vanita Gupta, President and Chief Executive Officer, Leadership Conference on Civil and Human Rights, at 2) [hereinafter "Gupta Testimony"].

and technical support to improve policies and procedures; and (3) high visibility episodes of police misconduct accompanied by substantial proof such as a video recording.

The DOJ typically sought to enjoin patterns or practices of unconstitutional conduct through judicially enforceable consent decrees or court orders that required the local law enforcement agency to end the misconduct at issue and change the policies and procedures that led to the violations. Examples of required policy changes included early intervention systems to monitor and intervene with officers at risk of serious misconduct, or more open administrative complaint procedures. Where violations were wide-spread and substantial, a consent decree and memorandum of agreement provided essential assurance that the reform effort would be monitored and enforced.

Relief secured by DOJ pursuant to its Section 12601 authority can have broad and lasting effects that encourage policing practices that reduce the risk of unconstitutional police-civilian encounters and build trust between law enforcement and the community. Section 12601 relief supports that goal by articulating best practices and demonstrating how to apply them while providing enforcement mechanisms which incentivize reform.

Unfortunately, under the Trump Administration, the DOJ has largely abdicated its responsibility to use its Section 12601 authority to address police abuses. As an early priority during his tenure, Attorney General Jeff Sessions reversed the DOJ's policy of pursuing consent decrees to resolve policing practices investigations. Within a month of his appointment, Attorney General Sessions ordered a review of the use of consent decrees to ensure that they advanced the safety and protection of the public.[38] He further asserted that consent decrees "reduce morale" among police officers and had the effect of increasing violent crime.[39] These principles

---

[38] Sheryl Gay Stolberg & Eric Lichtblau, *Sweeping Federal Review Could Affect Consent Decrees Nationwide*, N.Y. TIMES, Apr. 3, 2017, available at https://www.nytimes.com/2017/04/03/us/justice-department-jeff-sessions-baltimore-police.html.

[39] Katie Benner, *Sessions, in Last-Minute Act, Sharply Limits Use of Consent Decrees to Curb Police Abuses*, N.Y. TIMES, Nov. 8, 2018, available at https://www.nytimes.com/2018/11/08/us/politics/sessions-limits-consent-decrees.html.

were memorialized in a memorandum dated March 31, 2017 (the March 2017 Memo).[40]

In April 2017, the DOJ changed its position in a settlement agreement it had entered into with the Baltimore Police Depart ment during the Obama Administration. It filed a document in the district court seeking more time to "assess whether and how the provisions of the proposed consent decrees interact" with the principles outlined in the March 2017 Memo.[41]

The DOJ continued its non-decree policy in two notable investigations of Louisiana law enforcement agencies that were engaging in systemic abuses of constitutional rights. In December 2016, the Obama DOJ investigated the Ville Platte Police Department and Evangeline Parish Sheriff's Office in Louisiana and found that the agencies routinely arrested and detained individuals without probable cause.[42] In June 2018, the DOJ settled the cases out of court without a judicially enforceable consent decree and without community input.[43]

In October 2018, DOJ intervened in the State of Illinois' lawsuit against the Chicago Police Department (CPD), opposing a settlement even after the Obama Justice Department found rampant use of excessive force aimed at black and Latino individuals.[44] Finally, in November 2018, just prior to his resignation, Attorney General Sessions issued a second memorandum (the November 2018 Memo) making it more difficult for DOJ officials to obtain court-enforced agreements to stop civil rights

---

[40] Memorandum for Heads of Department Components and United States Attorneys, March 31, 2017, available at https://www.justice.gov/opa/press-release/file/954916/download.

[41] Motion for Continuance of Public Fairness Hearing, *USA* v. *Police Department of Baltimore City*, No. 1:17–cv–00099–JKB, (D. Md. Apr. 3, 2017), ECF No. 23.

[42] Department of Justice Investigation of the Ville Platte Police Department and the Evangeline Parish Sheriff's Office, December 19, 2016.

[43] Ian MacDougall, *How the Trump Administration Went Easy on Small-Town Police Abuses*, Pro Publica, Aug. 27, 2018, available at https://www.propublica.org/article/ville-platte-louisiana-police-consent-decree-trump-justice-department.

[44] Katie Benner, *Sessions, in Last-Minute Act, Sharply Limits Use of Consent Decrees to Curb Police Abuses*, N.Y. TIMES, Nov. 8, 2018, available at https://www.nytimes.com/2018/11/08/us/politics/sessions-limits-consent-decrees.html; *see also* United States' Statement of Interest Opposing Proposed Consent Decree, *Illinois* v. *Chicago*, No. 17–cv–06260 (N.D. Ill. Oct. 12, 2018), ECF No. 160.

abuses by local police departments.[45] The November 2018 Memo imposed three stringent requirements that will make it harder to negotiate and enforce consent decrees:

- DOJ lawyers must now provide evidence of violations beyond unconstitutional behavior;
- Consent decrees must have an identified sunset date, as opposed to being allowed to stay in place until the unlawful practices are remedied; Career DOJ lawyers can no longer approve consent decrees; approval from top political appointees is now required.[46]

Several witnesses raised concerns about the Trump Administration's failure to use its authority under Section 12601 at the Committee's hearing on policing practices. Vanita Gupta, President and Chief Executive Officer of the Leadership Conference on Civil and Human Rights (LCCHR) and the former Acting Assistant Attorney General for Civil Rights during the Obama Administration, testified that the current Administration had severely curtailed the DOJ's use of consent decrees to address police civil rights abuse.[47]

Similarly, Sherrilyn Ifill, President and Director-Counsel of the NAACP Legal Defense and Educational Fund, testified that the "Trump Administration has abdicated its authority to investigate police departments and instead has incited unlawful policing."[48] Ronald Davis, Chair of the Legislative Committee for the National Organization of Black Law Enforcement Executives (NOBLE), also proposed rescinding the Session

---

[45] Memorandum for Heads of Civil Litigation Components, United States Attorneys, Nov. 7, 2018, available at https://www.justice.gov/opa/press-release/file/1109681/download; Christy E. Lopez, *Here's Why Jeff Session's Parting Shot is Worse Than You Thought*, The Marshall Project, Nov. 19, 2018, available at https://www.themarshallproject.org/2018/11/19/here-s-why-jeff-sessions-parting-shot-is-worse-than-you-thought.

[46] Katie Benner, *Sessions, in Last-Minute Act, Sharply Limits Use of Consent Decrees to Curb Police Abuses*, N.Y. TIMES, Nov. 8, 2018, available at https://www.nytimes.com/2018/11/08/us/politics/sessions-limits-consent-decrees.html.

[47] Gupta Testimony at 3.

[48] Policing Practices Hearing (written testimony of Sherrilyn Ifill, President and Director-Counsel, NAACP Legal Defense and Educational Fund, at 3) [hereinafter "Ifill Testimony"].

memo pertaining to consent decrees.[49] The 2018 USCCR report recommended, among other things, that the DOJ return to vigorous pursuit of cases against local police departments for engaging in a "pattern or practice" of unconstitutional conduct and use consent decrees in such cases as necessary.[50]

H.R. 7120 strengthens the investigatory and enforcement mechanisms of Section 12601 in a number of ways. First, it grants the DOJ the authority to issue subpoenas in "pattern or practice" investigations of local law enforcement entities to compel the production of relevant information or documents in an investigation.[51] Obtaining such materials is critical to establishing the breadth of unconstitutional practices. Second, to provide an additional means of enforcement, it creates a cause of action allowing state attorneys general to pursue "pattern or practice" enforcement actions in federal court so that authority to pursue such actions would no longer be exclusively held by the DOJ.[52] Third, it expressly affirms the existing understanding and practice under Section 12601 that prosecutors are among those law enforcement officials subject to the statute's prohibition on engaging in a "pattern or practice" of conduct that deprives individuals of their constitutional or civil rights.[53] Finally, it authorizes appropriations for additional expenses related to the enforcement of Section 12601.[54]

---

[49] Davis Testimony at 8.

[50] USCCR Report at 4.

[51] H.R. 7120, the George Floyd Justice in Policing Act of 2020 (116th Cong. 2020), § 103(a)(3).

[52] *Id.*

[53] *Id.* For instance, the DOJ investigated the Missoula County (MT) Attorney's Office for allegations of gender bias in its handling of sexual assault cases. *See* Letter from Jocelyn Samuels, Acting Ass't Attn'y General et al. to Fred Van Valkenburg, County Attorney, Missoula County, MT, Feb. 14, 2014 available at https://www.justice.gov/sites/default/files/crt/legacy/2014/02/19/missoula_ltr_2-14-14.pdf. *See also* Memorandum of Understanding Between the Montana Attorney General, the Missoula County Attorney's Office, Missoula County, and the Dep't of Justice, *available at* https://www.justice.gov/sites/default/files/crt/legacy/2014/06/10/missoula_settle_6-10-14.pdf (outlining terms of settlement ending DOJ "pattern or practice" investigation of Missoula County Attorney's Office).

[54] *Id.* § 116.

Federal Criminal Enforcement Pursuant to 18 U.S.C. § 242

H.R. 7120 also strengthens an important criminal enforcement tool against police officers who violate a person's constitutional or civil rights. Among the criminal enforcement tools available to the DOJ to punish law enforcement officers that apply improper or excessive amounts of force against civilians is 18 U.S.C. § 242. Section 242 prohibits the willful deprivation of a person's federal civil or constitutional rights while acting under the color of law.[55]

Section 242 is a specific intent crime.[56] To sustain a conviction, the Justice Department must prove beyond a reasonable doubt that the defendant: (1) acted under color of law; (2) deprived an individual of a constitutional right; and (3) acted willfully.[57] To establish the third element, that a defendant acted "willfully," the government must demonstrate that the defendant intended to commit an act that results in a constitutional deprivation.[58] In the excessive force context, this means the government must prove that the defendant intentionally applied an amount of force that he or she *knew* was objectively unreasonable under the circumstances.[59] This required showing of willful intent on the defendant's part effectively makes prosecution of police officers who commit civil rights violations through their use of excessive force very difficult, if not impossible.

H.R. 7120 addresses the concern that the required showing of willfulness is too high a burden for prosecutors to meet by modifying the required showing of intent under Section 242. Under the bill, the government would only need to prove that an officer acted "knowingly or

---

[55] 18 U.S.C. § 242.

[56] *United States* v. *Proano*, 912 F.3d 431, 442 (7th Cir. 2019).

[57] The second element requires proof beyond a reasonable doubt that the defendant deprived the victim of their right to be free from excessive applications of force. The Supreme Court, in *Graham* v. *Connor*, 490 U.S. 386, 396–97 (1989), held that all applications of force by government agents prior to or during arrest must be governed by the Fourth Amendment, which prohibits "unreasonable searches and seizures." The reasonableness of a particular application of force is judged from the perspective of a reasonable officer on the scene in light of the totality of facts and circumstances confronting them at the moment force was applied.

[58] *Proano* at 442 (quoting *United States* v. *Bradley*, 196 F.3d 762, 770 (7th Cir. 1999).

[59] *Proano* at 442–443.

recklessly" in depriving a person of his or her constitutional rights.[60] At the hearing before the Committee, several witnesses, including Ronald Davis of NOBLE and Ms. Gupta of LCCHR, testified in favor of this change.[61] In addition, the bill would eliminate the death penalty from Section 242 and clarify that any act that was a substantial factor contributing to death of a person is considered an act resulting in death, subjecting the defendant to the strongest penalties under the statute.[62] Finally, the bill authorizes appropriations for additional expenses related to the enforcement of Section 242.[63]

Civil Action for Deprivation of Constitutional Rights

The civil counterpart to 18 U.S.C. § 242 is 42 U.S.C. § 1983, which authorizes a civil action against any "person who, under color of" state law, "subjects, or causes to be subjected, any citizen of the United States or other person within the jurisdiction thereof to the deprivation of" federal rights.[64] The law was first enacted during Reconstruction to combat systematic violence and abuse against African Americans.[65]

The text of Section 1983 contains no mention of official "immunities" or other defenses available to officers who are sued. However, over the past several decades, the Supreme Court has constructed a doctrine known as "qualified immunity." Qualified immunity shields officers from liability "unless they have 'violated a statutory or constitutional right that was clearly established at the time of the challenged conduct.'"[66] Thus, courts can (and often do) hold that an official's conduct violated the Constitution but that the plaintiff is nonetheless barred from recovering damages. The Supreme Court has described qualified immunity as an "exacting

---

60 H.R. 7120, § 101(1).

61 Davis Testimony at 6; Gupta Testimony at 6.

62 H.R. 7120, § § 101(2) & 101(3).

63 *Id.* § 116.

64 42 U.S.C. § 1983. A more limited cause of action is available against federal officers pursuant to *Bivens* v. *Six Unknown Named Agents*, 403 U.S. 388 (1971).

65 *See* An Act to Enforce the Provisions of the Fourteenth Amendment to the Constitution of the United States, and for Other Purposes, ch. 22, § 1, 17 Stat. 13 (1871).

66 *City and Cnty of San Francisco* v. *Sheehan*, 135 S. Ct. 1765, 1774 (2015) (quoting *Plumhoff* v. *Pickard*, 572 U.S. 765, 778 (2014)) (additional internal quotations omitted).

standard"[67] that "protects 'all but the plainly incompetent or those who knowingly violate the law.'"[68]

In the context of excessive force claims against police officers, qualified immunity has frequently barred victims of civil rights abuses from recovering in court. Even before qualified immunity is applied, a plaintiff alleging excessive force must demonstrate, by a preponderance of the evidence, that the officer caused injury or death to the victim by applying more force than "objectively reasonable" under the circumstances.[69] This reasonableness test "requires careful attention to the facts and circumstances of each particular case, including the severity of the crime at issue, whether the suspect poses an immediate threat to the safety of the officers or others, and whether he is actively resisting arrest or attempting to evade arrest by flight."[70] Qualified immunity imposes an additional and nearly insurmountable barrier: it requires the plaintiff to show that prior case law from an appellate court or the Supreme Court has already established that nearly identical conduct in nearly identical circumstances is unlawful.[71] For example, the Supreme Court recently denied review in a case holding that an officer who shot a child while aiming for a family dog—who posed no evident threat—was protected by qualified immunity, because no prior case law provided sufficiently " 'obvious clarity' to the unique and unfortunate circumstances" of the case.[72]

Qualified immunity has faced considerable criticism from a broad range of scholars,[73] practitioners,[74] civil rights advocates,[75] and even judges

---

[67] *Id.*

[68] *Ashcroft* v. *al-Kidd*, 563 U.S. 731, 743 (2011)) (quoting *Malley* v. *Briggs*, 475 U.S. 335, 341 (1986)).

[69] *Graham*, 490 U.S. at 397 (1989).

[70] *Id.* at 396.

[71] *See*, Ifill Testimony at 4–5; *e.g.*, *Kisela* v. *Hughes*, 138 S. Ct. 1148 (2018) (per curiam); *Mullenix* v. *Luna*, 136 S. Ct. 305 (2015) (per curiam).

[72] *Corbitt* v. *Vickers*, 929 F.3d 1304, 1316–17 (11th Cir. 2019), *cert denied*, No. 19–679, 2020 WL 3146693 (2020).

[73] *See, e.g.*, William Baude, *Is Qualified Immunity Unlawful?*, 106 CAL. L. REV. 45 (2018); David Rudovsky, *The Qualified Immunity Doctrine in the Supreme Court: Judicial Activism and the Restriction of Constitutional Rights*, 138 U. PA. L. REV. 23 (1989).

[74] *See, e.g.*, Policing Practices Hearing (written testimony of Benjamin Crump, at 1–2) [hereinafter "Crump Testimony"].

and Justices.[76] As Sherrilyn Ifill, Director-Counsel of the NAACP Legal Defense and Educational Fund, explained in her testimony before the Committee, qualified immunity "has been interpreted by courts so expansively that it now provides near-impunity for police officers who engage in unconstitutional acts of violence."[77] Section 102 of H.R. 7120 addresses the particular obstacles that qualified immunity imposes in civil rights suits against law enforcement officials. It expressly bars the defense of qualified immunity in Section 1983 suits against state and local law enforcement officers by prohibiting defenses based on the "good faith" of the official or on the purported absence of "clearly established" law.[78]

Section 102 also prohibits such defenses in suits against federal law enforcement officers. Although no federal statute expressly provides a right of action to seek damages against federal officials for violations of the plaintiff's constitutional rights, the Supreme Court in *Bivens* v. *Six Unknown Named Agents of the Federal Bureau of Narcotics* recognized that individuals may pursue such actions in certain circumstances.[79] In order to further ensure that federal officials are subject to the same accountability as their state and local counterparts, the Committee may also consider legislation in the future to expressly codify *Bivens*. In the meantime, Section 102 reflects the Committee's understanding that *Bivens* remains good law and that qualified immunity should not shield federal law enforcement officials in *Bivens* suits.

Although some have contended that eliminating qualified immunity would unfairly subject police officers to liability and could thereby harm police recruitment or cause officers to hesitate in performing their

---

[75] *See, e.g.*, Ifill Testimony at 4–5; Gupta Testimony at 6; Letter from Clark Neily, Vice President of Criminal Justice, Cato Institute, to Members of the H. Comm. on the Judiciary (June 16, 2020).

[76] *See, e.g.*, *Baxter* v. *Bracey*, No. 18–1287, 2020 WL 3146701, at *1 (2020) (Thomas, J., dissenting from denial of certiorari and observing that "our § 1983 qualified immunity doctrine appears to stray from the statutory text"); Jon. O. Newman, *Here's a Better Way to Punish the Police: Sue Them for Money*, WASH. POST (June 23, 2016).

[77] Ifill Testimony at 4.

[78] The "good faith" defense reflects an earlier iteration of qualified immunity doctrine in which the courts assessed whether the defendant subjectively believed his or her conduct was lawful. *See, e.g.*, *Wood* v. *Strickland*, 420 U.S. 308 (1975).

[79] 403 U.S. 388.

functions, the Committee finds these arguments unpersuasive. First, as an exhaustive study of police indemnification policies has demonstrated, police officers are almost never personally required to pay damages in civil rights suits.[80] Those costs are instead borne by the officers' employers. The elimination of qualified immunity will thus create appropriate incentives for cities and police departments to minimize instances of police brutality through proper training and disciplinary mechanisms. Second, even without the defense of qualified immunity, the existing "objective reasonableness" standard applied in excessive force cases already requires an intensive examination of "the facts and circumstances of each particular case."[81] The elimination of qualified immunity does not alter that underlying test.

Consistent with the overall purpose of addressing police misconduct, H.R. 7120 does not address qualified immunity in civil rights suits against other types of officials. As already noted, qualified immunity imposes a particularly high barrier to recovery in excessive force cases when combined with the fact-specific nature of the "objective reasonableness" test applied by the courts. Nonetheless, this legislation in no sense constitutes a ratification of qualified immunity in other contexts. The Committee shares the widespread concerns that have been raised regarding the doctrine, including its lack of foundation in the text of Section 1983 and the obstacles it presents to victims whose constitutional rights have been violated. In the future, the Committee may consider legislation to eliminate qualified immunity in cases against other types of officials, including by taking into account the nature of the officials' duties and the types of constitutional claims likely to arise. In addition, because qualified immunity reflects a judge-made doctrine and is not rooted in legislative text, the Supreme Court maintains ample authority to revise or eliminate it.

---

[80] Joanna C. Schwartz, *Police Indemnification*, 89 N.Y.U. L. REV. 885 (2014).

[81] *Graham*, 490 U.S. at 397.

Independent Investigations, Departmental Discipline, and Civilian Oversight

H.R. 7120 ensures independent investigations of police uses of force and independent civilian oversight of police departments. Police departments use internal disciplinary processes to sanction officers whose application of force deviates from departmental policies and procedures. Penalties can range from loss of leave to termination. Each state legislature has passed a set of administrative rules, typically called a "Law Enforcement Officers Bill of Rights (LEOBR)" that govern departmental disciplinary procedures. One key and controversial provision typically included in a LEOBR is the "cooling off" period, in which departmental investigators are prohibited from interviewing officers that have fatally applied force for a pre-determined period of time (typically 2–10 days) following the incident. The purpose of this provision is to allow for the psychological trauma typically involved in a fatal application of force to recede prior to compelling the officer to recount the events of the incident in detail.

Additionally, many police departments enter into contracts with police unions that allow officers that have engaged in serious or repeated misconduct to remain on the force, or transfer to other police forces. For example, 43 cities and 4 states erase records of misconduct making it difficult to discipline repeat offenders, or track officers with a propensity for misconduct if they switch departments.[82] One high profile example of how this failure ended in fatal consequences was when former Chicago Police Officer Jason Van Dyke, who had 20 complaints—half of which concerned use of force—fired 16 shots at Laquan McDonald, killing him.[83] Van Dyke was never disciplined or flagged as a potential problem and was later convicted of second degree murder for killing McDonald.

Critics argue that departmental disciplinary processes serve to protect officers from true accountability. For example, a study of the CPD showed that it sustained only 15 excessive force complaints out of 5,357 filed

---

[82] *See Police Union Contract Project*, CHECKTHEPOLICE.ORG, https://www.checkthepolice.org (last accessed May 29, 2020).

[83] *See* Stephen Rushin, *Police Union Contracts*, 66 DUKE L.J. 1191, 1195, n. 14 (2017).

between 2002 and 2004.[84] Additionally, a June 2019 NYPD Inspector General report showed that the NYPD failed to sustain any of the 2,495 complaints of racially biased policing made between 2014 and 2018.[85]

Many state and local law enforcement agencies have authorized civilian oversight over police departments. The idea behind civilian review is to provide a level of oversight and deterrence, separate and independent of the police departments, that carries legitimacy within the community. Typically, civilian oversight bodies use an adversarial fact-finding process to investigate individual claims of police misconduct.[86] They are also authorized to investigate patterns of police misconduct, engage in community outreach, and recommend policy reforms.[87] Critics of civilian oversight bodies point out that they often lack investigative resources and expertise, and the power to independently sanction police officers who are found responsible for engaging in misconduct.[88] In the typical model, although the civilian oversight body can recommend a sanction, any actual punishment is determined by the department.[89]

To address some of the concerns about the limitations of departmental disciplinary mechanisms and civilian oversight, including concern about police officers who have repeatedly engaged in misconduct being permitted to continue serving as officers, H.R. 7120 creates a grant program for state attorneys general to establish independent investigation processes for uses of deadly force by law enforcement officers, to address concerns about the lack of such independence in department-led investigations.[90] Both the President's Task Force and the USCCR

---

[84] Craig B. Futterman, H. Melissa Mather, and Melanie Miles, *The Use of Statistical Evidence to Address Police Supervisory and Disciplinary Practices: The Chicago Police Department's Broken System*, 1 DEPAUL J. FOR SOC. JUST., 251, 267 (Table 1) (2008).

[85] N.Y. DEP'T OF INVESTIGATION, COMPLAINTS OF BIASED POLICING IN NEW YORK CITY 2 (2019).

[86] Nathan Witkin, *The Police-Community Partnership: Civilian Oversight As An Evaluation Tool for Community Policing*, 18 Scholar: St. Mary's L. Rev. & Soc. Just. 181, 187 (2016).

[87] *Id.* at 187.

[88] *See id.* at 188–193.

[89] *See id.* at 192.

[90] H.R. 7210, § 104.

recommended such an independent investigation process for police misconduct.[91]

The bill also establishes a national police misconduct registry that would allow members of the public and law enforcement agencies to know about a particular officer's history of misconduct complaints, the officer's discipline or termination records, and records of lawsuits or settlements involving the officer and require agencies to certify hiring eligibility for law enforcement officers who change departments.[92] As Dr. Phillip Goff, Co-Founder and Chief Executive Officer of the Center for Policing Equity, testified, a national police misconduct registry is a reform that will increase transparency and the public's trust in law enforcement agencies. Doctors and lawyers, along with many other professions, are required to be licensed and their employment data are shared across state lines by appropriate entities. Why should a police officer who has been terminated for cause be able to move to another state or jurisdiction without undergoing an appropriate background check? The creation of a national clearinghouse with a list of those officers who have been terminated will empower state and local governments to decide what standards they want to set for officer conduct and character. Without it, many law enforcement agencies simply do not have the capacity to determine whether or not an officer was fired prior to seeking employment—and many, therefore, do not.[93] The bill also requires the Attorney General to conduct a study of the impact that any law, rule, or procedure that allows law enforcement officers to unreasonably delay answering questions from investigators of their misconduct.[94] This provision will help guide future efforts to address unreasonable or arbitrary delays by officers accused of misconduct in responding to investigators' inquiries.

---

[91] USCCR Report at 5; The President's Task Force at 16.
[92] H.R. 7120, § § 201, 202.
[93] Goff Testimony at 4.
[94] H.R. 7120, § 115.

Data Collection Measures

H.R. 7120 addresses the concern raised by the 2018 USCCR report and amplified by the testimony of several witnesses before the Committee on the need for robust data collection on police-community encounters and that a lack of comprehensive, publicly-available data about police use of force sharpens mistrust of the police in minority communities.[95] As the USCCR found, accurate and comprehensive data regarding police uses of force is generally not available to police departments or the American public, no comprehensive national database exists that captures rates of police use of force, and the lack of data on use of force is exacerbated by the absence of mandatory federal reporting and standardized reporting guidelines.[96] Similarly, the President's Task Force had recommended the collection and public availability of demographic data concerning police interactions with the public.[97]

The task of collecting data regarding the scope of excessive, but non-fatal, applications of force is made more complicated by the use of "cover charges" or arrests lacking in legal justification, to serve as a pretext for officers to apply excessive force or engage in other misconduct.[98] These offenses, often charged alone or in combination with other low-level charges, include battery, resisting arrest, disorderly conduct, and failure to obey a lawful order. In some instances, the cover charges arise from traffic stops or other minor encounters that escalate when an officer feels disrespected. This abusive conduct deters victims from reporting instances

---

[95] USCCR Report at 4; Acevedo Testimony at 5 ("robust data collection and analysis can help inform decision-making and identify problems"); Davis at 6 (emphasizing the need to require "robust data collection on police community encounters and law enforcement activities" that should capture all demographic categories and be disaggregated); Gupta Testimony at 5 (highlighting importance of disaggregated data and emphasizing that this data "allows communities and departments to analyze the effects of policies and practices, and to change and advocate against them if they are ineffective or disproportionately affect particular communities or groups).

[96] USCCR Report at 4.

[97] The President's Task Force at 16.

[98] *See* Jonah Newman, Chicago police use "cover charges" to justify excessive force, CHICAGO REPORTER, Oct. 23, 2018, https://www.chicagoreporter.com/chicago-police-use-cover-charges-to-justify-excessive-force/.

of excessive force or other misconduct and undermines investigations into misconduct.[99]

For example, research indicates the widespread use of cover charges to hide instances in which police applied excessive force in Chicago. Since 2004, 66% of reported CPD force applications resulted in the victim being arrested for aggravated assault against a police officer, aggravated battery against a police officer, or resisting arrest.[100] Between 2012 and September 2016, Chicago police made more than 1,300 arrests where the only charge was resisting arrest, and more than half of these cases were ultimately dismissed; the absence of an underlying offense raises red flags as to the legitimacy of the officer's decision to use force.[101] The burden then falls on the victim to determine how to use their limited time and resources; the options include defending the criminal charges, pleading guilty, hoping for diversion or dismissal by the prosecution, or filing an excessive force complaint. The evidence indicates that cover charge arrests cause direct and significant harm to those arrested, impact communities of color disproportionately, and exacerbate tensions between those communities and law enforcement.[102]

H.R. 7120 addresses the concern about the lack of adequate and consistent data collection regarding police conduct by requiring the Attorney General to collect data on use of force incidents from state and local law enforcement entities, disaggregated by race, ethnicity, national origin, age, disability, housing status, English language proficiency, and gender.[103] The reports from state and local agencies to the Attorney General must also include the date, time and location of the incident; whether the civilian was armed; the reason force was used; and a

---

[99] *See id.*
[100] *See id.*
[101] *See id.*
[102] *See generally*, Christy E. Lopez, *Disorderly (mis) Conduct: The Problem with "Contempt of Cop" Arrests*, AMERICAN CONSTITUTION SOCIETY FOR LAW AND POLICY, available at http://live-acslaw.pantheonsite.io/wp-content/uploads/2018/04/Lopez_Contempt_of_Cop.pdf.
[103] H.R. 7120, § 223.

description of any injuries.[104] This information is to be made available to the public.[105]

Pre-Incident Measures to Reduce Risk of Violent Police-Citizen Encounters

Use of Force Standards

H.R. 7120 establishes a uniform use-of-force standard for federal officers and conditions grants for state and local law enforcement agencies on their following those same use-of-force standards.[106] In terms of the substance of these standards, the bill requires that federal officers use deadly force only as a last resort to prevent imminent and serious bodily injury and requires officers to employ deescalation techniques.[107] The standard would also allow federal officers to use less lethal force only if necessary and proportional to effectuate an arrest.[108]

Law enforcement agencies generally have a set of directives or "general orders" that govern how they deliver services to the public, including the circumstances under which officers are authorized to use force. The standards provide officers with the tools they need to protect themselves and the public during encounters that are often emotionally charged and rapidly evolving. For example, the policy of the Metropolitan Police Department of Washington D.C., as expressed in its general orders, is to "value and preserve human life when using lawful authority to use force."[109] The policy provides guidance on when deadly force is authorized, provides a continuum for the level of non-deadly force appropriate for given situations, requires the provision of prompt medical attention to any injured subject, and requires notification and reporting for all applications of force involving injury.[110]

---

[104] *Id.*
[105] *Id.*
[106] H.R. 7120, § 364.
[107] *Id.*
[108] *Id.*
[109] D.C. METRO. POLICE DEP'T., Gen. Order GO–RAR–901.07 at 2, available at https://go.mpdconline.com/GO/GO_901_07.pdf.
[110] *See id.*

Such standards on use of force, however, vary from jurisdiction to jurisdiction in substance or in the manner of application. Testifying in support of H.R. 7120's uniform use-of-force standards, Professor Paul Butler of Georgetown University Law Center noted, "There are 18,000 different police departments in the United States, and the problem is that right now there are 18,000 different ways of policing. To establish accountability and transparency among the men and women who are licensed to kill, basic standards must be imposed."[111] Several other witnesses also testified in support of the bill's use-of-force standards.[112]

Accreditation

Law enforcement accreditation entities institutionalize best practices in the delivery of public safety services by establishing a professionalized set of policing standards, developed by public safety practitioners and other experts, that address core issues impacting community confidence while supporting police as an institution.[113] To maintain accreditation, law enforcement agencies voluntarily demonstrate that they meet the established standards. Accredited agencies must develop comprehensive, uniform directives linked to the accreditation standards, which are reinforced on an ongoing basis through data collection, onsite observation, agency reporting, community input, and public commission hearings.[114] Accreditation demonstrates a law enforcement agency's commitment to safety and professionalism which strengthens the agency's reputation in and relationship with the community. It also promotes a culture of compliance and accountability within the agency which, in turn, reduces its exposure to liability.[115] H.R. 7120 adopts this approach, in part, by

---

[111] Butler Testimony at 4–5.

[112] Crump Testimony at 1 (stating that police officers should "only use the level of force needed based on the level of threat actually posed by the circumstances); Davis Testimony at 6, 9 (stating NOBLE's support for bill's use of force provision); Gupta Testimony at 4 (stating support for bill's use of force provision).

[113] *Policing Strategies for the 21st Century: Hearing Before the H. Comm. On the Judiciary*, 114th Cong. 12–13 (2015) (testimony of W. Craig Hartley, Jr. Executive Director, Commission on Accreditation of Law Enforcement Agencies).

[114] See id. at 12.

[115] Matt Kenyon, Benefits of Police Accreditation, POWERDMS, Aug. 13, 2018, available at https://www.powerdms.com/blog/benefits-of-police-accreditation/.

requiring the Attorney General to create law enforcement accreditation standards based on recommendations by the President's Task Force.[116]

Training to End Racial Profiling and to Reduce Risk of Violent Interactions between Police and Racial and Other Minorities

H.R. 7120 creates several new training programs to reduce the risk of violent interactions between law enforcement officers and members of minority communities. Federal studies examining racial inequality dating back to the 1940s and 1960s cited inadequacies in officer training and professionalism as a contributing factor to disproportionate police violence against minorities and increased racial tensions.[117] More recently, the President's Task Force report made several detailed recommendations for improving police officer standards and training (POST) and reducing police violence against minorities. The 2015 report overall emphasized that POSTs should include "develop[ing] specialized knowledge and understanding that enable fair and procedurally just policing."[118] The 2015 report also noted that while "[t]actical skills are important" developing law enforcement officers' "attitude, tolerance, and interpersonal skills are equally" necessary to improved policing in minority communities.[119] The 2018 USCCR report similarly recommended that "[t]he Department of Justice should robustly support local efforts to develop and institute constitutional policing practices."[120]

The Committee also heard witness testimony at its June 10, 2020 oversight hearing on policing practices that echoed the 2015 and 2018 reports' recommendations that law enforcement officer training also include programs on racial and implicit bias and racial profiling as a means of improving policing in minority communities. Professor Paul Butler

---

[116] H.R. 7120, § 113.

[117] *See* Kerner Commission Report at 15 (suggesting that police departments "develop and adopt policy guidelines to assist officers in making critical decisions in cases where police conduct can create tension"); 1947 Report at 157 (recommending that "police training programs . . . should be oriented so as to indoctrinate officers with an awareness of civil rights problems).

[118] The President's Task Force at 52.

[119] *Id.*

[120] USCCR Report at 4.

stated, "[t]oo often police work seems to enforce the dehumanization of people of color. Understanding the history and reality of racism in the United States will make our men and women in blue more effective police officers."[121] LCCHR President Vanita Gupta recommended prohibiting racial profiling and the promotion of training programs that emphasize "[t]he equal treatment of all people, regardless of background, class, or characteristic" in order "to prevent and hold officers accountable for discriminatory policing and reduce and mitigate its disparate impact on marginalized communities."[122]

The legislation also supports the creation of training programs intended to address the inadequacies in law enforcement training and tactics that these studies have suggested factor into the disproportionate rate of police violence against racial minorities and other marginalized groups. Section 114 of H.R. 7120 authorizes the use of grant funding to support local law enforcement in developing policing best practices in areas including effective management, training, hiring, and oversight standards and programs to promote effective community and problem-solving strategies for law enforcement agencies.[123] To that end, section 114 also authorizes the development of pilot programs designed to implement policies, practices, and procedures addressing training and instruction to comply with accreditation standards in areas including: the use of force, and de-escalation tactics and techniques; investigation of officer misconduct and practices and procedures for referring to prosecuting authorities allegations of use of excessive force or racial profiling; interactions with youth, individuals with disabilities, individuals with limited English proficiency, and multi-cultural communities; and community relations and bias awareness.[124] This section also authorizes grants for pilot programs to develop policies, procedures, and practices for the recruitment, hiring, retention, and promotion of diverse law enforcement officers.[125]

---

[121] Butler Testimony at 5.
[122] Gupta Testimony at 4–5.
[123] H.R. 7120, § 114.
[124] *Id.*
[125] *Id.*

Section 334 authorizes the use of grant funding to support local law enforcement in the development and implementation of best practices for training to prevent racial profiling and to encourage more respectful interaction with the public.[126] Section 361 requires the Attorney General to establish a training program for law enforcement officers to cover racial profiling, implicit bias, and procedural justice.[127] It also requires the Attorney General to establish a clear duty for Federal law enforcement officers to intervene in cases where another law enforcement officer is using excessive force against a civilian, and to establish a training program that cover the duty to intervene.[128]

Ban on Chokeholds and Carotid Holds

In response to the cases of George Floyd, Eric Garner, and others, H.R. 7120 incentivizes state and local law enforcement agencies to ban the use of chokeholds and carotid holds.[129] It also defines a chokehold as a "punishment, pain, or penalty" for purposes of 18 U.S.C. § 242, the federal civil rights criminal statute discussed earlier in this report.[130] This definition makes chokeholds and carotid holds a federal civil rights crime under Section 242. Testifying in support of this provision, Vanita Gupta of LCCHR stated "Chokeholds are inherently dangerous, as we have seen in the horrific deaths of George Floyd and Eric Garner before. Recognizing the inherent danger of chokeholds and the threat they pose to human life, police departments in cities such as New York, Atlanta, and Miami prohibit them."[131] Other witnesses also testified in support of the bill's ban on chokeholds and similar maneuvers.[132]

Ban on No-Knock Warrants in Drug Cases

In response to the serious risk to lives that the use of no-knock warrants presents, as demonstrated by the tragic circumstances of Breonna

---

[126] H.R. 7120, § 334.
[127] H.R. 7120, § 361.
[128] *Id.*
[129] H.R. 7120, § 363(b).
[130] *Id.* § 363(c).
[131] Gupta Testimony at 5.
[132] Crump Testimony at 1; Davis Testimony at 6, 8; Goff Testimony at 2.

Taylor's death, Section 362 of H.R. 7120 bans no-knock warrants in drug cases at the federal level and conditions law enforcement funding for state and local law enforcement agencies on prohibition of the use of no-knock warrants in drug cases.[133] "No-knock" raids are a pernicious exception to the Fourth Amendment "knock and announce" rule that permits law enforcement officers to enter a residence without knocking or otherwise announcing their presence. In the course of securing a no knock warrant, law enforcement agencies must show that providing notice may be dangerous, futile, or result in the destruction of evidence.

During the George W. Bush Administration in 2002, the DOJ recognized that "although officers need not take affirmative steps to make an independent re-verification of the circumstances already recognized by a magistrate in issuing a no-knock warrant, such a warrant does not entitle officers to disregard reliable information clearly negating the existence of exigent circumstances when they actually receive such information before execution of the warrant."[134]

Over the course of the last few decades, the use of "no knock" warrants, which are primarily used in drug investigations, and typically justified by the belief that offenders will destroy drugs, have become more frequent, and these raids occur at an alarming rate in the U.S. every year. In the early 1980s, approximately 1,500 no-knock warrants were executed annually, and by 2010, about 45,000 such warrants were executed.[135] There exists, however, an increased risk of death or injury to children, bystanders, or others caught in the crossfire during these volatile execution of no-knock warrants. Between 2010 and 2016, at least 81 civilians and 13 law enforcement officers died as a result of executing no-knock warrants in drug cases.[136]

---

[133] H.R. 7120, § 362.

[134] Patrick F. Philbin, Deputy Assistant Attorney General Office of Legal Counsel, *Authority of Federal Judges and Magistrates to Issue "No-Knock" Warrants*, (Jun. 12, 2002), available at https://www.justice.gov/sites/default/files/olc/opinions/2002/06/31/op-olc-v026-p0044_0.pdf.

[135] Eric Foster, *Death and heartbreak caused by 'no-knock' warrants are impossible to justify*, (Jun 17, 2020), available at https://www.cleveland.com/opinion/2020/06/death-and-heartbreak-caused-by-no-knock-warrants-are-impossible-to-justify-eric-foster.html.

[136] *Id.*

As Ms. Gupta stated in her testimony in support of the bill's ban on no-knock warrants, No-knock warrants are inherently dangerous and have not proven to be more effective than search warrants that preserve the Fourth Amendment rule of knock-and-announce. When police burst into people's houses, unannounced, occupants are more likely to use weapons to try to defend themselves—endangering both the public and officers. We saw this exact scenario play out with Breonna Taylor's death. Furthermore, the increased risk of death or injury to children, bystanders, or others caught in the crossfire counsels against the use of no-knock warrants. Indeed, two states already outlaw no-knock warrants. Congress should likewise pass legislation prohibiting their use.[137]

Limit Transfers of Military Equipment for Police

Background on 1033 Program

Over the past ten years, the deployment by law enforcement of second-hand military equipment has become a fixture at protests throughout the United States. Following the 2014 protests in Ferguson, MO, law enforcement acquisition and use of military vehicles and firearms, through a program frequently referred to as the "1033 Program," came under increased scrutiny.[138] The use of surplus military equipment at recent protests has again refocused Congressional interest in oversight over the program.

The 1033 Program authorizes law enforcement agencies to receive surplus military property from the Department of Defense (DoD). Within DoD, the Defense Logistics Agency's (DLA) Law Enforcement Support Office (LESO) administers the Program and facilitates law enforcement agencies' receipt of excess military equipment. Currently, every state in the United States participates in the program, in addition to the District of

---

[137] Gupta Testimony at 5–6.

[138] *See* 10 U.S.C. § 2576a (2018). The reference to "1033" is to Section 1033 of the National Defense Authorization Act of 1997, the provision that granted permanent authority to the Secretary of Defense to transfer defense material to federal and state law enforcement agencies. Daniel H. Else, *The "1033" Program, Department of Defense Support to Law Enforcement*, Congressional Research Service Report to Congress 2, R43701 (Aug. 28, 2014).

Columbia, the Common-wealth of Puerto Rico, Guam and the U.S. Virgin Islands. Additionally, a number of federal agencies and Indian tribes also receive excess equipment. As of 2016, 6,536 law enforcement agencies participated in the program.[139] From 1991 to 2017, DoD reported that it transferred over $7 billion-worth of its excess controlled and non-controlled personal property to more than 8,600 federal, state, and local law enforcement agencies.[140] Participants in the 1033 Program may choose to receive a diverse set of equipment, from uniforms, boots, and personal protective gear to weapons, ammunition, armored personnel carriers, and aircraft.[141]

Regulation of the 1033 Program

Since its inception, the 1033 Program has been subject to intense oversight on account of the DoD's excessively lax administration of the Program.[142] Following the Ferguson protests, President Obama issued Executive Order 13688, which aimed to rein in law enforcement's use of military equipment.[143] In Executive Order 13688, President Obama directed an interagency group to develop guidelines that would impose "limitations or affirmative obligations imposed on the acquisition of controlled equipment or receipt of funds to purchase controlled equipment."[144]

---

[139] U.S. Gov. Accountability Office, DOD Excess Property (GAO–17–532), 8, Jul. 2017, available at https://www.gao.gov/assets/690/685916.pdf [hereinafter "GAO Report"].

[140] Brian Barrett, *The Pentagon's Hand-Me-Downs Helped Militarize Police. Here's How*, Wired, Jun. 6, 2020, https://www.wired.com/story/pentagon-hand-me-downs-militarize-police-1033-program/.

[141] By example, in 2014, Kentucky received generators, assault weapons, and socks. *See* Jonathan Meador, *Kentucky Police Get Guns, Aircraft and Socks from Military Surplus Program*, 89.3 WFPL News Louisville, Aug. 27, 2014, available at https://wfpl.org/kentucky-police-get-guns-aircraft-and-socks-from-military-surplus-program/.

[142] *See* DoD, DLA Office of the Inspector General, Audit of Law Enforcement Support Office Program Oversight, DLA OIG FY14–02 (Nov. 21, 2013); DLA Office of the Inspector General, Follow-up Audit of the Law Enforcement Support Office, DAO–12–26 (Apr. 4, 2013); DLA Accountability Office, Audit of Law Enforcement Support Office, Defense Reutilization and Marketing Service, DAO–09–01 (Mar. 1, 2010); and Office of the Inspector General, Logistics: Law Enforcement Support Office Excess Property Program, D–2003–101 (June 13, 2003).

[143] Exec. Order No. 13688, Federal Support for Local Law Enforcement Equipment Acquisition, 80 C.F.R. 3451 (2015).

[144] *Id.*

In 2015, the Law Enforcement Equipment Working Group convened pursuant to Executive Order 13688 issued a report that, among other recommendations, obliged Executive agencies to carry out reviews of compliance with "financial and programmatic obligations and adherence to civil rights statutes and requirements" by 1033 Program recipients.[145] Additionally, the report encouraged Executive agencies to consider whether a 1033 Program recipient had been found to be in violation of a federal civil rights statute or programmatic term during the previous three years when considering future provision of federal property. Two years later, the President's Task Force echoed the concern with misuse or abuse of controlled equipment, like that issued through the 1033 Program, and recommended compliance with civil rights requirements resulting from receipt of federal financial assistance.

In July 2017, the Government Accountability Office (GAO) issued a report that reviewed the 1033 Program, with a specific focus on accountability of controlled items and DoD's administration of the Program. As part of their review, the GAO posed as a law enforcement agency and applied for controlled items through the 1033 Program. GAO employees, who represented that they were representatives of the created law enforcement agency were about to obtain "over 100 controlled items with an estimated value of $1.2 million, including nightvision goggles, simulated rifles, and simulated pipe bombs, which could be potentially lethal items if modified with commercially available items."[146] Not surprisingly, the GAO's testing identified that DLA has deficiencies in its processes for verification and approval of federal law enforcement agency applications and in the transfer of controlled property. The GAO also found that DoD had not conducted a fraud risk assessment and lacked internal controls that could prevent, detect, and respond to potential fraud and minimize associated security risks. On August 28, 2017, President Donald J. Trump revoked Executive Order 13688 and lifted many of the

---

[145] Law Enforcement Equipment Working Group, Recommendations Pursuant to Executive Order 13688: Federal Support for Local Law Enforcement Equipment Acquisition, May 2015, https://obamawhitehouse.archives.gov/sites/default/files/docs/le_equipment_wg_final_report_final.pdf.

[146] GAO Report.

accountability measures that were instituted on account of President Obama's order.

In light of the foregoing, H.R. 7120 limits transfers under the 1033 Program from the U.S. military to federal and state law enforcement agencies. Despite the opposition from members of the Minority to this provision, there is good reason to restrict transfers of firearms and military-grade equipment. The record of mismanagement of the 1033 program is well-documented, as outlined above. The GAO found poor management by DoD over the transfer of controlled items, such as firearms. Furthermore, contrary to what the Minority asserts, the bill's language does not prohibit the transfer of items that are not made for military use, such as office supplies and clothing. These items make up the overwhelming majority of items transferred through the 1033 program. The bill simply prohibits the transfer of military vehicles, firearms, and surveillance equipment.

The Minority's attempt to allow transfer of military equipment for use in border control and enforcement was also misguided. The Congress already provides hundreds of millions of dollars for border enforcement. Studies suggest that agencies that receive such equipment see no measurable improvement in officer safety or crime rates, and, rather, there is a correlation with higher rates of officer-involved shootings and reduced public trust. There's no evidence that additional military-grade equipment will improve border security. This alone serves as justification for the transfer limitations in the bill. Sending additional military equipment for use in border enforcement also further militarizes the Canadian and Mexican borders, communities where tens of millions of Americans live.

Body Cameras and Limits on Facial Recognition Technology

Law Enforcement and Body Cameras

Over the past several years, body cameras have come to be regarded as a key police accountability tool. A 2015 poll found that 88 percent of

Americans supported the use of body cameras by law enforcement.[147] Beginning in 2015, the DOJ under the Obama Administration began awarding grants to local law enforcement agencies to aid in financing the initial purchase of body cameras.[148] In 2016, DOJ surveys found that 95 percent of law enforcement agencies in large cities had already launched or planned to launch body camera programs in the future.[149]

Although the adoption of body camera programs by law enforcement agencies appears to be growing—if not widespread among major law enforcement agencies—there are no uniform standards with respect to protocols for the use of body cameras that balance law enforcement needs with personal privacy interests, as well as the processing and retention of data. Similarly, some small and medium-sized law enforcement departments are reportedly ending their body camera programs due to the costs associated with the retention and processing of body camera footage.[150]

H.R. 7120 addresses these issues by requiring federal uniformed police officers to wear body cameras and to have dashboard cameras in marked federal patrol vehicles, setting forth rules governing retention and dissemination of footage and describing ways in which footage can be used to investigate misconduct or as evidence in criminal proceedings.[151] With respect to state and local law enforcement, the bill requires that they use existing federal funds to ensure the use of body cameras by officers and requires grant recipients to establish policies and procedures for safe use of such cameras.[152] Specifically, it authorizes DOJ to award grants and to provide technical assistance related to body camera programs, and to condition such awards on the adoption of uniform standards described in

---

[147] Peter Moore, *Overwhelming support for police body cameras*, YouGov.Com, May 7, 2015 *available at* https://today.yougov.com/topics/politics/articles-reports/2015/05/07/body-cams.

[148] Kimberly Kindy, *Some U.S. police departments dump body-camera programs amid high costs*, Wash. Post, Jan. 21, 2019.

[149] P.R. Lockhart, *Why some police departments are dropping their body camera programs*, Vox, Jan. 25, 2019 available at https://www.vox.com/2019/1/24/18196097/police-body-cameras-storage-cost-washington-post.

[150] *Id.*

[151] H.R. 7120, §§ 371–373, 375–377.

[152] H.R. 7120, §§ 381–382.

the legislation.[153] The grant program is also intended to ensure that small and medium-sized law enforcement agencies are able to acquire funding to maintain their body-camera programs.

Facial Recognition Technology

Facial recognition systems use computer algorithms to pick out specific details about a person's face, such as the distance between the eyes or the shape of a chin, and converts these details into a mathematical representation.[154] This information is then compared to data on faces already collected in the facial recognition database.[155] Facial recognition technology can identify people in photos, videos, or in real-time. Face recognition has been used in airports, at border crossings, and during events such as the Super Bowl.[156]

Federal Government Use of Facial Recognition Technology

The Federal Bureau of Investigation (FBI) mainly uses two types of facial recognition software, Next General Identification–Interstate Photo System (NGI–ISP) and Facial Analysis, Comparison and Evaluation (FACE) Services. The NGI–ISP database contains over 30 million face recognition records pulled from state criminal sources, such as mug shots, and is shared with state and local governments.[157] In addition to the FBI, a select group of state and local agencies can also submit a request to use NGI–ISP to help them identify an unknown person during an investigation. According to the FBI, in fiscal year, NGI–ISP returned about 50,000 face

---

[153] *Id.*

[154] Jennifer Lynch, *Face Off: Law Enforcement Use of Facial Recognition Technology*, Electronic Frontier Foundation, 4–5 (2019), *available at*, https://www.eff.org/wp/law-enforcement-use-face-recognition.

[155] *Id* at 5.

[156] Niraj Chokshi, *Facial Recognition's Many Controversies: From Stadium Surveillance to Racist Software*, N. Y. Times, May 1, 2019 (noting that the city of Tampa, Florida, used facial recognition software during the 2001 Superbowl and identified 19 people with outstanding warrants). *See also* Franchesca Street, *How Facial Recognition is Taking Over Airports*, CNN Oct. 8, 2019) (noting that some airlines are using a facial scan instead of boarding passes).

[157] Memorandum from Kimberly Del Greco, Criminal Justice Info. Serv., FBI to Comm. on Oversight & Reform Staff (May 30, 2019), *available at* https://oversight.house.gov/sites/democrats.oversight.house.gov/files/documents/2019.05.31.%20Hearing%20Memo%20for%20the%20Facial%20Recognition%20Technology%20%28Part%20II%29.pdf.

recognition search results to law enforcement agencies.[158] The FBI also has a team of employees working in FACE Services.[159] Unlike NGI–ISP, FACE Services use non-criminal photos, pulled mostly from driver's license photos, passports, and visa applications. The FBI has agreements with 21 states as well as the Department of State to allow it to search its systems. The total number of photos available to FACE Services is more than 411 million.[160]

Facial Recognition's Shortcomings

The use of this technology is troubling because studies have shown that these identification systems have a high error rate when it comes to correctly identifying women and people of color.[161] A 2019 study conducted by the National Institute of Standards and Technology on the reliability of facial recognition systems found that there was a higher rate of false positives for black people than for whites.[162] The study also showed that false positives were up to 100 times more likely for black people than for white people.[163] Additionally, the rate of false positives were higher for women than men across all races.[164] Not surprisingly, since African Americans are more likely to be arrested (and subsequently photographed), the high propensity of false positives has a disproportionate impact on the group.[165]

Despite the fact that the FBI has been using these recognition systems for many years, there is little transparency and oversight within the FBI

---

[158] Statement of Gretta L. Goodwin, Director, Homeland Security and Justice Team, U.S. Gov't Accountability Office, Before the Comm. on Oversight & Reform, H. of Rep., June 4, 2010, *available at* https://docs.house.gov/meetings/GO/GO00/20190604/109578/HHRG-116-GO00-Wstate-GoodwinG-20190604.pdf.

[159] Lynch, *Face Off*, *supra* note 1, at 15.

[160] Government Accountability Office, *Face Recognition Technology; FBI Should Better Ensure Privacy and Accuracy* (May 2016), *available at* www.gao.gov/productus/GAO-16-267).

[161] Patrick Grother Mei Ngan Kayee Hanaoka, *Face Recognition Vendor Test* (FRVT) Part 3: Demographic Effects, NIST, 2019, *available at* https://nvlpubs.nist.gov/nistpubs/ir/2019/NIST.IR.8280.pdf.

[162] *See id.*

[163] *Id.*

[164] *Id.*

[165] Megan Stevenson, & Sandra Gabriel Mayson, *The Scale of Misdemeanor Justice*. 98 BOSTON UNIV. L. REV 731, 759 (2018).

regarding its facial recognition systems.[166] A GAO report found that the FBI had not yet conducted the necessary audits of its newest facial recognition system to ensure that the system can correctly identify individuals.[167] Nor has the FBI studied how states have used the information gleaned from FBI's facial recognition systems.[168]

H.R. 7120's body-camera provisions also contain limitations on the use of facial recognition technology. Specifically, the bill prohibits the use of facial recognition technology in body cameras worn by federal officers, prohibits footage from such cameras from being subjected to facial recognition technology, and imposes the same restrictions on dashboard cameras and footage.[169] Additionally, it prohibits states from using federal funds for expenses related to facial recognition technology.[170]

Incentivizing Public Safety Innovations

In addition to providing program support for training and mechanisms of accountability for police misconduct, H.R. 7120 also authorizes the use of federal grant money to foster innovation in areas of public safety. The Committee recognizes that a potent mix of interconnected societal ills such as racism and poverty—which federal and state governments have failed to adequately address for decades—have long shaped law enforcement officers' interactions with minority communities, especially in poverty-stricken communities, contributing to incidences of police violence.[171] Societal issues like poverty, chronic homelessness, untreated substance abuse, and unaddressed mental illness, while not exclusive to communities of color, disproportionately affect them.

Several witnesses at the Committee's June 10, 2020 hearing recommended that the federal government support efforts to develop alternative means to address public safety concerns stemming from societal problems that are too often left to law enforcement officers to manage.

---

[166] GAO, *Face Recognition Technology*; *supra* note 7.
[167] *Id.*
[168] *Id.*
[169] H.R. 7120, §§ 372(g), 374.
[170] *Id.* § 382(b).
[171] *See* Kerner Commission Report; 1947 Report.

LCCHR President Vanita Gupta noted in her written testimony that "[m]any factors contribute to crises relating to disabilities and substance use disorders, such as inadequate social services and supports, high rates of poverty, income inequality, housing insecurity, and an ongoing opioid epidemic."[172] Yet because of the lack of investment in mental health and other social services "[m]any of these same issues are generally the basis for police encounters that often escalate to the use of force or turn deadly."[173] NAACP Legal Defense and Educational Fund President Sherrilyn Ifill suggested in her testimony that "a revised vision of public safety that prioritizes social services, youth development, mental health, reentry support, and meaningful provisions for homeless individuals that strengthen community resources to proactively address underlying factors that can contribute to public safety concerns."[174]

To this end, Section 366 of H.R. 7120 authorizes the use of grant funding for law enforcement programs that include the development of best practices for and the creation of local task forces on public safety innovation charged with exploring and developing new strategies for public safety, including non-law enforcement strategies.[175]

Criminalizing Conspiracy to Engage in Lynching

Title IV of H.R. 7120 is the "Emmett Till Justice for Victims of Lunching Act," which would make it a federal crime to conspire to engage in a number of hate crimes, including lynching.[176] This legislation has already passed the House and the Senate, but for parliamentary reasons, it must be passed by both chambers again. It is appropriate that it be added to

---

[172] Gupta Testimony at 6.

[173] *Id.*; *see also* Goff Testimony at 4 ("Even police agree that they are ill-equipped to perform a number of services that currently fall to them. For example, underfunding of mental health resources often leaves police departments as the only state agents left to respond to serious mental health crises. No one thinks this is ideal, but often police are all communities have. Investment in community mental health resources is a logical solve for this specific problem, allow police to focus on crime reduction."); Davis Testimony at 11 (suggesting that policymakers "stop the over-reliance of police to address social issues" and develop community reinvestment strategies).

[174] Ifill Testimony at 7–8.

[175] H.R. 7120, § 366.

[176] H.R. 7120, §§ 401–402.

this legislation because it would have addressed a number of the recent incidents outlined earlier in this report. For instance, the killing of Ahmaud Arbery by two white civilians appears to have been the kind of racially-motivated act of vigilantism that would have been punishable under this Act.

Alternative Proposals Offered by President Trump and Senator Scott Are Insufficient

While the Committee appreciates the fact that both President Trump and Senator Tim Scott (R–SC) have attempted to engage the conversation over policing reform by offering their own proposals, it is the Committee's view that these proposals fall far short of what is necessary to effect meaningful improvements with respect to police misconduct and the reduction of police-community tensions. To be sure, there are some points of commonality among all three proposals. For example, President Trump's Executive Order, issued on June 16, 2020, would, like H.R. 7120, establish a national police misconduct registry and require the Attorney General to certify law enforcement accreditation agencies, and all three proposals would make conspiracy to engage in lynching a federal crime.

The proposals offered by President Trump and Senator Scott, however, are completely missing many significant law enforcement accountability and reform measures that are contained in H.R. 7120 or otherwise take too narrow an approach compared to H.R. 7120, falling far short of the comprehensive steps needed for meaningful change. For example, neither the Executive Order nor Senator Scott's bill: ban no-knock warrants, ban racial profiling by law enforcement, ban chokeholds without exception, have use of force standards that prohibit the use of deadly force by law enforcement except as a last resort, abolish qualified immunity, enhance "pattern or practice" enforcement authority under 34 U.S.C. § 12601, and do not modify the overly burdensome mens rea requirement in 18 U.S.C. § 242.

Key Distinctions between H.R. 7120, the Scott Bill, and the Executive Order

- *No-Knock Warrants*—While H.R. 7120 bans "no knock" warrants in drug cases at the federal level and conditions funding for state and local law enforcement agencies on prohibiting their use; Senator Scott's legislation merely requires states to compile data for use of such no-knock warrants and President Trump's Executive Order completely ignores the problem, which has cost many lives, including most recently Breonna Taylor in Louisville.
- *Chokeholds*—In light of the tragic deaths of George Floyd, Eric Garner and others, H.R. 7120 bans chokeholds and carotid holds at the federal level and conditions law enforcement funding for state and local law enforcement agencies on prohibiting their use. By contrast, Senator Scott's bill has no federal ban and mere merely encourages chokehold bans, and even that is limited where "deadly force [is] authorized" and the President's Executive Order simply seeks standards that take the use of chokeholds into account, also with the exception of cases where "the use of deadly force is authorized by law."
- *Racial Profiling*—H.R. 7120 contains the first ever outright ban on racial and religious profiling and mandates that law enforcement entities provide training on racial, religious, and discriminatory profiling. By contrast Senator Scott's bill does not include any outright ban and merely seeks to study and develop best practices on profiling and the Executive Order ignores this important issue.
- *Public Grants to Reimagine Community Policing*—This much-needed program to reimagine policing in the wake of all too many cases of violence and death involving police misconduct is included in H.R. 7120, but ignored in the Scott legislation and the President's Executive Order.
- *Criminal Intent Standard*—While H.R. 7120 modifies the criminal intent or *mens rea* standard to provide for accountability in cases of knowing or reckless misconduct, Senator Scott's legislation and President Trump's recent Executive Order would leave the status quo in place.

- *Qualified Immunity in Civil Cases*—While H.R. 7120 eliminates the dubious and controversial court-made doctrine of qualified immunity in civil cases which have made it nearly impossible for many victims to obtain recourse, Senator Scott's legislation and President Trump's Executive Order leave the doctrine in place.
- *Pattern and Practice Investigations*—While H.R. 7120 strengthens pattern and practice investigations at the federal level and authorizes and incentivizes state attorney general investigations, the question is ignored under Senator Scott's legislation and President Trump's Executive Order.
- *Independent Prosecution of Misconduct*—While H.R. 7120 incentivizes independent investigations of police misconduct by states attorneys general, Senator Scott's bill and President Trump's Executive Order leave in place a system that too often discourages police investigations.
- *Accreditation*—H.R. 7120 requires the Attorney General to create law enforcement accreditation standard recommendations based on President Obama's Taskforce on 21st Century policing and creates law enforcement development programs to develop policing best practices and improve training, hiring, and retention programs. Senator Scott's bill, however, only addresses law enforcement agency hiring and training programs by providing grant eligibility for recruiters and academy candidates, and President Trump's Executive Order provides for an accreditation system, though it lacks any statutory force of law.
- *Misconduct Registry*—H.R. 7120 addresses a fundamental deficiency in police hiring processes by creating a federal registry of misconduct involving federal, state and local law enforcement officers—which would help ensure officers who were fired, or left the agency due to misconduct, are not re-circulated through the hiring process in other jurisdictions—and would allow for public disclosure incidents involving use of force or racial profiling. By contrast, Senator Scott's legislation merely provides for

information sharing among agencies, and President Trump's Executive Order is limited to the category of "deadly use of force."

- *Deadly Force*—H.R. 7120 requires that deadly force be used by federal officers only as a last resort to prevent imminent and serious bodily injury and conditions grants on state and local law enforcement agencies doing the same while also establishing duty to intervene standards; and setting up a data collection system; while Senator Scott's bill and the President's Executive Order merely require states to report cases of use of force that leads to death or serious injury. Senator Scott's bill does seek to develop a duty to intervene standard as well.
- *Transfer of Military Equipment*—H.R. 7120 limits the transfer of military-grade equipment to state and local law enforcement, while both Senator Scott's bill and Trump's Executive Order leave the status quo in place.
- *Body Cameras*—H.R. 7120 requires federal uniformed police officers to wear body cameras and marked federal police vehicles to have dashboard cameras and incentivizes states to do the same (so long as the dashboard cameras and body cameras do not employ facial recognition technology), while Senator Scott's bill merely incentivizes their use at the state and local level while ignoring the concern about facial recognition technology and President Trump's Executive Order ignores the issue entirely.

HEARINGS

For the purposes of section 103(i) of H. Res. 6 of the 116th Congress, the following hearing was used to consider H.R. 7120: Hearing on "Policing Practices and Law Enforcement Accountability" held before the full Committee on June 10, 2020, during which there was extensive discussion of H.R. 7120. The witnesses were Art Acevedo, Chief of the Houston Police Department and President, Major City Chiefs Association; Paul Butler, Albert Brick Professor in Law, Georgetown University Law

Center; Benjamin Crump, Attorney for the Family of George Floyd; Ron Davis, National Organization of Black Law Enforcement Executives; Philonise Floyd, Brother of George Floyd; Phillip Goff, Franklin A. Thomas Professor of Policing Equality, John Jay College of Criminal Justice and President, Center for Policing Equity; Vanita Gupta, President and Chief Executive Officer, Leadership Conference on Civil and Human Rights; Sherrilyn Ifill, President and Director-Counsel, NAACP Legal Defense and Educational Fund; and Marc Morial, President, National Urban League; Daniel Bongino, Political Commentator and Former Secret Service Agent; Darrell Scott, Pastor and Co-Founder, New Spirit Revival Center; and Angela Underwood Jacobs, Sister of Federal Protective Officer David Underwood.

Committee Consideration

On June 17, 2020, the Committee met in open session and ordered the bill, H.R. 7120, favorably reported as an amendment in the nature of a substitute, by a rollcall vote of 24 to 14, a quorum being present.

Committee Votes

In compliance with clause 3(b) of rule XIII of the Rules of the House of Representatives, the Committee advises that the following rollcall votes occurred during the Committee's consideration of H.R. 7120:

1. An amendment by Mr. Armstrong to add a section regarding audio recording of interviews conducted by certain federal law enforcement officers was defeated by a rollcall vote of 13 to 25.

Roll Call No. **Date:** 6/17/20

COMMITTEE ON THE JUDICIARY

House of Representatives

116th Congress

Amendment # 1 ( ) to ANS HR7120 offered by Rep. Armstrong

☐ PASSED

☑ FAILED

	AYES	NOS	PRES.
Jerrold Nadler (NY-10)		✓	
Zoe Lofgren (CA-19)		✓	
Sheila Jackson Lee (TX-18)		✓	
Steve Cohen (TN-09)		✓	
Hank Johnson (GA-04)		✓	
Ted Deutch (FL-22)		✓	
Karen Bass (CA-37)		✓	
Cedric Richmond (LA-02)		✓	
Hakeem Jeffries (NY-08)		✓	
David Cicilline (RI-01)		✓	
Eric Swalwell (CA-15)		✓	
Ted Lieu (CA-33)		✓	
Jamie Raskin (MD-08)		✓	
Pramila Jayapal (WA-07)		✓	
Val Demings (FL-10)		✓	
Lou Correa (CA-46)		✓	
Mary Gay Scanlon (PA-05)		✓	
Sylvia Garcia (TX-29)		✓	
Joseph Neguse (CO-02)		✓	
Lucy McBath (GA-06)		✓	
Greg Stanton (AZ-09)		✓	
Madeleine Dean (PA-04)		✓	
Debbie Mucarsel-Powell (FL-26)		✓	
Veronica Escobar (TX-16)		✓	
	AYES	NOS	PRES
Jim Jordan (OH-04)	✓		
James F. Sensenbrenner (WI-05)			
Steve Chabot (OH-01)	✓		
Louie Gohmert (TX-01)	✓		
Doug Collins (GA-27)	✓		
Ken Buck (CO-04)			
Martha Roby (AL-02)		✓	
Matt Gaetz (FL-01)	✓		
Mike Johnson (LA-04)	✓		
Andy Biggs (AZ-05)	✓		
Tom McClintock (CA-04)	✓		
Debbie Lesko (AZ-08)	✓		
Guy Reschenthaler (PA-14)	✓		
Ben Cline (VA-06)	✓		
Kelly Armstrong (ND-AL)	✓		
Greg Steube (FL-17)	✓		
	AYES	NOS	PRES.
TOTAL	13	25	

2. An amendment by Mr. Reschenthaler to add a section regarding findings and study regarding Antifa was defeated by a rollcall vote of 13 to 25.

Roll Call No. **Date:** 6/17/20

COMMITTEE ON THE JUDICIARY

House of Representatives

116th Congress

Amendment # 2 ( ) to ANS HR 7120 offered by Rep. Reschenthaler

☐ PASSED

☑ FAILED

	AYES	NOS	PRES.
Jerrold Nadler (NY-10)		✓	
Zoe Lofgren (CA-19)		✓	
Sheila Jackson Lee (TX-18)		✓	
Steve Cohen (TN-09)		✓	
Hank Johnson (GA-04)		✓	
Ted Deutch (FL-22)		✓	
Karen Bass (CA-37)		✓	
Cedric Richmond (LA-02)		✓	
Hakeem Jeffries (NY-08)		✓	
David Cicilline (RI-01)		✓	
Eric Swalwell (CA-15)		✓	
Ted Lieu (CA-33)		✓	
Jamie Raskin (MD-08)		✓	
Pramila Jayapal (WA-07)		✓	
Val Demings (FL-10)		✓	
Lou Correa (CA-46)		✓	
Mary Gay Scanlon (PA-05)		✓	
Sylvia Garcia (TX-29)		✓	
Joseph Neguse (CO-02)		✓	
Lucy McBath (GA-06)		✓	
Greg Stanton (AZ-09)		✓	
Madeleine Dean (PA-04)		✓	
Debbie Mucarsel-Powell (FL-26)		✓	
Veronica Escobar (TX-16)		✓	
	AYES	NOS	PRES
Jim Jordan (OH-04)	✓		
James F. Sensenbrenner (WI-05)			
Steve Chabot (OH-01)	✓		
Louie Gohmert (TX-01)	✓		
Doug Collins (GA-27)	✓		
Ken Buck (CO-04)	✓		
Martha Roby (AL-02)		✓	
Matt Gaetz (FL-01)	✓		
Mike Johnson (LA-04)	✓		
Andy Biggs (AZ-05)	✓		
Tom McClintock (CA-04)	✓		
Debbie Lesko (AZ-08)	✓		
Guy Reschenthaler (PA-14)	✓		
Ben Cline (VA-06)	✓		
Kelly Armstrong (ND-AL)			
Greg Steube (FL-17)	✓		
	AYES	NOS	PRES.
TOTAL	13	25	

3. An amendment by Mr. Gohmert to strike page 135 lines 16–35 and insert "Whoever commits murder in the commission of a kidnaping shall be punished by any term of years including life or death" was defeated by a rollcall vote of 15 to 23.

Roll Call No. **Date:** 6/17/20

COMMITTEE ON THE JUDICIARY

House of Representatives

116th Congress

Amendment # 3 ( ) to ANS HR7120 offered by Rep. Gohmert

☐ PASSED

☑ FAILED

	AYES	NOS	PRES.
Jerrold Nadler (NY-10)		✓	
Zoe Lofgren (CA-19)		✓	
Sheila Jackson Lee (TX-18)		✓	
Steve Cohen (TN-09)		✓	
Hank Johnson (GA-04)		✓	
Ted Deutch (FL-22)		✓	
Karen Bass (CA-37)		✓	
Cedric Richmond (LA-02)			
Hakeem Jeffries (NY-08)		✓	
David Cicilline (RI-01)		✓	
Eric Swalwell (CA-15)		✓	
Ted Lieu (CA-33)		✓	
Jamie Raskin (MD-08)		✓	
Pramila Jayapal (WA-07)		✓	
Val Demings (FL-10)		✓	
Lou Correa (CA-46)		✓	
Mary Gay Scanlon (PA-05)		✓	
Sylvia Garcia (TX-29)		✓	
Joseph Neguse (CO-02)		✓	
Lucy McBath (GA-06)		✓	
Greg Stanton (AZ-09)		✓	
Madeleine Dean (PA-04)		✓	
Debbie Mucarsel-Powell (FL-26)		✓	
Veronica Escobar (TX-16)		✓	
	AYES	NOS	PRES
Jim Jordan (OH-04)	✓		
James F. Sensenbrenner (WI-05)			
Steve Chabot (OH-01)	✓		
Louie Gohmert (TX-01)	✓		
Doug Collins (GA-27)	✓		
Ken Buck (CO-04)	✓		
Martha Roby (AL-02)	✓		
Matt Gaetz (FL-01)	✓		
Mike Johnson (LA-04)	✓		
Andy Biggs (AZ-05)	✓		
Tom McClintock (CA-04)	✓		
Debbie Lesko (AZ-08)	✓		
Guy Reschenthaler (PA-14)	✓		
Ben Cline (VA-06)	✓		
Kelly Armstrong (ND-AL)	✓		
Greg Steube (FL-17)	✓		
	AYES	NOS	PRES.
TOTAL	15	23	

4. An amendment by Mr. Buck to strike section 102 was defeated by a rollcall vote of 13 to 23.

Roll Call No. **Date:** 6/17/20

COMMITTEE ON THE JUDICIARY

House of Representatives

116th Congress

Amendment # 4 ( ) to ANS HR7120 offered by Rep. BUCK

☐ PASSED

☑ FAILED

	AYES	NOS	PRES.
Jerrold Nadler (NY-10)		✓	
Zoe Lofgren (CA-19)		✓	
Sheila Jackson Lee (TX-18)		✓	
Steve Cohen (TN-09)		✓	
Hank Johnson (GA-04)		✓	
Ted Deutch (FL-22)		✓	
Karen Bass (CA-37)			
Cedric Richmond (LA-02)		✓	
Hakeem Jeffries (NY-08)			
David Cicilline (RI-01)		✓	
Eric Swalwell (CA-15)		✓	
Ted Lieu (CA-33)		✓	
Jamie Raskin (MD-08)		✓	
Pramila Jayapal (WA-07)		✓	
Val Demings (FL-10)		✓	
Lou Correa (CA-46)		✓	
Mary Gay Scanlon (PA-05)		✓	
Sylvia Garcia (TX-29)		✓	
Joseph Neguse (CO-02)		✓	
Lucy McBath (GA-06)		✓	
Greg Stanton (AZ-09)		✓	
Madeleine Dean (PA-04)		✓	
Debbie Mucarsel-Powell (FL-26)		✓	
Veronica Escobar (TX-16)		✓	
	AYES	NOS	PRES
Jim Jordan (OH-04)	✓		
James F. Sensenbrenner (WI-05)			
Steve Chabot (OH-01)	✓		
Louie Gohmert (TX-01)	✓		
Doug Collins (GA-27)	✓		
Ken Buck (CO-04)	✓		
Martha Roby (AL-02)	✓		
Matt Gaetz (FL-01)	✓		
Mike Johnson (LA-04)	✓		
Andy Biggs (AZ-05)			
Tom McClintock (CA-04)		✓	
Debbie Lesko (AZ-08)	✓		
Guy Reschenthaler (PA-14)	✓		
Ben Cline (VA-06)	✓		
Kelly Armstrong (ND-AL)	✓		
Greg Steube (FL-17)	✓		
	AYES	NOS	PRES.
TOTAL	13	23	

5. An amendment by Ms. Lesko to add a section regarding prohibition of autonomous zones was defeated by a rollcall vote of 12 to 23.

Roll Call No. **Date:** 6/17/20

COMMITTEE ON THE JUDICIARY

House of Representatives

116th Congress

Amendment # 5 ( ) to ANS HR 7120 offered by Rep. LESKO

☐ PASSED

☑ FAILED

	AYES	NOS	PRES.
Jerrold Nadler (NY-10)		✓	
Zoe Lofgren (CA-19)		✓	
Sheila Jackson Lee (TX-18)		✓	
Steve Cohen (TN-09)		✓	
Hank Johnson (GA-04)			
Ted Deutch (FL-22)		✓	
Karen Bass (CA-37)		✓	
Cedric Richmond (LA-02)		✓	
Hakeem Jeffries (NY-08)		✓	
David Cicilline (RI-01)		✓	
Eric Swalwell (CA-15)		✓	
Ted Lieu (CA-33)			
Jamie Raskin (MD-08)		✓	
Pramila Jayapal (WA-07)		✓	
Val Demings (FL-10)		✓	
Lou Correa (CA-46)		✓	
Mary Gay Scanlon (PA-05)		✓	
Sylvia Garcia (TX-29)		✓	
Joseph Neguse (CO-02)		✓	
Lucy McBath (GA-06)		✓	
Greg Stanton (AZ-09)		✓	
Madeleine Dean (PA-04)		✓	
Debbie Mucarsel-Powell (FL-26)		✓	
Veronica Escobar (TX-16)		✓	
	AYES	NOS	PRES
Jim Jordan (OH-04)	✓		
James F. Sensenbrenner (WI-05)			
Steve Chabot (OH-01)	✓		
Louie Gohmert (TX-01)			
Doug Collins (GA-27)	✓		
Ken Buck (CO-04)	✓		
Martha Roby (AL-02)		✓	
Matt Gaetz (FL-01)	✓		
Mike Johnson (LA-04)	✓		
Andy Biggs (AZ-05)			
Tom McClintock (CA-04)	✓		
Debbie Lesko (AZ-08)	✓		
Guy Reschenthaler (PA-14)	✓		
Ben Cline (VA-06)	✓		
Kelly Armstrong (ND-AL)	✓		
Greg Steube (FL-17)	✓		
	AYES	NOS	PRES.
TOTAL	12	23	

6. An amendment by Mr. Steube to strike section 365 was defeated by a rollcall vote of 10 to 24.

Roll Call No. **Date:** 6/17/20

COMMITTEE ON THE JUDICIARY

House of Representatives

116th Congress

Amendment #6 ( ) to ANS HR7120 offered by Rep. Steube

☐ PASSED

☒ FAILED

	AYES	NOS	PRES.
Jerrold Nadler (NY-10)		✓	
Zoe Lofgren (CA-19)		✓	
Sheila Jackson Lee (TX-18)		✓	
Steve Cohen (TN-09)		✓	
Hank Johnson (GA-04)			
Ted Deutch (FL-22)		✓	
Karen Bass (CA-37)		✓	
Cedric Richmond (LA-02)		✓	
Hakeem Jeffries (NY-08)			
David Cicilline (RI-01)		✓	
Eric Swalwell (CA-15)		✓	
Ted Lieu (CA-33)		✓	
Jamie Raskin (MD-08)		✓	
Pramila Jayapal (WA-07)		✓	
Val Demings (FL-10)		✓	
Lou Correa (CA-46)		✓	
Mary Gay Scanlon (PA-05)		✓	
Sylvia Garcia (TX-29)		✓	
Joseph Neguse (CO-02)		✓	
Lucy McBath (GA-06)		✓	
Greg Stanton (AZ-09)		✓	
Madeleine Dean (PA-04)		✓	
Debbie Mucarsel-Powell (FL-26)		✓	
Veronica Escobar (TX-16)		✓	
	AYES	NOS	PRES
Jim Jordan (OH-04)	✓		
James F. Sensenbrenner (WI-05)			
Steve Chabot (OH-01)	✓		
Louie Gohmert (TX-01)			
Doug Collins (GA-27)	✓		
Ken Buck (CO-04)	✓		
Martha Roby (AL-02)	✓		
Matt Gaetz (FL-01)		✓	
Mike Johnson (LA-04)	✓		
Andy Biggs (AZ-05)			
Tom McClintock (CA-04)		✓	
Debbie Lesko (AZ-08)	✓		
Guy Reschenthaler (PA-14)			
Ben Cline (VA-06)	✓		
Kelly Armstrong (ND-AL)	✓		
Greg Steube (FL-17)	✓		
	AYES	NOS	PRES.
TOTAL	10	24	

7. An amendment by Mr. Gaetz to add a section regarding a study on no-knock warrants was defeated by a rollcall vote of 12 to 24.

Roll Call No. **Date:** 6/17/20

COMMITTEE ON THE JUDICIARY

House of Representatives

116th Congress

Amendment # 7 ( ) to ANS HR 7120 offered by Rep. Gaetz

☐ PASSED

☑ FAILED

	AYES	NOS	PRES.
Jerrold Nadler (NY-10)		✓	
Zoe Lofgren (CA-19)		✓	
Sheila Jackson Lee (TX-18)		✓	
Steve Cohen (TN-09)		✓	
Hank Johnson (GA-04)		✓	
Ted Deutch (FL-22)		✓	
Karen Bass (CA-37)		✓	
Cedric Richmond (LA-02)		✓	
Hakeem Jeffries (NY-08)			
David Cicilline (RI-01)		✓	
Eric Swalwell (CA-15)		✓	
Ted Lieu (CA-33)		✓	
Jamie Raskin (MD-08)		✓	
Pramila Jayapal (WA-07)		✓	
Val Demings (FL-10)		✓	
Lou Correa (CA-46)		✓	
Mary Gay Scanlon (PA-05)		✓	
Sylvia Garcia (TX-29)		✓	
Joseph Neguse (CO-02)		✓	
Lucy McBath (GA-06)		✓	
Greg Stanton (AZ-09)		✓	
Madeleine Dean (PA-04)		✓	
Debbie Mucarsel-Powell (FL-26)		✓	
Veronica Escobar (TX-16)		✓	
	AYES	NOS	PRES
Jim Jordan (OH-04)	✓		
James F. Sensenbrenner (WI-05)			
Steve Chabot (OH-01)	✓		
Louie Gohmert (TX-01)			
Doug Collins (GA-27)	✓		
Ken Buck (CO-04)	✓		
Martha Roby (AL-02)	✓		
Matt Gaetz (FL-01)	✓		
Mike Johnson (LA-04)	✓		
Andy Biggs (AZ-05)			
Tom McClintock (CA-04)	✓		
Debbie Lesko (AZ-08)	✓		
Guy Reschenthaler (PA-14)	✓		
Ben Cline (VA-06)	✓		
Kelly Armstrong (ND-AL)	✓		
Greg Steube (FL-17)		✓	
	AYES	NOS	PRES.
TOTAL	12	24	

8. An amendment by Mr. Cline to add a section on limitations on collective bargaining agreements was defeated by a rollcall vote of 12 to 23.

Roll Call No. **Date:** 6/17/20

COMMITTEE ON THE JUDICIARY

House of Representatives

116th Congress

Amendment # 8 (__) to ANS HR 7120 offered by Rep. Cline

☐ PASSED

☑ FAILED

	AYES	NOS	PRES.
Jerrold Nadler (NY-10)		✓	
Zoe Lofgren (CA-19)		✓	
Sheila Jackson Lee (TX-18)		✓	
Steve Cohen (TN-09)		✓	
Hank Johnson (GA-04)		✓	
Ted Deutch (FL-22)		✓	
Karen Bass (CA-37)		✓	
Cedric Richmond (LA-02)		✓	
Hakeem Jeffries (NY-08)			
David Cicilline (RI-01)		✓	
Eric Swalwell (CA-15)		✓	
Ted Lieu (CA-33)		✓	
Jamie Raskin (MD-08)		✓	
Pramila Jayapal (WA-07)		✓	
Val Demings (FL-10)		✓	
Lou Correa (CA-46)		✓	
Mary Gay Scanlon (PA-05)		✓	
Sylvia Garcia (TX-29)		✓	
Joseph Neguse (CO-02)		✓	
Lucy McBath (GA-06)		✓	
Greg Stanton (AZ-09)		✓	
Madeleine Dean (PA-04)		✓	
Debbie Mucarsel-Powell (FL-26)		✓	
Veronica Escobar (TX-16)		✓	
	AYES	NOS	PRES
Jim Jordan (OH-04)	✓		
James F. Sensenbrenner (WI-05)			
Steve Chabot (OH-01)	✓		
Louie Gohmert (TX-01)			
Doug Collins (GA-27)	✓		
Ken Buck (CO-04)	✓		
Martha Roby (AL-02)	✓		
Matt Gaetz (FL-01)	✓		
Mike Johnson (LA-04)	✓		
Andy Biggs (AZ-05)			
Tom McClintock (CA-04)	✓		
Debbie Lesko (AZ-08)	✓		
Guy Reschenthaler (PA-14)			
Ben Cline (VA-06)	✓		
Kelly Armstrong (ND-AL)	✓		
Greg Steube (FL-17)	✓		
	AYES	NOS	PRES.
TOTAL	12	23	

9. An amendment by Mr. Steube to strike section 362 was defeated by a rollcall vote of 13 to 25.

Roll Call No. **Date:** 6/17/20

COMMITTEE ON THE JUDICIARY

House of Representatives

116th Congress

Amendment #9 (__) to ANS HR 7120 offered by Rep. Steube

☐ PASSED

☑ FAILED

	AYES	NOS	PRES.
Jerrold Nadler (NY-10)		✓	
Zoe Lofgren (CA-19)		✓	
Sheila Jackson Lee (TX-18)		✓	
Steve Cohen (TN-09)		✓	
Hank Johnson (GA-04)		✓	
Ted Deutch (FL-22)		✓	
Karen Bass (CA-37)		✓	
Cedric Richmond (LA-02)		✓	
Hakeem Jeffries (NY-08)		✓	
David Cicilline (RI-01)		✓	
Eric Swalwell (CA-15)		✓	
Ted Lieu (CA-33)		✓	
Jamie Raskin (MD-08)		✓	
Pramila Jayapal (WA-07)		✓	
Val Demings (FL-10)		✓	
Lou Correa (CA-46)		✓	
Mary Gay Scanlon (PA-05)		✓	
Sylvia Garcia (TX-29)		✓	
Joseph Neguse (CO-02)		✓	
Lucy McBath (GA-06)		✓	
Greg Stanton (AZ-09)		✓	
Madeleine Dean (PA-04)		✓	
Debbie Mucarsel-Powell (FL-26)		✓	
Veronica Escobar (TX-16)		✓	
	AYES	NOS	PRES
Jim Jordan (OH-04)	✓		
James F. Sensenbrenner (WI-05)			
Steve Chabot (OH-01)	✓		
Louie Gohmert (TX-01)			
Doug Collins (GA-27)	✓		
Ken Buck (CO-04)	✓		
Martha Roby (AL-02)	✓		
Matt Gaetz (FL-01)	✓		
Mike Johnson (LA-04)	✓		
Andy Biggs (AZ-05)	✓		
Tom McClintock (CA-04)		✓	
Debbie Lesko (AZ-08)	✓		
Guy Reschenthaler (PA-14)	✓		
Ben Cline (VA-06)	✓		
Kelly Armstrong (ND-AL)	✓		
Greg Steube (FL-17)	✓		
	AYES	NOS	PRES.
TOTAL	13	25	

10. An amendment by Mr. Gaetz to strike subparagraph A on page 85 and strike line 23 on page 86 was defeated by a rollcall vote of 14 to 24.

Roll Call No. **Date:** 6/17/20

COMMITTEE ON THE JUDICIARY

House of Representatives

116th Congress

Amendment # 10 ( ) to ANS HR 7120 offered by Rep. Gaetz

☐ PASSED

☐ FAILED

	AYES	NOS	PRES.
Jerrold Nadler (NY-10)		✓	
Zoe Lofgren (CA-19)		✓	
Sheila Jackson Lee (TX-18)		✓	
Steve Cohen (TN-09)		✓	
Hank Johnson (GA-04)		✓	
Ted Deutch (FL-22)		✓	
Karen Bass (CA-37)		✓	
Cedric Richmond (LA-02)		✓	
Hakeem Jeffries (NY-08)		✓	
David Cicilline (RI-01)		✓	
Eric Swalwell (CA-15)		✓	
Ted Lieu (CA-33)		✓	
Jamie Raskin (MD-08)		✓	
Pramila Jayapal (WA-07)		✓	
Val Demings (FL-10)		✓	
Lou Correa (CA-46)		✓	
Mary Gay Scanlon (PA-05)		✓	
Sylvia Garcia (TX-29)		✓	
Joseph Neguse (CO-02)		✓	
Lucy McBath (GA-06)		✓	
Greg Stanton (AZ-09)		✓	
Madeleine Dean (PA-04)		✓	
Debbie Mucarsel-Powell (FL-26)		✓	
Veronica Escobar (TX-16)		✓	
	AYES	NOS	PRES
Jim Jordan (OH-04)	✓		
James F. Sensenbrenner (WI-05)			
Steve Chabot (OH-01)	✓		
Louie Gohmert (TX-01)			
Doug Collins (GA-27)	✓		
Ken Buck (CO-04)	✓		
Martha Roby (AL-02)	✓		
Matt Gaetz (FL-01)	✓		
Mike Johnson (LA-04)	✓		
Andy Biggs (AZ-05)	✓		
Tom McClintock (CA-04)	✓		
Debbie Lesko (AZ-08)	✓		
Guy Reschenthaler (PA-14)	✓		
Ben Cline (VA-06)	✓		
Kelly Armstrong (ND-AL)	✓		
Greg Steube (FL-17)	✓		
	AYES	NOS	PRES.
TOTAL	14	24	

11. An amendment by Mr. Biggs to add a section regarding deescalation tactics and techniques was defeated by a rollcall vote of 9 to 26.

Roll Call No. **Date:** 6/17/20

COMMITTEE ON THE JUDICIARY

House of Representatives

116th Congress

Amendment #11 ( ) to ANS HR 7120 offered by Rep. Biggs

☐ PASSED

☑ FAILED

	AYES	NOS	PRES.
Jerrold Nadler (NY-10)		✓	
Zoe Lofgren (CA-19)		✓	
Sheila Jackson Lee (TX-18)		✓	
Steve Cohen (TN-09)		✓	
Hank Johnson (GA-04)		✓	
Ted Deutch (FL-22)		✓	
Karen Bass (CA-37)		✓	
Cedric Richmond (LA-02)		✓	
Hakeem Jeffries (NY-08)			
David Cicilline (RI-01)		✓	
Eric Swalwell (CA-15)		✓	
Ted Lieu (CA-33)		✓	
Jamie Raskin (MD-08)		✓	
Pramila Jayapal (WA-07)		✓	
Val Demings (FL-10)		✓	
Lou Correa (CA-46)		✓	
Mary Gay Scanlon (PA-05)		✓	
Sylvia Garcia (TX-29)		✓	
Joseph Neguse (CO-02)		✓	
Lucy McBath (GA-06)		✓	
Greg Stanton (AZ-09)		✓	
Madeleine Dean (PA-04)		✓	
Debbie Mucarsel-Powell (FL-26)		✓	
Veronica Escobar (TX-16)		✓	
	AYES	NOS	PRES
Jim Jordan (OH-04)	✓		
James F. Sensenbrenner (WI-05)			
Steve Chabot (OH-01)	✓		
Louie Gohmert (TX-01)			
Doug Collins (GA-27)			
Ken Buck (CO-04)	✓		
Martha Roby (AL-02)		✓	
Matt Gaetz (FL-01)	✓		
Mike Johnson (LA-04)	✓		
Andy Biggs (AZ-05)	✓		
Tom McClintock (CA-04)	✓		
Debbie Lesko (AZ-08)	✓		
Guy Reschenthaler (PA-14)	✓		
Ben Cline (VA-06)		✓	
Kelly Armstrong (ND-AL)		✓	
Greg Steube (FL-17)			
	AYES	NOS	PRES.
TOTAL	9	26	

12. An amendment by Ms. Lesko to add a section on no COPS grants for jurisdictions that defund the police was defeated by a rollcall vote of 13 to 25.

Roll Call No. **Date:** 6/17/20

COMMITTEE ON THE JUDICIARY

House of Representatives

116th Congress

Amendment #12 (___) to ANS HR7120 offered by Rep. Lesko

☐ PASSED

☑ FAILED

	AYES	NOS	PRES.
Jerrold Nadler (NY-10)		✓	
Zoe Lofgren (CA-19)		✓	
Sheila Jackson Lee (TX-18)		✓	
Steve Cohen (TN-09)		✓	
Hank Johnson (GA-04)		✓	
Ted Deutch (FL-22)		✓	
Karen Bass (CA-37)		✓	
Cedric Richmond (LA-02)		✓	
Hakeem Jeffries (NY-08)			
David Cicilline (RI-01)		✓	
Eric Swalwell (CA-15)		✓	
Ted Lieu (CA-33)		✓	
Jamie Raskin (MD-08)		✓	
Pramila Jayapal (WA-07)		✓	
Val Demings (FL-10)		✓	
Lou Correa (CA-46)		✓	
Mary Gay Scanlon (PA-05)		✓	
Sylvia Garcia (TX-29)		✓	
Joseph Neguse (CO-02)		✓	
Lucy McBath (GA-06)		✓	
Greg Stanton (AZ-09)		✓	
Madeleine Dean (PA-04)		✓	
Debbie Mucarsel-Powell (FL-26)		✓	
Veronica Escobar (TX-16)		✓	
	AYES	NOS	PRES
Jim Jordan (OH-04)	✓		
James F. Sensenbrenner (WI-05)			
Steve Chabot (OH-01)	✓		
Louie Gohmert (TX-01)			
Doug Collins (GA-27)	✓		
Ken Buck (CO-04)	✓		
Martha Roby (AL-02)		✓	
Matt Gaetz (FL-01)	✓		
Mike Johnson (LA-04)	✓		
Andy Biggs (AZ-05)	✓		
Tom McClintock (CA-04)	✓		
Debbie Lesko (AZ-08)	✓		
Guy Reschenthaler (PA-14)	✓		
Ben Cline (VA-06)	✓		
Kelly Armstrong (ND-AL)	✓		
Greg Steube (FL-17)	✓		
	AYES	NOS	PRES.
TOTAL	13	24	

13. Motion to report H.R. 7120, as amended, favorably was agreed to by a rollcall vote of 24 to 14.

Roll Call No.

Date: 6/17/20

COMMITTEE ON THE JUDICIARY

House of Representatives

116th Congress

Final Passage on HR 7120

☑ PASSED

☐ FAILED

	AYES	NOS	PRES.	
Jerrold Nadler (NY-10)	✓			
Zoe Lofgren (CA-19)	✓			
Sheila Jackson Lee (TX-18)	✓			
Steve Cohen (TN-09)	✓			
Hank Johnson (GA-04)	✓			
Ted Deutch (FL-22)	✓			
Karen Bass (CA-37)	✓			
Cedric Richmond (LA-02)	✓			
Hakeem Jeffries (NY-08)	✓			
David Cicilline (RI-01)	✓			
Eric Swalwell (CA-15)	✓			
Ted Lieu (CA-33)	✓			
Jamie Raskin (MD-08)	✓			
Pramila Jayapal (WA-07)	✓			
Val Demings (FL-10)	✓			
Lou Correa (CA-46)	✓			
Mary Gay Scanlon (PA-05)	✓			
Sylvia Garcia (TX-29)	✓			
Joseph Neguse (CO-02)	✓			
Lucy McBath (GA-06)	✓			
Greg Stanton (AZ-09)	✓			
Madeleine Dean (PA-04)	✓			
Debbie Mucarsel-Powell (FL-26)	✓			
Veronica Escobar (TX-16)	✓			
	AYES	NOS	PRES	
Jim Jordan (OH-04)		✓		
James F. Sensenbrenner (WI-05)				
Steve Chabot (OH-01)		✓		
Louie Gohmert (TX-01)				
Doug Collins (GA-27)		✓		
Ken Buck (CO-04)		✓		
Martha Roby (AL-02)		✓		
Matt Gaetz (FL-01)		✓		
Mike Johnson (LA-04)		✓		
Andy Biggs (AZ-05)		✓		
Tom McClintock (CA-04)		✓		
Debbie Lesko (AZ-08)		✓		
Guy Reschenthaler (PA-14)		✓		
Ben Cline (VA-06)		✓		
Kelly Armstrong (ND-AL)		✓		
Greg Steube (FL-17)		✓		
	AYES	NOS	PRES.	
TOTAL	24	14		

Committee Oversight Findings

In compliance with clause 3(c)(1) of rule XIII of the Rules of the House of Representatives, the Committee advises that the findings and recommendations of the Committee, based on oversight activities under clause 2(b)(1) of rule X of the Rules of the House of Representatives, are incorporated in the descriptive portions of this report.

New Budget Authority and Tax Expenditures and Congressional Budget Office Cost Estimate

With respect to the requirements of clause 3(c)(2) of rule XIII of the Rules of the House of Representatives and section 308(a) of the Congressional Budget Act of 1974 and with respect to requirements of clause (3)(c)(3) of rule XIII of the Rules of the House of Representatives and section 402 of the Congressional Budget Act of 1974, the Committee has requested but not received a cost estimate for this bill from the Director of Congressional Budget Office. The Committee has requested but not received from the Director of the Congressional Budget Office a statement as to whether this bill contains any new budget authority, spending authority, credit authority, or an increase or decrease in revenues or tax expenditures.

Duplication of Federal Programs

No provision of H.R. 7120 establishes or reauthorizes a program of the federal government known to be duplicative of another federal program, a program that was included in any report from the Government Accountability Office to Congress pursuant to section 21 of Public Law 111–139, or a program related to a program identified in the most recent Catalog of Federal Domestic Assistance.

Performance Goals and Objectives

The Committee states that pursuant to clause 3(c)(4) of rule XIII of the Rules of the House of Representatives, H.R. 7120 would create new statutory provisions and amend existing statutes to ensure greater accountability for and transparency of law enforcement uses of force, create uniform standards, and ensure better training for law enforcement to minimize the risk of unnecessary or excessive uses of force, and study possible public safety innovations.

Advisory on Earmarks

In accordance with clause 9 of rule XXI of the Rules of the House of Representatives, H.R. 7120 does not contain any congressional earmarks, limited tax benefits, or limited tariff benefits as defined in clause 9(d), 9(e), or 9(f) of rule XXI.

Section-by-Section Analysis

The following discussion describes the bill as reported by the Committee.

Section 1. Short Title; Table of Contents. Section 1 sets forth the short title "George Floyd Justice in Policing Act of 2020" and contains the table of contents.

Section 2. Definitions. Section 2 contains the definitions used under the Act.

Title I—Police Accountability

Subtitle A—Holding Police Accountable in the Courts

Section 101. Deprivation of Rights under Color of Law. Section 101 amends 18 U.S.C. 242, a criminal statute under which law enforcement officers can be charged for willful violation of rights under color of law. Section 101(1) changes the statute's *mens rea* requirement from "willfully" to "knowingly or recklessly." Section 101(2) strikes the death penalty from the sentences currently permitted under 18 U.S.C. 242. Section 101(3) adds a new sentence to the end of the statute that defines an act under 18 U.S.C. 242 to be considered to have resulted in death if the act was a substantial factor contributing to the death of the person.

Section 102. Qualified Immunity Reform

Section 102 amends 42 U.S.C. 1983, a statute that allows individuals to bring suit for harms resulting from a deprivation of a constitutional right, to prohibit law enforcement officers from asserting a defense or immunity that (1) the defendant was acting in good faith, or that the defendant believed, reasonably or otherwise, that his or her conduct was lawful at the time when the conduct was committed; or (2) the rights, privileges, or immunities secured by the Constitution and laws were not clearly established at the time of their deprivation by the defendant, or that at such time, the state of the law was otherwise such that the defendant could not reasonably have been expected to know whether his or her conduct was lawful.

Section 103. Pattern and Practice Investigations

Section 103 amends 34 U.S.C. 12601, a statute that prohibits a government authority or official from engaging in a pattern or practice of conduct that deprives persons of their constitutional rights and permits the Attorney General to file a civil action to eliminate the pattern or practice.

Section 103(a)(1) adds language making explicit the existing understanding and practice that 34 U.S.C. 12601(a) prohibits prosecutors from engaging in a pattern or practice of conduct that deprives persons of their constitutional rights.

Section 103(a)(2) amends section 34 U.S.C. 12601(b) by changing a reference to paragraph (1) to subsection (a).

Section 103(a)(3) creates new subsections (c) through (f) under 34 U.S.C. 12601:

New subsection (c) provides the Attorney General with subpoena authority to carry out pattern or practice investigations under 34 U.S.C. 12601(b).

New subsection (d) permits state attorneys general or other such official as a state may designate to bring a civil action in the appropriate federal district court to obtain appropriate equitable and declaratory relief to eliminate a pattern or practice, and grants states attorneys general or official carrying out the authority in this subsection the same subpoena authority granted to the Attorney General under new subsection (c).

New subsection (e) adds a rule of construction stating that nothing in this section may be construed to limit the authority of the Attorney General under 34 U.S.C. 12601(b) in any case in which a state attorney general brought a civil action under new subsection (d).

New subsection (f) adds a requirement that one year after the date of enactment and annually thereafter, the Civil Rights Division shall make publicly available on an internet website a report on, during the previous year: (1) the number of preliminary investigations of violations of subsection (a) that were commenced; (2) the number of preliminary investigations of violations of subsection (a) that were resolved; and (3) the status of any pending investigations of violations of subsection (a).

Section 103(b)(1) authorizes the Attorney General to award grants to assist a state in conducting pattern and practice investigations under 34 U.S.C. 12601. Grants authorized under this subsection may be used only to investigate a pattern or practice of misconduct by law enforcement officers, including prosecutor's offices, or by officials or employees of any governmental agency with responsibility for the administration of juvenile justice or the incarceration of juveniles.

Section 103(b)(2) requires that a state seeking a grant under paragraph (1) must submit an application in such form, at such time, and containing such information required by the Attorney General.

Section(b)(3) authorizes an appropriation of $100M to the Attorney General for each of FY 2021 through 2023 to carry out this subsection.

Section 103(c) amends 34 U.S.C. 12602, a statute that permits the Attorney General, through appropriate means, to collect data about the use of excessive force by law enforcement officers.

Section 103(c)(1)(A) amends 34 U.S.C. 12602(a) to create a new subsection (a)(1) by striking Attorney General and inserting "(1) Federal Collection of Data—Attorney General."

Section 103(c)(1)(B) also amends 34 U.S.C. 12602(a) by adding a new subparagraph (2) to permit state attorneys general, through appropriate means, to acquire data about the use of excessive force by law enforcement officers and to allow such data to be used in conducting pattern or practice investigations permitted under 34 U.S.C. 12601. It also prohibits data collected under this paragraph from containing any information that may reveal the identity of the victim or any law enforcement officers.

Section 103(c)(2) amends 34 U.S.C. 12602(b), which limits the use of data acquired by the Attorney General under 34 U.S.C. 12602(a), to reference new subsection (a)(1).

Section 104. Independent Investigations

Section 104 authorizes the Attorney General to award grants to eligible states and Indian Tribes to assist in implementing independent investigation of law enforcement statute. It also amends 34 U.S.C. 10381 et seq. to permit the Community Oriented Policing Services (COPS) program to fund grants to develop best practices for and to create civilian review boards.

Section 104(a)(1) contains definitions that apply in this subsection.

Section 104(a)(2) authorizes the Attorney General to award grants to eligible states or Indian Tribes under this subsection. Grants authorized under this subsection may be used only to implement such a statute or conduct independent investigations into the use of deadly force by law enforcement officers.

Section 104(a)(3) requires a state or Indian Tribe to have in effect an independent investigation of law enforcement statute to be eligible for a grant under this subsection.

Section 104(a)(4) authorizes an appropriation to the Attorney General of $750M for FY 2021 through 2023 to carry out this subsection.

Section 104(b) amends 34 U.S.C. 10381 et seq. to permit the COPS program to fund grants to develop best practices for and to create civilian review boards.

Subtitle B—Law Enforcement Trust and Integrity Act

Section 111. Short Title

Section 111 sets forth the short title of the subtitle as the "Law Enforcement Trust and Integrity Act of 2020."

Section 112. Definitions

Section 112 contains the definitions used under the subtitle.

Section 113. Accreditation of Law Enforcement Agencies

Section 113 requires the Attorney General to study existing law enforcement accreditation standards nationwide and then recommend the adoption of additional standards that will result in greater community accountability of law enforcement agencies.

Section 113(a)(1) requires the Attorney General to perform an analysis of existing law enforcement accreditation standards developed by law enforcement accreditation organizations nationwide.

Section 113(a)(2)(A) requires the Attorney General, following the completion of the analysis described in section 113(a)(1), to recommend in consultation with law enforcement accreditation organizations and community-based organizations, the adoption of additional standards that will result in greater community accountability of law enforcement agencies and an increased focus on policing with a guardian mentality.

Included must be standards related to early warning systems and related intervention programs; use of force procedures; civilian review procedures; traffic and pedestrian stop and search procedures; data collection and transparency; administrative due process requirements; video monitoring technology; youth justice and school safety; and recruitment, hiring, and training.

Section 113(a)(2)(B) also requires the Attorney General to recommend additional areas for the development of national standards for the accreditation of law enforcement agencies in consultation with existing law enforcement accreditation organizations, professional law enforcement associations, labor organizations, and professional civilian oversight organizations.

Section 113(a)(3) requires the Attorney General to adopt policies and procedures to partner with existing law enforcement accreditation organizations, professional law enforcement associations, labor organizations, and professional civilian oversight organizations to continue development of further accreditation standards consistent with Section 113(a)(2)(b); to encourage the pursuit of accreditation of federal, state, local, and tribal law enforcement agencies by certified law enforcement accreditation organizations; and to develop recommendations for implementation of a national accreditation requirement tied to federal grant eligibility.

Section 113(b) amends 34 U.S.C. 10153(a) to add a new paragraph (7) that requires that a grant application made under this part include an assurance that for each fiscal year covered by an application, the applicant will use not less than 5 percent of the total amount of the grant award for the fiscal year to assist law enforcement agencies of the applicant, including campus public safety departments, gain or maintain accreditation from certified law enforcement accreditation organizations in accordance with section 113 of the Law Enforcement Trust and Integrity Act of 2020.

Section 114. Law Enforcement Grants

Section 114(a) amends 34 U.S.C. 10153(a), as amended by section 113, by adding a new paragraph (8) that requires that a grant application made under this part include an assurance that for each fiscal year covered by an application, the applicant will use not less than 5 percent of the total amount of the grant award for the fiscal year to study and implement effective management, training, recruiting, hiring, and oversight standards and programs to promote effective community and problem solving strategies for law enforcement agencies in accordance with section 114 of the Law Enforcement Trust and Integrity Act of 2020.

Section 114(b) authorizes the Attorney General to make grants to community-based organizations to study and implement (1) effective management, training, recruiting, hiring, and oversight standards and programs to promote effective community and problem solving strategies for law enforcement agencies; or (2) effective strategies and solutions to public safety, including strategies that do not rely on federal and local law enforcement agency response. Section 114(c) requires that grant amounts described in new paragraph (8) added to 34 U.S.C. 10153(a) by section 114(a) and grant amounts awarded under section 114(b) of this section be used to: (1) study management and operations standards for law enforcement agencies, including standards relating to administrative due process, residency requirements, compensation and benefits, use of force, racial profiling, early warning and intervention systems, youth justice, school safety, civil review boards or analogous procedures, or research into the effectiveness of existing programs, projects, or other activities designed to address misconduct and (2) to develop pilot program and implement effective standards and programs in the areas of training, hiring and recruitment, and oversight that are designed to improve management and address misconduct by law enforcement officers.

Section 114(d) requires that a pilot program developed under section 114(c)(2) include implementation of the following: (1) Training;

(2) Recruitment, Hiring, Retention, and Promotion of Diverse Law Enforcement Officers; (3) Oversight; (4) Youth Justice and School Safety; and (5) Victim Services.

Section 114(e) permits (1) the Attorney general to provide technical assistance to states and community-based organizations in furtherance of this section; and (2) the technical assistance provided by the Attorney

General may include the development of models for states and community-based organizations to reduce law enforcement officer misconduct. Any development of such models shall be in consultation with community-based organizations.

Section 114(f) permits the Attorney General to use any component or components of the Department of Justice in carrying out this section.

Section 114(g) requires an application for a grant under 114(b) to be submitted in such form and contain such information as the Attorney General may prescribe by rule.

Section 114(h) requires each program, project, or activity funded under this section to contain a monitoring component, which shall be developed pursuant to rules made by the Attorney General.

Section 114(i) permits the Attorney General, as a result of monitoring under section 114(h) or otherwise, to revoke or suspend funding of a grant made under the Byrne grant program or under section 114(b) if the Attorney General determines that the grant is not in substantial compliance with the requirements of this section.

Section 114(j) defines for the purposes of this section the term "civilian review board."

Section 114(k) authorizes an appropriation to the Attorney General of $25M for Fiscal Year 2021 to carry out the grant program authorized under section 114(b).

Section 115. Attorney General to Conduct Study

Section 115(a)(1) requires the Attorney General to conduct a nationwide study of the prevalence and effect of any law, rule, or procedure that allows a law enforcement officer to delay the response to questions posed by local internal affairs officer, or review board on the investigative integrity and prosecution of law enforcement misconduct, including pre-interview warnings and termination policies. As part of the study, the Attorney General is required to conduct an initial analysis as described in section 115(a)(2) followed by a nationwide data collection as described in section 115(a)(3). Section 115(b)(1) requires the Attorney General to submit a report to Congress and the public 120 days after enactment containing the results of the initial analysis prescribed by this section and identify the jurisdictions for which the study is to be conducted. Section 115(b)(2) requires the Attorney General not less than 2 years after enactment to submit a report to Congress containing the results of the data collection prescribed under this section and publish the report in the Federal Register.

Section 116. Authorization of Appropriations

Section 116 authorizes for fiscal year 2021, in addition to any other sums authorized to be appropriated: (1) $25M for additional expenses related to the enforcement of 34 U.S.C. 12601, criminal enforcement under 18 241 and 242, and administrative enforcement by the Department of Justice of such sections, including compliance with consent decrees or judgments; and (2) $3.3M for additional expenses related to conflict resolution by the Department of Justice's Community Relations Service.

Section 117. National Task Force on Law Enforcement Oversight

Section 117(a) establishes within the Department of Justice a Task Force on Law Enforcement Oversight. Section 117(b) requires that the Task Force be composed of individuals appointed by the Attorney General who is required to appoint not less than 1 individual from the DOJ components described under this section. Section 117(c) outlines the powers and duties of the Task Force and re quires that it consult with professional law enforcement associations, labor organizations, and community-based organizations to coordinate the process of the detection and referral of complaints regarding incidents of alleged law enforcement misconduct. Section 117(d) authorizes an appropriation of $5M for each fiscal year to carry out this section.

Section 118. Federal Data Collection Law Enforcement Practices

Section 118(a) requires each federal, state, tribal, and local law enforcement agency to report data of the practices enumerated in section 118(c) of that agency to the Attorney General.

Section 118(b) requires that for each practice enumerated in section 118(c), the reporting law enforcement agency must provide a breakdown of the number of incidents of that practice by race, ethnicity, age, and gender of the officers of the agency and of members of the public involved in the practice.

Section 118(c) enumerates the practices to be reported to the Attorney General.

Section 118(d) requires that each law enforcement agency required to report data under this section must maintain records relating to any matter reported for 4 years after the creation of the records.

Section 118(e) enacts a penalty on states for failing to report as required under this section. A state shall not receive any amount that would otherwise be allocated to that state under 34 U.S.C. 10156(a) or any amount from any other DOJ law enforcement assistance program unless the state has assured to the satisfaction of the Attorney General that the state and each of its local law enforcement agencies is in substantial compliance with the requirements of this section.

Section 118(f) authorizes the Attorney General to prescribe regulations to carry out this section.

Title II—Policing Transparency through Data

Subtitle A—Misconduct Registry

Section 201. Establishment of National Police Misconduct Registry

Section 201(a) requires the Attorney General not less than 180 days after enactment of this Act to establish a National Police Misconduct Registry to be compiled and maintained by the Department of Justice.

Section 201(b) sets forth the contents of the registry. With respect to all federal and local law enforcement officers, the registry must contain:

(1) each complaint filed against a law enforcement officer aggregated by (A) complaints found credible or that resulted in disciplinary action against the officer; (B) complaints that are pending review; and (C)

complaints for which the officer was exonerated or that were determined to be unfounded or not sustained. All complaints must be disaggregated by whether the complaint involved a use of force or racial profiling.

(2) Discipline records disaggregated by whether the complaint involved a use of force or racial profiling.

(3) Termination records, including the reason for each termination, by whether the complaint involved a use of force or racial profiling.

(4) Records of certification in accordance with Section 202.

(5) Records of lawsuits against law enforcement officers and settlements of such lawsuits.

Section 201(c) requires that the head of each federal law enforcement agency shall submit to the Attorney General the information described in Section 201(b) not later than 1 year after the date of enactment of this Act, and every 6 months thereafter.

Section 201(d) requires a state that receives funds under the Byrne grant program to submit the information described under 201(b) for the state and each local law enforcement agency within the state to the Attorney General every 180 days beginning in the first fiscal year that begins after the date that is one year after the enactment of this Act and each fiscal year thereafter in which the state receives funds under the Byrne grant program.

Section 201(e) requires the Attorney General to make the registry available to the public on a website of the Attorney General in a manner that allows the public to search an individual law enforcement officer's records of misconduct as described in Section 201(b) involving the use of force or racial profiling. Nothing in this subsection shall be construed to supersede the requirements or limitations under the Privacy Act of 1974.

Section 202. Certification Requirements for Hiring of Law Enforcement Officers

Section 202(a) states that a state or unit of local government, other than an Indian Tribe, may not receive funds under the Byrne grant program for that fiscal year if, on the day before that first day of the fiscal year, the state or unit of local government has not: (1) submitted to the Attorney

General evidence that the state or unit of local government has a certification or decertification program for the purposes of employment as a law enforcement officer in that state or unit of local government; and (2) submitted to the registry established under section 201 records demonstrating that all law enforcement officers of the state or unit of local government have completed all state certification requirements during the 1 year period preceding the fiscal year.

Section 202(b) requires the Attorney General to make available to law enforcement agencies all information in the registry under section 201 for purposes of compliance with certification and decertification programs described in section 202(a) and considering applications of employment.

Section 202 (c) authorizes the Attorney General to make rules to carry out section 202 and section 201, including uniform reporting standards.

Subtitle B—Police Reporting Information Data and Evidence (Pride) Act

Section 221. Short Title

Section 221 sets forth the short title of this subtitle as the "Police Reporting Information, Data, and Evidence Act of 2020" or "PRIDE Act of 2020."

Section 222. Definitions

Section 222 sets forth definitions of various terms used in this subtitle.

Section 223. Use of Force Reporting

Section 223(a) requires any state or Indian tribe receiving Byrne grant funds to report to the Attorney General on a quarterly basis, any incident involving use of deadly force or shooting against a civilian by a state, local, or tribal law enforcement officer employed by the grant recipient jurisdiction, any incident involving the death or arrest of an officer, any incident involving use of force by or against an officer, any death in custody, and any use of force in arrests and bookings. Also requires a grant recipient to establish a system and policies to ensure that all use of force incidents are reported by state, local, and tribal law enforcement officers and that they submit to the Attorney General a plan for the required data collection.

The report must contain at least the following information: (1) the national origin, race, sex, ethnicity, age, disability, English language proficiency, and housing status of each civilian against whom state, local, or tribal law enforcement officer used force; (2) the date, time, and location, including whether on school grounds, and zip code of the incident and whether the jurisdiction allows for open-carry or concealed-carry of a firearm; (3) whether the civilian was armed and, if so, the type of weapon the civilian had; (4) the type of force and weapons used against either the officer or the civilian; (5) the reason force was used; (6) a description of injuries sustained because of the incident; (7) the number of officers involved in the incident; and (9) a brief description of the circumstances surrounding the incident. A grant recipient jurisdiction is not required to include in this report an incident reported pursuant to 34 USC 12105(a)(2)). Each law enforcement agency reporting data under this section must maintain records relating to any reportable matter for a minimum of 4 years. In addition, prior to submitting a report, the jurisdiction must compare the information with publicly available sources and revise the report if any incident is determined to be missing.

Section 223(a) further requires that each grant recipient jurisdiction must conduct an annual audit of its use-of-force incident reporting system and submit a report on the audit to the Attorney General.

Section 223(b) reduces by up to 10 percent any amount of Byrne grant funds that a jurisdiction would have received should it fail to comply with the reporting requirements of Section 223(a). That money must instead be reallocated to other jurisdictions that have complied with those requirements. A grant recipient jurisdiction must also ensure that schools and local education agencies provide the required information to the jurisdiction regarding school resources officers.

Section 223(c) requires the Attorney General to publish and make publicly available a report containing the data required to be reported to the Attorney General under Section 223, subject to privacy protections, and further requires the Attorney General to issue guidance on best practices related to establishing standard data collection systems for the required information.

Section 224. Use of Force Data Reporting

Section 224 allows the Attorney General to make grants available to local law enforcement agencies to cover the costs of compliance with Section 223, public awareness campaigns on use of force by or against law enforcement officers, and use of force training for law enforcement agencies and personnel. To be eligible for a grant under this section, the agency must be in a jurisdiction that receives Byrne grant funding, employ 100 or fewer officers, demonstrate that its use of force policy is publicly available, and establish and maintain a complaint system that meets certain requirements.

Section 225. Compliance with Reporting Requirements

Section 225 requires the Attorney General to conduct an audit and review of the information provided by grant recipient jurisdictions pursuant to Section 223. Any data reported must be collected and reported consistent with existing Justice Department data collection programs regarding police-civilian encounters and with civil rights laws governing public dissemination of information. It also requires the Attorney General to issue guidelines for the Section 223 reporting requirement and to seek public comment on those guidelines before issuing them.

Section 226. Federal Law Enforcement Reporting

Section 226 requires each federal law enforcement agency to submit the information outlined in Section 223 to the Attorney General on a quarterly basis.

Section 227. Authorization of Appropriations

Section 227 authorizes appropriations to carry out this subtitle.

Title III—Improving Police Training and Policies

Subtitle A—End Racial and Religious Profiling Act

Section 301. Short Title

Section 301 sets forth the short title of Subtitle A of Title III as the "End Racial and Religious Profiling Act of 2020," or "ERRPA."

Section 302. Definitions

Section 302 provides definitions used within ERRPA. Among other things, subsection 302(6) defines "racial profiling" to include any reliance by law enforcement on a person's "actual or perceived race, ethnicity, national origin, religion, gender, gender identity, or sexual orientation" in making decisions with respect to law enforcement activity. Section 302 provides exceptions where relevant and trustworthy information links a person with a particular characteristic described, and for purposes of tribal law enforcement officers making jurisdictional determinations.

Part I—Prohibition of Racial Profiling

Section 311. Prohibition

Section 311 prohibits all federal, state, and local law enforcement agents and agencies from engaging in racial profiling.

Section 312. Enforcement

Section 312 provides a cause of action for the United States or any injured individual to enforce this prohibition. It also provides that a disparate impact on individuals with characteristics defined in subsection 302(6) constitutes prima facie evidence of racial profiling. Finally, it permits prevailing plaintiffs other than the United States to obtain attorney's fees.

Part II—Programs to Eliminate Racial Profiling by Federal Law Enforcement Agencies

Section 321. Policies to Eliminate Racial Profiling

Section 321 requires federal law enforcement agencies to maintain policies prohibiting racial profiling, including by providing adequate training, collecting relevant data in accordance with Section 341, and implementing procedures to investigate and respond to allegations of racial profiling.

Part III—Programs to Eliminate Racial Profiling by State and Local Law Enforcement Agencies

Section 331. Policies Required for Grants

Section 331 requires any state or local entity applying for a grant under any covered program (defined in subsection 302(1) to include any Byrne grant program or any COPS grant program) to certify that the recipient maintains adequate policies prohibiting racial profiling. Such policies must, among other things, provide for adequate training and collection of relevant data in accordance with Section 341, and include participation in a complaint or audit program to investigate and respond to allegations of racial profiling.

Section 332. Involvement of Attorney General

Section 332 requires the Attorney General within six months of enactment to issue regulations regarding complaint procedures and auditing programs to respond to allegations of racial profiling. It also directs the Attorney General to withhold funds from grant recipients that fail to comply and requires the Attorney General to create a mechanism by which private parties may present evidence that a recipient is not in compliance.

Section 333. Data Collection Demonstration Project

Section 333 creates a $5 million grant program for technical assistance for up to five recipients to engage in data collection regarding law enforcement agencies' "hit rates" (defined in subsection 302(3) as the percentage of stops and searches that yield contraband), disaggregated by race, ethnicity, national origin, gender, and religion. This section also authorizes $500,000 for the Attorney General to conduct an evaluation of the data collected by grantees.

Section 334. Development of Best Practices

Section 334 requires applications for Byrne grants to include an assurance that the applicant will use at least 10 percent of the grant award to develop best practices to eliminate racial profiling.

Section 335. Authorization of Appropriations

Section 335 authorizes funds to the Attorney General as necessary to implement this part.

Part IV—Data Collection

Section 341. Attorney General to Issue Regulations

Section 341 requires the Attorney General within six months of enactment to issue regulations for the collection of relevant data from federal, state, and local law enforcement entities, as provided in sections 321 and 331. It requires, among other things, that the regulations provide for collection of data regarding routine and spontaneous investigatory activities; that the data be disaggregated by race, ethnicity, national origin, gender, disability, and religion; and that the data contain sufficient detail to permit an analysis of whether a law enforcement agency is engaging in racial profiling. It also requires law enforcement agencies to maintain this data for at least four years and requires the Bureau of Justice Statistics to analyze the data for certain statistical disparities and to publish an annual report of its findings, beginning three years after enactment.

Section 342. Publication of Data

Section 342 requires the Bureau of Justice Statistics to provide the data collected under this subtitle to Congress and to the public, together with the report required under Section 341, excluding any personally identifiable information.

Section 343. Limitations on Publication of Data

Section 343 prohibits disclosure of the names or identifying information of law enforcement agents, complainants, or other individuals except under certain specified circumstances. It exempts this information from disclosure under the Freedom of Information Act, except for disclosures of information regarding a particular person to that person.

Part V—Department of Justice Regulations and Reports on Racial Profiling in the United States

Section 351. Attorney General to Issue Regulations and Reports

Section 351 requires the Attorney General to issue such other regulations as may be necessary and requires the Attorney General to issue an annual report to Congress on racial profiling, beginning two years after enactment. The report must include, among other things, a summary of the data collected by the Attorney General from federal, state, and local law enforcement agencies, the status of policies to eliminate racial profiling, and a description of any other policies the Attorney General believes would facilitate the elimination of racial profiling.

Subtitle B—Additional Reforms

Section 361. Training on Racial Bias and Duty to Intervene

Section 361(a) Requires the Attorney General to establish a training program for law enforcement officers to cover racial profiling, implicit bias, and procedural justice. It also requires the Attorney General to establish a duty for federal law enforcement officers to intervene in cases where another officer uses excessive force and requires training program for this duty to intervene. Section 361(b) requires each federal law enforcement officer to complete the training programs established under subsection (a). Section 361(c) conditions Byrne grants for state and local governments on those jurisdictions requiring law enforcement officers to complete the training programs established under subsection (a). Section 361(d) allows grants for training programs for law enforcement officers on use of force and duty to intervene.

Section 362. Ban on No-Knock Warrants in Drug Cases

Section 362(a) amends the Controlled Substances Act to prohibit no-knock warrants by federal law enforcement officers in a drug case. Section 362(b) conditions COPS grants to state and local governments on their having in effect a law that prohibits the issuance of a no-knock warrant in a drug case. Section 362(c) defines "no-knock warrant" as a warrant that allows a law enforcement officer to enter a property without announcing the presence of the officer or the intention of the officer to enter the property.

Section 363. Incentivizing Banning of Chokeholds and Carotid Holds

Section 363(a) defines "chokehold or carotid hold" to mean the application of any pressure to the throat or windpipe, the use of maneuvers restricting blood or oxygen flow to the brain, or carotid artery restraints that prevent or hinder breathing or reduce intake of air. Section 363(b) conditions Byrne grants and COPS grants for state and local governments on that state and local government having in effect a law prohibiting law enforcement officers from using a chokehold or carotid hold. Section 363(c) amends 18 U.S.C. § 242 to define "chokehold or carotid hold" as a "punishment, pain, or penalty." Section 242 makes it a federal crime to, among other things, willfully subject someone to such "punishments, pains, or penalties."

Section 364. PEACE Act

Section 364(a) sets forth the short title of this section as the "Police Exercising Absolute Care with Everyone Act of 2020" or "PEACE Act of

2020." Section 364(b) establishes a use-of-force standard for federal law enforcement officers. Section 364(b)(1) provides definitions of various terms as used in this section. Section 364(b)(2) prohibits a federal law enforcement officer from using less lethal force unless such force is necessary and proportional in order to effectuate an arrest of a person who the officer has probable cause to believe has committed a crime and reasonable alternatives to the less lethal force have been exhausted.

Section 364(b)(3) prohibits a federal law enforcement officer from using deadly force unless the use of deadly force is necessary as a last resort to prevent imminent and serious bodily injury, the use of such force does not create a substantial risk of injury to a third person, and reasonable alternatives have been exhausted.

Section 364(b)(4) requires a federal law enforcement officer, when feasible, to identify himself or herself as a federal law enforcement officer and give a verbal warning prior to using force. The warning must include a request that the suspect surrender and notify that person that the officer will use force if the person resists arrest or flees.

Section 364(b)(5) requires the Attorney General to issue guidance to federal law enforcement agencies on types of less lethal and deadly force prohibited by this section and ways the officer can assess whether use of force is appropriate and necessary and use the least amount of force when interacting with certain types of individuals. Section 364(b)(6) requires the Attorney General to provide training for federal law enforcement officers on how to interact with these categories of individuals.

Section 364(b)(7) disallows a federal law enforcement officer to raise the justification defense in a civil rights prosecution under 18 U.S.C. § § 1111 or 1112 if that officer's use of force violates the standards set forth in Section 364(b) or the officer's gross negligence contributed to the necessity to use such force.

Section 364(c) conditions a state or local government's receipt of Byrne grant funds on the jurisdiction having in effect a law setting forth the same use-of-force standards provided in Section 364(b). A jurisdiction that has had funds withheld and then subsequently enacts a law conforming with this requirement and demonstrates substantial efforts to enforce such a law, would once again be eligible in the follow fiscal year the total amount of funds that were withheld, subject to a 5-fiscal-year cap. Finally, the Attorney General is required to issue guidance to state and local governments on the criteria for determining whether a jurisdiction has enacted law conforming with this section.

Section 365. Stop Militarizing Law Enforcement Act

Section 365(a) contains findings regarding the transfer of military equipment to local law enforcement agencies. Section 365(b) restricts the Defense Department program allowing transfer of equipment to local law enforcement agencies by striking "counterdrug" and "border security activities" as permissible uses for such property. It also adds new conditions for transfer of such property to a local law enforcement agency, including that the recipient submits to the Department a description of how it expects to use the property; the recipient certifies that if the property exceed the recipient's needs, it will return the property to the Department; the recipient certifies that it has notified the local community of the request for the property; and the recipient has received the approval of the local governing body to acquire the property sought from the Department. Section 365(b) also strikes the existing preference for counterdrug, counterterrorism, and border security uses by the recipient agency. Section 365(b) also requires the Secretary of Defense to certify annually that each recipient agency has provided the Secretary a documented accounting for all controlled property, including arms and ammunition, and carried out the bill's other certification requirements. It also requires the Secretary to submit an annual report to Congress describing property to be transferred with a certification that the transfer will not be unlawful. It also prohibits certain types of items from being transferred, including controlled firearms, ammunition, grenade launchers, grenades, and explosives; controlled vehicles, trucks, highly mobile multi-wheeled vehicles, mine-resistant ambush-protected vehicles; drones; controlled aircraft that are combat configured or have no commercial use; silencers; and long-range acoustic devices. It prohibits the Secretary from requiring that a recipient agency demonstrate the use of any small arms or ammunition, and clarifies that the bill's various limitations also apply to property previously transferred by the Defense Department to an agency from that agency to another. This section, however, allows the Secretary to waive the annual certification requirement under certain emergency circumstances. It also prohibits the extension of the military property transfer program unless the Secretary certifies to Congress that: each recipient of controlled property under the program has demonstrated complete accountability for all such property or has been suspended from the program and also certifies that various other actions related to accounting for such property have been taken, and that any recipient for which 100 percent of the property was not accounted for has been suspended from the program. Also, no recipient agency may take ownership of any property transferred under the surplus military property program. Finally, Section 365 requires the Secretary to make a number of reports to Congress regarding various aspects of the property transfer program.

Section 366. Public Safety Innovation Grants

Section 366(a) amends the Byrne grant program statute by adding a new provision concerning local task forces on public safety innovation. That provision states that a law enforcement program eligible to receive Byrne grants may include the development of best practices for and the creation of local task forces on public safety innovation, charged with exploring and developing new strategies for public safety, including non-law enforcement strategies. This section also defines "local task force on public safety innovation" to mean an "administrative entity, created from partnerships between community-based organizations and other local stakeholders, that may develop innovative law enforcement and non-law enforcement strategies to enhance just and equitable public safety, repair breaches of trust between law enforcement agencies and the community they pledge to serve, and enhance accountability of law enforcement officers."

Section 366(b) adds a requirement of a report on best practices for crisis intervention as part of a program assessment of crisis intervention teams.

Section 366(c) adds as a permissible use of COPS grants the recruitment, hiring, retention and training of law enforcement officers who live in or are willing to relocate to (1) communities where relations between police and community residents are poor or where there is a high incidence of crime and (2) are the communities or close to the communities where these officers serve. Such grants may also be used to collect data on the number of officers willing to relocate to communities where they serve and whether such relocations have impacted crime in those communities, and to develop and publicly report strategies and timelines for recruiting, hiring, promoting, and retaining a diverse and inclusive law enforcement workforce.

Subtitle C—Law Enforcement Body Cameras

Part I—Federal Police Camera and Accountability Act

Section 371. Short Title

Section 371 sets forth the short title of this part as the "Federal Police Camera and Accountability Act."

Section 372. Requirements for Federal Law Enforcement Officers Regarding the Use of Body Cameras

Section 372(a) sets forth definitions for various terms used in this part. Section 372(b)(1) requires federal law enforcement officers to wear a body camera. Section 372(b)(2) sets forth the minimum requirements for the camera. Section 372(c) sets forth the requirement that the body camera's video and audio functions be activated whenever a federal law enforcement officer responds to a service call or at the initiation of any other law enforcement or investigative stop involving a member of the public, except when an imminent threat to the officer's life or safety makes activating the camera impossible or dangerous. Under such circumstances, the officer must activate the camera at the first reasonable opportunity. The officer may deactivate the camera after the stop is concluded and the officer leaves the scene.

Section 372(d) requires a federal law enforcement officer to notify a subject of the recording that he or she is being recorded by a body camera as close to the inception of the stop as reasonably possible. Section 372(e) outlines a number of additional requirements with respect to a federal law enforcement officer's use of a body camera with respect to giving notice to a subject of the camera recording and an opportunity for the subject to have the camera discontinue recording. Section 372(f) requires a recording of each offer to discontinue body camera use.

Section 372(g) prohibits the use of body cameras to "gather intelligence information based on First Amendment protected speech, association, or religion, or to record activity that is unrelated to" a legitimate law enforcement activity, and the body camera may not be equipped with or employ any real time facial recognition technologies.

Section 372(h) outlines exceptions to the requirement that a federal law enforcement officer wear a body camera.

Section 372(i) outlines footage retention requirements for body cameras. It requires that the agency employing an officer retain footage for 6 months after it is recorded, and then to delete it permanently. During this 6-month period, certain persons have a right to inspect the footage, including anyone who is a subject of the footage or their legal counsel; the parent or legal guardian of a minor subject or their legal counsel; the spouse, next of kin, or legal authorized designee of a deceased subject of the footage or their legal counsel; the officer whose body camera recorded the footage or their legal counsel; the officer's superior officer; or any defense counsel who claims to have a reasonable basis for believing that the footage contains exculpatory evidence. The right to review the footage does not include the right to possess a copy except when authorized.

Section 372(j) outlines additional retention and deletion requirements for body camera footage, including minimum 3-year retention if the footage captures any use of force or a stop about which the subject of the footage has made a complaint. The footage must be retained for at least 3 years when the footage has been requested by an officer under certain circumstances or by the subject of the footage, a parent or legal guardian of a minor who is a subject of the footage, or a deceased subject's spouse, next of kin, or legally authorized designee.

Section 372(k) provides that any subject of footage, parent or guardian of a minor subject, or deceased subject's next of kin or legally authorized designee must be allowed to review the specific footage to make a determination whether to request a 3-year retention of the footage.

Section 372(l) provides that all video footage of an interaction or event must be provided to any member of the public making a request for it if the interaction or event is identified with reasonable specificity. This section also outlines a number of exceptions to this rule and prioritizes requests for footage where the subject is killed, shot, or grievously injured. It also allows for the use of redaction technology to protect personal privacy of persons appearing in the video footage.

Section 372(m) prohibits withholding body camera footage from the public because it is an investigatory record if any person under investigation is a police officer or other law enforcement employee and the video relates to their official capacity conduct. Section 372(n) provides that any footage retained for six months as required by this part shall not be admissible as evidence in a criminal or civil proceeding. Section 372(o) prohibits public disclosure of body camera footage unless expressly authorized by law. Sections 372(p) and (q) place limitations on the use of body camera footage. Section 372(r) prohibits a third-party agent who maintains body camera footage from independently accessing, viewing, or altering footage except to delete footage as required. Section 372(s) outlines disciplinary procedures for any federal law enforcement officer or employee who fails to follow the requirements regarding body camera recording or footage retention. Section 372(t) provides that where an officer is involved in, a witness to, or in viewable range of a use of force by another officer that results in death, a firearm discharge results in injury, or another officer's conduct becomes the subject of a criminal investigation, the agency must take possession of the camera and any data on it, a copy of the data must be made, and the data must be made publicly available according to the procedures outlined in Section 372(l). Section 372(u) limits footage that violates any law may not be offered as evidence in any criminal or civil action against a member of the public. Section 372(v) requires public disclosure of any agency policy or guidance regarding the use of body cameras or video footage. Section 372(w) is a rule of construction providing that nothing in this part shall be construed to preempt laws governing handling evidence in criminal investigation and prosecutions.

Section 373. Patrol Vehicles with In-Car Video Recording Cameras

Section 373(a) provides definitions to be used in this section. Section 373(b) requires that each federal law enforcement agency install in-car video camera recording equipment in all patrol vehicles with certain recording capabilities. It requires that the equipment be capable of recording for 10 hours or more and that it record certain specified activities, including whenever a patrol vehicle is assigned to patrol duty, certain activities outside a patrol vehicle, and inside the vehicle when transporting an arrestee or when the officer reasonably believes that recording may assist with prosecution, enhance safety, or for some other lawful purpose. Section 373(b)(3) requires a federal law enforcement officer to start recording at the start of an enforcement or investigative stop until the stop is completed and either the officer or the subject has left the scene or when the patrol vehicle emergency lights are activated. Section 373(c) requires that in-car camera footage must be retained for at least 90 days and prohibits footage from being altered or deleted during that time. Section 373(d) requires that audio or video recordings be made available to the public under administrative procedures. Finally, Section 373(e) requires an agency to ensure proper maintenance and care of in-car cameras.

Section 374. Facial Recognition Technology

Section 374 prohibits a camera or recording device required or authorized by this part from being equipped with or employing real time facial recognition technology and also prohibits footage from such camera or recording device from being subjected to such technology.

Section 375. GAO Study

Section 375 requires the GAO to conduct a study within one year of the date of enactment on federal law enforcement officer training, vehicle pursuits, use of force, and interaction with citizens, and to submit such report to the House and Senate Judiciary Committees, the House Oversight and Reform Committee, and the Senate Homeland Security and Governmental Affairs Committee.

Section 376. Regulations

Section 376 requires the Attorney General to issue regulations to carry out this part.

Section 377. Rule of Construction

Section 377 provides that nothing in this part be construed to impose any requirement on a federal law enforcement officer outside of the officer's course of duty.

Part 2—Police Camera Act

Section 381. Short Title

Section 381 sets forth the short title of the part as the "Police Creating Accountability by Making Effective Recording Available Act of 2020" or the "Police CAMERA Act of 2020."

Section 382. Law Enforcement Body-Worn Camera Requirements

Section 382(a) adds a new Byrne grant requirement for a state or local government seeking a grant provide an assurance that for each fiscal year covered by the application, the jurisdiction will use at least 5 percent of the grant award for the fiscal year to develop policies and protocols to comply with the body camera requirements in Section 382(b).

Section 382(b) adds a new "Part OO" to Title I of the Omnibus Crime Control and Safe Streets Act of 1968, to govern use of Byrne grant funds regarding body-worn cameras by state and local law enforcement. It provides, in proposed new Section 3051, that funds provided pursuant to the requirement outlined in Section 382(a) of the bill must be used to purchase or lease body-worn cameras for use by state, local, and tribal law enforcement officers, for expenses related to a body-worn camera program, and to implement certain policies and procedures. It also prohibits the use of expenses for facial recognition technology.

The required policies and procedures for a grant for body-worn cameras include adoption of data collection and retention protocols before the use of body cameras; the development of policies and protocols, with community input, for safe and effective use of cameras; secure storage, handling, and destruction of recorded data; the protection of privacy rights; the release of recorded data from a body camera in accordance with state open records laws; and making recorded data available to prosecutors, defense attorneys, and other court officers. The bill also specifies the issues that the data collection and retention protocols must address, including required uses, such as for the collection and reporting of statistical data on use of force incidents disaggregated by race, ethnicity, gender, and age of the victim, the number of complaints filed against law enforcement officers, the disposition of such complaints, and any other statistical evidence. The protocols must also allow an individual to file a complaint relating to an improper use of body cameras. Proposed Section 3051 also limits use of body camera footage for officer misconduct investigation to those cases where there is a reasonable suspicion that the recording contains evidence of a crime or for limited training purposes and prohibits transfer of any recorded data by a grant recipient to another law enforcement or intelligence agency, with certain exceptions for criminal investigations and civil rights claims.

Proposed Section 3051 requires an audit of the use of funds for body-worn cameras and the development of policies and protocols for their use by grant recipients and requires each grant recipient to file a report with the Director of the Office of Audit, Assessment, and Management. The Director, in turn, must evaluate the policies and protocols of grantees and take steps to ensure compliance with program requirements.

New proposed Section 3052 requires the Director to establish a training toolkit for body-worn cameras. Section 3053 requires the Director to conduct a study within 2 years of the date of enactment of this part on the efficacy of body-worn cameras in deterring police excessive force; the impacts of body-worn cameras on police accountability and transparency, on responses to and adjudications of excessive force complaints, and on evidence collection for criminal investigations; the effects of body-worn cameras on the safety of both law enforcement officers and the public; and on various other issues relating to privacy, individual constitutional rights, limitations on facial recognition technology, public access to body camera footage, and law enforcement body camera use and training. The Director must submit a report to Congress on the study, including any policy recommendations, within 180 days after the study is completed.

Title IV—Justice for Victims of Lynching Act

Section 401. Short Title

Section 401 sets forth the short title of Title IV as the "Emmett Till Anti-Lynching Act."

Section 402. Findings

Section 402 contains findings regarding lynching.

Section 403. Lynching

Section 403 adds at the end of title 18, chapter 13 of the United States Code a new Section 250, making it a crime to conspire with another person to violate existing federal hate crimes statutes.

Title V—Miscellaneous Provisions

Section 501. Severability

Section 501 provides that if any provision of the George Floyd Justice in Policing Act or particular application of it is held to be unconstitutional, the remainder of the Act or any other application shall not be affected.

Section 502. Savings Clause

Section 502 provides that nothing in the Act shall be construed: (1) to limit remedies under 42 U.S.C. 1983 or certain other statutes; affect any laws that apply to an Indian Tribe because of its political status; or waive an Indian Tribe's sovereign immunity without the Tribe's consent.

CHANGES IN EXISTING LAW MADE BY THE BILL, AS REPORTED

In compliance with clause 3(e) of rule XIII of the Rules of the House of Representatives, changes in existing law made by the bill, H.R. 5, as reported, are shown as follows:

Changes in Existing Law Made by the Bill, as Reported

In compliance with clause 3(e) of rule XIII of the Rules of the House of Representatives, changes in existing law made by the bill, as reported, are shown as follows (existing law proposed to be omitted is enclosed in black brackets, new matter is printed in italic, and existing law in which no change is proposed is shown in roman):

Title 18, United States Code

Part I—Crimes

Chapter 13—Civil Rights

Sec.

241. Conspiracy against rights.

250. Lynching

§ 242. Deprivation of Rights under Color of Law

Whoever, under color of any law, statute, ordinance, regulation, or custom, willfully, *knowingly or recklessly* subjects any person in any State, Territory, Commonwealth, Possession, or District to the deprivation of any rights, privileges, or immunities secured or protected by the Constitution or laws of the United States, or to different punishments, pains, or penalties, on account of such person being an alien, or by reason of his color, or race, than are prescribed for the punishment of citizens, shall be fined under this title or imprisoned not more than one year, or both; and if bodily injury results from the acts committed in violation of this section or if such acts include the use, attempted use, or threatened use of a dangerous weapon, explosives, or fire, shall be fined under this title or imprisoned not more than ten years, or both; and if death results from the acts committed in violation of this section or if such acts include kidnapping or an attempt to kidnap, aggravated sexual abuse, or an attempt to commit aggravated sexual abuse, or an attempt to kill, shall be fined under this title, or imprisoned for any term of years or for life, or bothø, or may be sentenced to death¿. For purposes of this section, an act shall be considered to have resulted in death if the act was a substantial factor contributing to the death of the person. For the purposes of this section, the application of any pressure to the throat or windpipe, use of maneuvers that restrict blood or oxygen flow to the brain, or carotid artery restraints which prevent or hinder breathing or reduce intake of air is a punishment, pain, or penalty.

§ 250. Lynching

Whoever conspires with another person to violate section 245, 247, or 249 of this title or section 901 of the Civil Rights Act of 1968 (42 U.S.C. 3631) shall be punished in the same manner as a completed violation of such section, except that if the maximum term of imprisonment for such completed violation is less than 10 years, the person may be imprisoned for not more than 10 years.

Chapter 51—Homicide

Sec. 1111. Murder.

1123. Limitation on justification defense for Federal law enforcement officers.

§ 1123. Limitation on Justification Defense for Federal Law Enforcement Officers

(a) IN GENERAL.—It is not a defense to an offense under section 1111 or 1112 that the use of less lethal force or deadly force by a Federal law enforcement officer was justified if—

(1) that officer's use of use of such force was inconsistent with section 364(b) of the George Floyd Justice in Policing Act of 2020; or

(2) that officer's gross negligence, leading up to and at the time of the use of force, contributed to the necessity of the use of such force.

(b) DEFINITIONS.—In this section—

(1) the terms "deadly force" and "less lethal force" have the meanings given such terms in section 2 and section 364 of the George Floyd Justice in Policing Act of 2020; and

(2) the term "Federal law enforcement officer" has the meaning given such term in section 115.

Revised Statutes of the United States

Title XXIV

SEC. 1979. Every person who, under color of any statute, ordinance, regulation, custom, or usage, of any State or Territory or the District of Columbia, subjects, or causes to be subjected, any citizen of the United States or other person within the jurisdiction thereof to the deprivation of any rights, privileges, or immunities secured by the Constitution and laws, shall be liable to the party injured in an action at law, suit in equity, or other proper proceeding for redress, except that in any action brought against a judicial officer for an act or omission taken in such officer's judicial capacity, injunctive relief shall not be granted unless a declaratory decree was violated or declaratory relief was unavailable. For the purposes of this section, any Act of Congress applicable exclusively to the District of Columbia shall be considered to be a statute of the District of Columbia. It shall not be a defense or immunity in any action brought under this section against a local law enforcement officer (as such term is defined in section 2 of the George Floyd Justice in Policing Act of 2020), or in any action under any source of law against a Federal investigative or law enforcement officer (as such term is defined in section 2680(h) of title 28, United States Code), that—

(1) the defendant was acting in good faith, or that the defendant believed, reasonably or otherwise, that his or her conduct was lawful at the time when the conduct was committed; or

(2) the rights, privileges, or immunities secured by the Constitution and laws were not clearly established at the time of their deprivation by the defendant, or that at such time, the state of the law was otherwise such that the defendant could not reasonably have been expected to know whether his or her conduct was lawful.

Violent Crime Control and Law Enforcement Act of 1994

Title XXI—State and Local Law Enforcement

Subtitle D—Police Pattern or Practice

Sec. 210401. Cause of Action

(a) UNLAWFUL CONDUCT.—It shall be unlawful for any governmental authority, or any agent thereof, or any person acting on behalf of a governmental authority, to engage in a pattern or practice of conduct by law enforcement officers, *by prosecutors,* or by officials or employees of any governmental agency with responsibility for the administration of juvenile justice or the incarceration of juveniles that deprives persons of rights, privileges, or immunities secured or protected by the Constitution or laws of the United States.

(b) CIVIL ACTION BY ATTORNEY GENERAL.—Whenever the Attorney General has reasonable cause to believe that a violation of øparagraph (1)¿ *subsection (a)* has occurred, the Attorney General, for or in the name of the United States, may in a civil action obtain appropriate equitable and declaratory relief to eliminate the pattern or practice.

(c) SUBPOENA AUTHORITY.—In carrying out the authority in subsection (b), the Attorney General may require by subpoena the production of all information, documents, reports, answers, records, accounts, papers, and other data in any medium (including electronically stored information), as well as any tangible thing and documentary evidence, and the attendance and testimony of witnesses necessary in the performance of the Attorney General under subsection (b). Such a subpoena, in the case of contumacy or refusal to obey, shall be enforceable by order of any appropriate district court of the United States.

(d) CIVIL ACTION BY STATE ATTORNEYS GENERAL.—Whenever it shall appear to the attorney general of any State, or such other official as a State may designate, that a violation of subsection (a) has occurred within their State, the State attorney general or official, in the name of the State, may bring a civil action in the appropriate district court of the United States to obtain appropriate equitable and declaratory relief to eliminate the pattern or practice. In carrying out the authority in this subsection, the State attorney general or official shall have the same subpoena authority as is available to the Attorney General under subsection (c).

(e) RULE OF CONSTRUCTION.—Nothing in this section may be construed to limit the authority of the Attorney General under subsection (b) in any case in which a State attorney general has brought a civil action under subsection (d).

(f) REPORTING REQUIREMENTS.—On the date that is one year after the enactment of the George Floyd Justice in Policing Act of 2020, and annually thereafter, the Civil Rights Division of the Department of Justice shall make publicly available on an internet website a report on, during the previous year—

(1) the number of preliminary investigations of violations of subsection (a) that were commenced;

(2) the number of preliminary investigations of violations of subsection (a) that were resolved; and

(3) the status of any pending investigations of violations of subsection (a).

Sec. 210402. Data on Use of Excessive Force

(a) ATTORNEY GENERAL TO COLLECT.—The Attorney General

(1) FEDERAL COLLECTION OF DATA.—The Attorney General shall, through appropriate means, acquire data about the use of excessive force by law enforcement officers.

(2) STATE COLLECTION OF DATA.—The attorney general of a State may, through appropriate means, acquire data about the use of excessive force by law enforcement officers and such data may be used by the attorney general in conducting investigations under section 210401. This data may not contain any information that may reveal the identity of the victim or any law enforcement officer.

(b) LIMITATION ON USE OF DATA.—Data acquired under this section shall be used only for research or statistical purposes and may not contain any information that may reveal the identity of the victim or any law enforcement officer.¿

(b) LIMITATION ON USE OF DATA ACQUIRED BY THE ATTORNEY GENERAL.—Data acquired under subsection (a)(1) shall be used only for research or statistical purposes and may not contain any information that may reveal the identity of the victim or any law enforcement officer.

(c) ANNUAL SUMMARY.—The Attorney General shall publish an annual summary of the data acquired under this section.

Omnibus Crime Control and Safe Streets Act of 1968

Title I—Justice System Improvement

Part E—Bureau of Justice Assistance Grant Programs

Subpart 1—Edward Byrne Memorial Justice Assistance Grant Program

Sec. 501. Description

(a) GRANTS AUTHORIZED.—

(1) IN GENERAL.—From amounts made available to carry out this subpart, the Attorney General may, in accordance with the formula established under section 505, make grants to States and units of local government, for use by the State or unit of local government to provide additional personnel, equipment, supplies, contractual support, training, technical assistance, and information systems for criminal justice, including for any one or more of the following programs:

(A) Law enforcement programs.

(B) Prosecution and court programs.

(C) Prevention and education programs.

(D) Corrections and community corrections programs.

(E) Drug treatment and enforcement programs.

(F) Planning, evaluation, and technology improvement programs.

(G) Crime victim and witness programs (other than compensation).

(H) Mental health programs and related law enforcement and corrections programs, including behavioral programs and crisis intervention teams.

(I) *Training programs for law enforcement officers, including training programs on use of force and a duty to intervene.*

(2) RULE OF CONSTRUCTION.—Paragraph (1) shall be construed to ensure that a grant under that paragraph may be used for any purpose for which a grant was authorized to be used under either or both of the programs specified in section 500(b), as those programs were in effect immediately before the enactment of this paragraph.

(3) *LOCAL TASK FORCES ON PUBLIC SAFETY INNOVATION.—*

(A) *IN GENERAL.—A law enforcement program under paragraph (1)(A) may include the development of best practices for and the creation of local task forces on public safety innovation, charged with exploring and developing new strategies for public safety, including non-law enforcement strategies.*

(B) *DEFINITION.—The term "local task force on public safety innovation" means an administrative entity, created from partnerships between community-based organizations and other local stakeholders, that may develop innovative law enforcement and non-law enforcement strategies to enhance just and equitable public safety, repair breaches of trust between law enforcement agencies and the community they pledge to serve, and enhance accountability of law enforcement officers.*

(b) CONTRACTS AND SUBAWARDS.—A State or unit of local government may, in using a grant under this subpart for purposes authorized by subsection (a), use all or a portion of that grant to contract with or make one or more subawards to one or more—

(1) neighborhood or community-based organizations that are private and nonprofit; or

(2) units of local government.

(c) PROGRAM ASSESSMENT COMPONENT; WAIVER.—

(1) Each program funded under this subpart shall contain a program assessment component, developed pursuant to guidelines established by the Attorney General, in coordination with the National Institute of Justice.

(2) The Attorney General may waive the requirement of paragraph (1) with respect to a program if, in the opinion of the Attorney General, the program is not of sufficient size to justify a full program assessment.

(3) *In the case of crisis intervention teams funded under subsection (a)(1)(H), a program assessment under this subsection shall contain a report on best practices for crisis intervention.*

(d) PROHIBITED USES.—Notwithstanding any other provision of this Act, no funds provided under this subpart may be used, directly or indirectly, to provide any of the following matters:

(1) Any security enhancements or any equipment to any nongovernmental entity that is not engaged in criminal justice or public safety.

(2) Unless the Attorney General certifies that extraordinary and exigent circumstances exist that make the use of such funds to provide such matters essential to the maintenance of public safety and good order—

(A) vehicles (excluding police cruisers), vessels (excluding police boats), or aircraft (excluding police helicopters);

(B) luxury items;

(C) real estate;

(D) construction projects (other than penal or correctional institutions); or

(E) any similar matters.

(e) ADMINISTRATIVE COSTS.—Not more than 10 percent of a grant made under this subpart may be used for costs incurred to administer such grant.

(f) PERIOD.—The period of a grant made under this subpart shall be four years, except that renewals and extensions beyond that period may be granted at the discretion of the Attorney General.

(g) RULE OF CONSTRUCTION.—Subparagraph (d)(1) shall not be construed to prohibit the use, directly or indirectly, of funds provided under this subpart to provide security at a public event, such as a political convention or major sports event, so long as such security is provided under applicable laws and procedures.

Sec. 502. Applications

(a) IN GENERAL.—To request a grant under this subpart, the chief executive officer of a State or unit of local government shall submit an application to the Attorney General within 120 days after the date on which funds to carry out this subpart are appropriated for a fiscal year, in such form as the Attorney General may require. Such application shall include the following:

(1) A certification that Federal funds made available under this subpart will not be used to supplant State or local funds, but will be used to increase the amounts of such funds that would, in the absence of Federal funds, be made available for law enforcement activities.

(2) An assurance that, not fewer than 30 days before the application (or any amendment to the application) was submitted to the Attorney General, the application (or amendment) was submitted for review to the governing body of the State or unit of local government (or to an organization designated by that governing body).

(3) An assurance that, before the application (or any amendment to the application) was submitted to the Attorney General—

(A) the application (or amendment) was made public; and

(B) an opportunity to comment on the application (or amendment) was provided to citizens and to neighborhood or community-based organizations, to the extent applicable law or established procedure makes such an opportunity available.

(4) An assurance that, for each fiscal year covered by an application, the applicant shall maintain and report such data, records, and information (programmatic and financial) as the Attorney General may reasonably require.

(5) A certification, made in a form acceptable to the Attorney General and executed by the chief executive officer of the applicant (or by another officer of the applicant, if qualified under regulations promulgated by the Attorney General), that—

(A) the programs to be funded by the grant meet all the requirements of this subpart;

(B) all the information contained in the application is correct;

(C) there has been appropriate coordination with affected agencies; and

(D) the applicant will comply with all provisions of this subpart and all other applicable Federal laws.

(6) A comprehensive Statewide plan detailing how grants received under this section will be used to improve the administration of the criminal justice system, which shall—

(A) be designed in consultation with local governments, and representatives of all segments of the criminal justice system, including judges, prosecutors, law enforcement personnel, corrections personnel, and providers of indigent defense services, victim services, juvenile justice delinquency prevention programs, community corrections, and reentry services;

(B) include a description of how the State will allocate funding within and among each of the uses described in subparagraphs (A) through (G) of section 501(a)(1);

(C) describe the process used by the State for gathering evidence-based data and developing and using evidence-based and evidence-gathering approaches in support of funding decisions;

(D) describe the barriers at the State and local level for accessing data and implementing evidence-based approaches to preventing and reducing crime and recidivism; and

(E) be updated every 5 years, with annual progress reports that—

(i) address changing circumstances in the State, if any;

(ii) describe how the State plans to adjust funding within and among each of the uses described in sub-paragraphs (A) through (G) of section 501(a)(1);

(iii) provide an ongoing assessment of need;

(iv) discuss the accomplishment of goals identified in any plan previously prepared under this paragraph; and

(v) reflect how the plan influenced funding decisions in the previous year.

(7) An assurance that, for each fiscal year covered by an application, the applicant will use not less than 5 percent of the total amount of the grant award for the fiscal year to assist law enforcement agencies of the applicant, including campus public safety departments, gain or maintain accreditation from certified law enforcement accreditation organizations in accordance with section 113 of the Law Enforcement Trust and Integrity Act of 2020.

(8) An assurance that, for each fiscal year covered by an application, the applicant will use not less than 5 percent of the total amount of the

grant award for the fiscal year to study and implement effective management, training, recruiting, hiring, and oversight standards and programs to promote effective community and problem solving strategies for law enforcement agencies in accordance with section 114 of the Law Enforcement Trust and Integrity Act of 2020.

(9) An assurance that, for each fiscal year covered by an application, the applicant will use not less than 10 percent of the total amount of the grant award for the fiscal year to develop and implement best practice devices and systems to eliminate racial profiling in accordance with section 334 of the End Racial and Religious Profiling Act of 2020.

(10) An assurance that, for each fiscal year covered by an application, the applicant will use not less than 5 percent of the total amount of the grant award for the fiscal year to develop policies and protocols in compliance with part OO.

(b) TECHNICAL ASSISTANCE.—

(1) STRATEGIC PLANNING.—Not later than 90 days after the date of enactment of this subsection, the Attorney General shall begin to provide technical assistance to States and local governments requesting support to develop and implement the strategic plan required under subsection (a)(6). The Attorney General may enter into agreements with 1 or more non-governmental organizations to provide technical assistance and training under this paragraph.

(2) PROTECTION OF CONSTITUTIONAL RIGHTS.—Not later than 90 days after the date of enactment of this subsection, the Attorney General shall begin to provide technical assistance to States and local governments, including any agent thereof with responsibility for administration of justice, requesting support to meet the obligations established by the Sixth Amendment to the Constitution of the United States, which shall include—

(A) public dissemination of practices, structures, or models for the administration of justice consistent with the requirements of the Sixth Amendment; and

(B) assistance with adopting and implementing a system for the administration of justice consistent with the requirements of the Sixth Amendment.

(3) AUTHORIZATION OF APPROPRIATIONS.—For each of fiscal years 2017 through 2021, of the amounts appropriated to carry out this subpart, not less than $5,000,000 and not more than $10,000,000 shall be used to carry out this subsection.

Part Q—Public Safety and Community Policing; "Cops on the Beat"

Sec. 1701. Authority to Make Public Safety and Community Policing Grants.

(a) GRANT AUTHORIZATION.—The Attorney General shall carry out a single grant program under which the Attorney General makes grants to States, units of local government, Indian tribal governments, other public and private entities, and multi-jurisdictional or regional consortia for the purposes described in subsection (b).

(b) USES OF GRANT AMOUNTS.—The purposes for which grants made under subsection (a) may be made are—

(1) to rehire law enforcement officers who have been laid off as a result of State, tribal, or local budget reductions for deployment in community-oriented policing;

(2) to hire and train new, additional career law enforcement officers for deployment in community-oriented policing across the Nation, including by prioritizing the hiring and training of veterans (as defined in section 101 of title 38, United States Code);

(3) to procure equipment, technology, or support systems, or pay overtime, to increase the number of officers deployed in community-oriented policing;

(4) to award grants to pay for offices hired to perform intelligence, anti-terror, or homeland security duties;

(5) to increase the number of law enforcement officers involved in activities that are focused on interaction with members of the community

on proactive crime control and prevention by redeploying officers to such activities;

(6) to provide specialized training to law enforcement officers to enhance their conflict resolution, mediation, problem solving, service, and other skills needed to work in partnership with members of the community;

(7) to increase police participation in multidisciplinary early intervention teams;

(8) to develop new technologies, including interoperable communications technologies, modernized criminal record technology, and forensic technology, to assist State, tribal, and local law enforcement agencies in reorienting the emphasis of their activities from reacting to crime to preventing crime and to train law enforcement officers to use such technologies;

(9) to develop and implement innovative programs to permit members of the community to assist State, tribal, and local law enforcement agencies in the prevention of crime in the community, such as a citizens' police academy, including programs designed to increase the level of access to the criminal justice system enjoyed by victims, witnesses, and ordinary citizens by establishing decentralized satellite offices (including video facilities) of principal criminal courts buildings;

(10) to establish innovative programs to reduce, and keep to a minimum, the amount of time that law enforcement officers must be away from the community while awaiting court appearances;

(11) to establish and implement innovative programs to increase and enhance proactive crime control and prevention programs involving law enforcement officers and young persons in the community;

(12) to establish school-based partnerships between local law enforcement agencies and local school systems by using school resource officers who operate in and around elementary and secondary schools to combat school-related crime and disorder problems, gangs, and drug activities, including the training of school resource officers in the prevention of human trafficking offenses;

(13) to develop and establish new administrative and managerial systems to facilitate the adoption of community-oriented policing as an organization-wide philosophy;

(14) to assist a State or Indian tribe in enforcing a law throughout the State or tribal community that requires that a convicted sex offender register his or her address with a State, tribal, or local law enforcement agency and be subject to criminal prosecution for failure to comply;

(15) to establish, implement, and coordinate crime prevention and control programs (involving law enforcement officers working with community members) with other Federal programs that serve the community and community members to better address the comprehensive needs of the community and its members;

(16) to support the purchase by a law enforcement agency of no more than 1 service weapon per officer, upon hiring for deployment in community-oriented policing or, if necessary, upon existing officers' initial redeployment to community-oriented policing;

(17) to participate in nationally recognized active shooter training programs that offer scenario-based, integrated response courses designed to counter active shooter threats or acts of terrorism against individuals or facilities;

(18) to provide specialized training to law enforcement officers to—

(A) recognize individuals who have a mental illness; and

(B) properly interact with individuals who have a mental illness, including strategies for verbal de-escalation of crises;

(19) to establish collaborative programs that enhance the ability of law enforcement agencies to address the mental health, behavioral, and substance abuse problems of individuals encountered by law enforcement officers in the line of duty;

(20) to provide specialized training to corrections officers to recognize individuals who have a mental illness;

(21) to enhance the ability of corrections officers to address the mental health of individuals under the care and custody of jails and prisons, including specialized training and strategies for verbal de-escalation of crises;

(22) to develop best practices for and to create civilian review boards;

(23) to recruit, hire, incentivize, retain, develop, and train new, additional career law enforcement officers or current law enforcement officers who are willing to relocate to communities—

(A) where there are poor or fragmented relationships between police and residents of the community, or where there are high incidents of crime; and

(B) that are the communities that the law enforcement officers serve, or that are in close proximity to the communities that the law enforcement officers serve;

(24) to collect data on the number of law enforcement officers who are willing to relocate to the communities where they serve, and whether such law enforcement officer relocations have impacted crime in such communities;

(25) to develop and publicly report strategies and timelines to recruit, hire, promote, retain, develop, and train a diverse and inclusive law enforcement workforce, consistent with merit system principles and applicable law;

ø(22)¿ (26) to permit tribal governments receiving direct law enforcement services from the Bureau of Indian Affairs to access the program under this section for use in accordance with paragraphs (1) through ø(21)¿ (25); and

ø(23)¿ *(27)* to establish peer mentoring mental health and wellness pilot programs within State, tribal, and local law enforcement agencies.

(c) PREFERENTIAL CONSIDERATION OF APPLICATIONS FOR CERTAIN GRANTS.—In awarding grants under this part, the Attorney General may give preferential consideration, where feasible, to an application—

(1) for hiring and rehiring additional career law enforcement officers that involves a non-Federal contribution exceeding the 25 percent minimum under subsection (g);

(2) from an applicant in a State that has in effect a law that—

(A) treats a minor who has engaged in, or has attempted to engage in, a commercial sex act as a victim of a severe form of trafficking in persons;

(B) discourages or prohibits the charging or prosecution of an individual described in subparagraph (A) for a prostitution or sex trafficking offense, based on the conduct described in subparagraph (A); and

(C) encourages the diversion of an individual described in subparagraph (A) to appropriate service providers, including child welfare services, victim treatment programs, child advocacy centers, rape crisis centers, or other social services; or

(3) from an applicant in a State that has in effect a law—

(A) that—

(i) provides a process by which an individual who is a human trafficking survivor can move to vacate any arrest or conviction records for a non-violent offense committed as a direct result of human trafficking, including prostitution or lewdness;

(ii) establishes a rebuttable presumption that any arrest or conviction of an individual for an offense associated with human trafficking is a result of being trafficked, if the individual—

(I) is a person granted nonimmigrant status pursuant to section 101(a)(15)(T)(i) of the Immigration and Nationality Act (8 U.S.C. 1101(a)(15)(T)(i));

(II) is the subject of a certification by the Secretary of Health and Human Services under section 107(b)(1)(E) of the Trafficking Victims Protection Act of 2000 (22 U.S.C. 7105(b)(1)(E)); or

(III) has other similar documentation of trafficking, which has been issued by a Federal, State, or local agency; and

(iii) protects the identity of individuals who are human trafficking survivors in public and court records; and

(B) that does not require an individual who is a human trafficking survivor to provide official documentation as described in subclause (I), (II), or (III) of subparagraph (A)(ii) in order to receive protection under the law.

(d) TECHNICAL ASSISTANCE.—

(1) IN GENERAL.—The Attorney General may provide technical assistance to States, units of local government, Indian tribal governments,

and to other public and private entities, in furtherance of the purposes of the Public Safety Partnership and Community Policing Act of 1994.

(2) MODEL.—The technical assistance provided by the Attorney General may include the development of a flexible model that will define for State and local governments, and other public and private entities, definitions and strategies associated with community or problem-oriented policing and methodologies for its implementation.

(3) TRAINING CENTERS AND FACILITIES.—The technical assistance provided by the Attorney General may include the establishment and operation of training centers or facilities, either directly or by contracting or cooperative arrangements. The functions of the centers or facilities established under this paragraph may include instruction and seminars for police executives, managers, trainers, supervisors, and such others as the Attorney General considers to be appropriate concerning community or problem-oriented policing and improvements in police-community interaction and cooperation that further the purposes of the Public Safety Partnership and Community Policing Act of 1994.

(e) UTILIZATION OF COMPONENTS.—The Attorney General may utilize any component or components of the Department of Justice in carrying out this part.

(f) MINIMUM AMOUNT.—Unless all applications submitted by any State and grantee within the State pursuant to subsection (a) have been funded, each qualifying State, together with grantees within the State, shall receive in each fiscal year pursuant to subsection

(a) not less than 0.5 percent of the total amount appropriated in the fiscal year for grants pursuant to that subsection. In this subsection, "qualifying State" means any State which has submitted an application for a grant, or in which an eligible entity has submitted an application for a grant, which meets the requirements prescribed by the Attorney General and the conditions set out in this part.

(g) MATCHING FUNDS.—The portion of the costs of a program, project, or activity provided by a grant under subsection (a) may not exceed 75 percent, unless the Attorney General waives, wholly or in part, the requirement under this subsection of a non-Federal contribution to the costs of a program, project, or activity. In relation to a grant for a period exceeding 1 year for hiring or rehiring career law enforcement officers, the Federal share shall decrease from year to year for up to 5 years, looking toward the continuation of the increased hiring level using State or local sources of funding following the conclusion of Federal support, as provided in an approved plan pursuant to section 1702(c)(8).

(h) ALLOCATION OF FUNDS.—The funds available under this part shall be allocated as provided in section 1001(a)(11)(B).

(i) TERMINATION OF GRANTS FOR HIRING OFFICERS.—Except as provided in subsection (j), the authority under subsection (a) of this section to make grants for the hiring and rehiring of additional career law enforcement officers shall lapse at the conclusion of 6 years from the date of enactment of this part. Prior to the expiration of this grant authority, the Attorney General shall submit a report to Congress concerning the experience with and effects of such grants. The report may include any recommendations the Attorney General may have for amendments to this part and related provisions of law in light of the termination of the authority to make grants for the hiring and rehiring of additional career law enforcement officers.

(j) GRANTS TO INDIAN TRIBES.—

(1) IN GENERAL.—Notwithstanding subsection (i) and section 1703, and in acknowledgment of the Federal nexus and distinct Federal responsibility to address and prevent crime in Indian country, the Attorney General shall provide grants under this section to Indian tribal governments, for fiscal year 2011 and any fiscal year thereafter, for such period as the Attorney General determines to be appropriate to assist the Indian tribal governments in carrying out the purposes described in subsection (b).

(2) PRIORITY OF FUNDING.—In providing grants to Indian tribal governments under this subsection, the Attorney General shall take into consideration reservation crime rates and tribal law enforcement staffing needs of each Indian tribal government.

(3) FEDERAL SHARE.—Because of the Federal nature and responsibility for providing public safety on Indian land, the Federal share of the cost of any activity carried out using a grant under this subsection—

(a) shall be 100 percent; and

(B) may be used to cover indirect costs.

(4) AUTHORIZATION OF APPROPRIATIONS.—There is authorized to be appropriated to carry out this subsection $40,000,000 for each of fiscal years 2011 through 2015.

(k) COPS ANTI-METH PROGRAM.—The Attorney General shall use amounts otherwise appropriated to carry out this section for a fiscal year (beginning with fiscal year 2019) to make competitive grants, in amounts of not less than $1,000,000 for such fiscal year, to State law enforcement agencies with high seizures of precursor chemicals, finished methamphetamine, laboratories, and laboratory dump seizures for the purpose of locating or investigating illicit activities, such as precursor diversion, laboratories, or methamphetamine traffickers.

(1) COPS ANTI-HEROIN TASK FORCE PROGRAM.—The Attorney General shall use amounts otherwise appropriated to carry out this section, or other amounts as appropriated, for a fiscal year (beginning with fiscal year 2019) to make competitive grants to State law enforcement agencies in States with high per capita rates of primary treatment admissions, for the purpose of locating or investigating illicit activities, through Statewide collaboration, relating to the distribution of heroin, fentanyl, or carfentanil or relating to the unlawful distribution of prescription opioids.

(m) REPORT.—Not later than 180 days after the date of enactment of this subsection, the Attorney General shall submit to Congress a report describing the extent and effectiveness of the Community Oriented Policing (COPS) initiative as applied in Indian country, including particular references to—

(1) the problem of intermittent funding;

(2) the integration of COPS personnel with existing law enforcement authorities; and

(3) an explanation of how the practice of community policing and the broken windows theory can most effectively be applied in remote tribal locations.

Sec. 1709. Definitions

In this part—

(1) "career law enforcement officer" means a person hired on a permanent basis who is authorized by law or by a State or local public agency to engage in or supervise the prevention, detection, or investigation of violations of criminal laws.

(2) "citizens' police academy" means a program by local law enforcement agencies or private nonprofit organizations in which citizens, especially those who participate in neighborhood watch programs, are trained in ways of facilitating communication between the community and local law enforcement in the prevention of crime.

(3) "Indian tribe" means a tribe, band, pueblo, nation, or other organized group or community of Indians, including an Alaska Native village (as defined in or established under the Alaska Native Claims Settlement Act (43 U.S.C. 1601 et seq.)), that is recognized as eligible for the special programs and services provided by the United States to Indians because of their status as Indians.

(4) "school resource officer" means a career law enforcement officer, with sworn authority, deployed in community-oriented policing, and assigned by the employing police department or agency to work in collaboration with schools and community-based organizations—

(A) to address crime and disorder problems, gangs, and drug activities affecting or occurring in or around an elementary or secondary school;

(B) to develop or expand crime prevention efforts for students;

(C) to educate likely school-age victims in crime prevention and safety;

(D) to develop or expand community justice initiatives for students;

(E) to train students in conflict resolution, restorative justice, and crime awareness;

(F) to assist in the identification of physical changes in the environment that may reduce crime in or around the school; and

(G) to assist in developing school policy that addresses crime and to recommend procedural changes.

(5) "commercial sex act" has the meaning given the term in section 103 of the Victims of Trafficking and Violence Protection Act of 2000 (22 U.S.C. 7102).

(6) "minor" means an individual who has not attained the age of 18 years.

(7) "severe form of trafficking in persons" has the meaning given the term in section 103 of the Victims of Trafficking and Violence Protection Act of 2000 (22 U.S.C. 7102).

(8) "civilian review board" means an administrative entity that investigates civilian complaints against law enforcement officers and—

(A) is independent and adequately funded;

(B) has investigatory authority and subpoena power;

(C) has representative community diversity;

(D) has policy making authority;

(E) provides advocates for civilian complainants;

(F) may conduct hearings; and

(G) conducts statistical studies on prevailing complaint trends.

Part OO—Law Enforcement Body-Worn Cameras and Recorded Data

Sec. 3051. Use of Grant Funds

(a) IN GENERAL.—Grant amounts described in paragraph (10) of section 502(a) of this title—

(1) shall be used—

(A) to purchase or lease body-worn cameras for use by State, local, and tribal law enforcement officers (as defined in section 2503);

(B) for expenses related to the implementation of a bodyworn camera program in order to deter excessive force, improve accountability and transparency of use of force by law enforcement officers, assist in responding to complaints against law enforcement officers, and improve evidence collection; and

(C) to implement policies or procedures to comply with the requirements described in subsection (b); and

(2) may not be used for expenses related to facial recognition technology.

(b) REQUIREMENTS.—A recipient of a grant under subpart 1 of part E of this title shall—

(1) establish policies and procedures in accordance with the requirements described in subsection (c) before law enforcement officers use of body-worn cameras;

(2) adopt recorded data collection and retention protocols as described in subsection (d) before law enforcement officers use of body-worn cameras;

(3) make the policies and protocols described in paragraphs

(1) and (2) available to the public; and

(4) comply with the requirements for use of recorded data under subsection (f).

(c) REQUIRED POLICIES AND PROCEDURES.—A recipient of a grant under subpart 1 of part E of this title shall—

(1) develop with community input and publish for public view policies and protocols for—

(A) the safe and effective use of body-worn cameras;

(B) the secure storage, handling, and destruction of recorded data collected by body-worn cameras;

(C) protecting the privacy rights of any individual who may be recorded by a body-worn camera;

(D) the release of any recorded data collected by a bodyworn camera in accordance with the open records laws, if any, of the State; and

(E) making recorded data available to prosecutors, defense attorneys, and other officers of the court in accordance with subparagraph (E); and

(2) conduct periodic evaluations of the security of the storage and handling of the body-worn camera data.

(d) RECORDED DATA COLLECTION AND RETENTION PROTOCOL.— The recorded data collection and retention protocol described in this paragraph is a protocol that—

(1) requires—

(A) a law enforcement officer who is wearing a body-worn camera to provide an explanation if an activity that is required to be recorded by the body-worn camera is not recorded;

(B) a law enforcement officer who is wearing a body-worn camera to obtain consent to be recorded from a crime victim or witness before interviewing the victim or witness;

(C) the collection of recorded data unrelated to a legitimate law enforcement purpose be minimized to the greatest extent practicable;

(D) the system used to store recorded data collected by body-worn cameras to log all viewing, modification, or deletion of stored recorded data and to prevent, to the greatest extent practicable, the unauthorized access or disclosure of stored recorded data;

(E) any law enforcement officer be prohibited from accessing the stored data without an authorized purpose; and

(F) the law enforcement agency to collect and report statistical data on—

(i) incidences of use of force, disaggregated by race, ethnicity, gender, and age of the victim;

(ii) the number of complaints filed against law enforcement officers;

(iii) the disposition of complaints filed against law enforcement officers;

(iv) the number of times camera footage is used for evidence collection in investigations of crimes; and

(v) any other additional statistical data that the Director determines should be collected and reported;

(2) allows an individual to file a complaint with a law enforcement agency relating to the improper use of body-worn cameras; and

(3) complies with any other requirements established by the Director.

(e) REPORTING.—Statistical data required to be collected under subsection (d)(1)(D) shall be reported to the Director, who shall—

(1) establish a standardized reporting system for statistical data collected under this program; and

(2) establish a national database of statistical data recorded under this program.

(f) USE OR TRANSFER OF RECORDED DATA.—

(1) IN GENERAL.—Recorded data collected by an entity receiving a grant under a grant under subpart 1 of part E of this title from a body-worn camera shall be used only in internal and external investigations of misconduct by a law enforcement agency or officer, if there is reasonable suspicion that a recording contains evidence of a crime, or for limited training purposes. The Director shall establish rules to ensure that the recorded data is used only for the purposes described in this paragraph.

(2) PROHIBITION ON TRANSFER.—Except as provided in paragraph (3), an entity receiving a grant under subpart 1 of part E of this title may not transfer any recorded data collected by the entity from a body-worn camera to another law enforcement or intelligence agency.

(3) EXCEPTIONS.—

(A) CRIMINAL INVESTIGATION.—An entity receiving a grant under subpart 1 of part E of this title may transfer recorded data collected by the entity from a body-worn camera to another law enforcement agency or intelligence agency for use in a criminal investigation if the requesting law enforcement or intelligence agency has reasonable suspicion that the requested data contains evidence relating to the crime being investigated.

(B) CIVIL RIGHTS CLAIMS.—An entity receiving a grant under subpart 1 of part E of this title may transfer recorded data collected by the law enforcement agency from a body-worn camera to another law enforcement agency for use in an investigation of the violation of any right, privilege, or immunity secured or protected by the Constitution or laws of the United States.

(g) AUDIT AND ASSESSMENT.—

(1) IN GENERAL.—Not later than 2 years after the date of enactment of this part, the Director of the Office of Audit, Assessment, and Management shall perform an assessment of the use of funds under this section and the policies and protocols of the grantees.

(2) REPORTS.—Not later than September 1 of each year, beginning 2 years after the date of enactment of this part, each recipient of a grant under subpart 1 of part E of this title shall submit to the Director of the Office of Audit, Assessment, and Management a report that—

(A) describes the progress of the body-worn camera program; and

(B) contains recommendations on ways in which the Federal Government, States, and units of local government can further support the implementation of the program.

(3) REVIEW.—The Director of the Office of Audit, Assessment, and Management shall evaluate the policies and protocols of the grantees and take such steps as the Director of the Office of Audit, Assessment, and Management determines necessary to ensure compliance with the program.

Sec. 3052. Body-Worn Camera Training Toolkit

(a) IN GENERAL.—The Director shall establish and maintain a body-worn camera training toolkit for law enforcement agencies, academia, and other relevant entities to provide training and technical assistance, including best practices for implementation, model policies and procedures, and research materials.

(b) MECHANISM.—In establishing the toolkit required to under subsection (a), the Director may consolidate research, practices, templates, and tools that been developed by expert and law enforcement agencies across the country.

Sec. 3053. Study

(a) IN GENERAL.—Not later than 2 years after the date of enactment of the Police CAMERA Act of 2020, the Director shall conduct a study on—

(1) the efficacy of body-worn cameras in deterring excessive force by law enforcement officers;

(2) the impact of body-worn cameras on the accountability and transparency of the use of force by law enforcement officers;

(3) the impact of body-worn cameras on responses to and adjudications of complaints of excessive force;

(4) the effect of the use of body-worn cameras on the safety of law enforcement officers on patrol;

(5) the effect of the use of body-worn cameras on public safety;

(6) the impact of body-worn cameras on evidence collection for criminal investigations;

(7) issues relating to the secure storage and handling of recorded data from the body-worn cameras;

(8) issues relating to the privacy of individuals and officers recorded on body-worn cameras;

(9) issues relating to the constitutional rights of individuals on whom facial recognition technology is used;

(10) issues relating to limitations on the use of facial recognition technology;

(11) issues relating to the public's access to body-worn camera footage;

(12) the need for proper training of law enforcement officers that use body-worn cameras;

(13) best practices in the development of protocols for the safe and effective use of body-worn cameras;

(14) a review of law enforcement agencies that found bodyworn cameras to be unhelpful in the operations of the agencies; and

(15) any other factors that the Director determines are relevant in evaluating the efficacy of body-worn cameras.

(b) REPORT.—Not later than 180 days after the date on which the study required under subsection (a) is completed, the Director shall submit to Congress a report on the study, which shall include any policy recommendations that the Director considers appropriate.

Controlled Substances Act

Title II—Control and Enforcement

Part E—Administrative and Enforcement Provisions

Search Warrants

SEC. 509. A search warrant relating to offenses involving controlled substances may be served at any time of the day or night if the judge or United States magistrate issuing the warrant is satisfied that there is probable cause to believe that grounds exist for the warrant and for its service at such time. A search warrant authorized under this section shall require that a law enforcement officer execute the search warrant only after providing notice of his or her authority and purpose.

Title 10, United States Code

Subtitle A—General Military Law

Part IV—Service, Supply, and Procurement

Chapter 153—Exchange of Material and Disposal of Obsolete, Surplus, or Unclaimed Property

§ 2576a. Excess Personal Property: Sale or Donation for Law Enforcement Activities

(a) TRANSFER AUTHORIZED.—(1) Notwithstanding any other provision of law and subject to subsection (b), the Secretary of Defense may transfer to Federal and State agencies personal property of the Department of Defense, including small arms and ammunition, that the Secretary determines is—

(A) suitable for use by the agencies in law enforcement activities, including counterdrug, counterterrorism, and border security activities¿ counterterrorism; and

(B) excess to the needs of the Department of Defense.

(2) The Secretary shall carry out this section in consultation with the Attorney General, the Director of National Drug Control Policy, and the Secretary of Homeland Security, as appropriate.

(b) CONDITIONS FOR TRANSFER.—The Secretary of Defense may transfer personal property under this section only if—

(1) the property is drawn from existing stocks of the Department of Defense;

(2) the recipient accepts the property on an as-is, where-is basis;

(3) the transfer is made without the expenditure of any funds available to the Department of Defense for the procurement of defense equipment;

(4) all costs incurred subsequent to the transfer of the property are borne or reimbursed by the recipient;

(5) the recipient, on an annual basis, and with the authorization of the relevant local governing body or authority, certifies that it has adopted publicly available protocols for the appropriate use of controlled property, the supervision of such use, and the evaluation of the effectiveness of such use, including auditing and accountability policies; and

(6) after the completion of the assessment required by section 1051(e) of the National Defense Authorization Act for Fiscal Year 2016, the recipient, on an annual basis, certifies that it provides annual training to relevant personnel on the maintenance, sustainment, and appropriate use of controlled property;

(7) the recipient submits to the Department of Defense a description of how the recipient expects to use the property;

(8) the recipient certifies to the Department of Defense that if the recipient determines that the property is surplus to the needs of the recipient, the recipient will return the property to the Department of Defense;

(9) with respect to a recipient that is not a Federal agency, the recipient certifies to the Department of Defense that the recipient notified the local community of the request for personal property under this section by—

(A) publishing a notice of such request on a publicly accessible Internet website;

(B) posting such notice at several prominent locations in the jurisdiction of the recipient; and

(C) ensuring that such notices were available to the local community for a period of not less than 30 days; and

(10) the recipient has received the approval of the city council or other local governing body to acquire the personal property sought under this section.

(c) CONSIDERATION.—Subject to subsection (b)(4), the Secretary may transfer personal property under this section without charge to the recipient agency.

(d) PREFERENCE FOR CERTAIN TRANSFERS.—In considering applications for the transfer of personal property under this section, the Secretary shall give a preference to those applications indicating that the transferred property will be used in the counterdrug, counterterrorism, or border security activities of the recipient agency.

(d) ANNUAL CERTIFICATION ACCOUNTING FOR TRANSFERRED PROPERTY.—(1) For each fiscal year, the Secretary shall submit to Congress certification in writing that each Federal or State agency to which the Secretary has transferred property under this section—

(A) has provided to the Secretary documentation accounting for all controlled property, including arms and ammunition, that the Secretary has transferred to the agency, including any item described in subsection (f) so transferred before the date of the enactment of the George Floyd Justice in Policing Act of 2020; and

(B) with respect to a non-Federal agency, carried out each of paragraphs (5) through (8) of subsection (b).

(2) If the Secretary does not provide a certification under paragraph (1) for a Federal or State agency, the Secretary may not transfer additional property to that agency under this section.

(e) ANNUAL REPORT ON EXCESS PROPERTY.—Before making any property available for transfer under this section, the Secretary shall annually submit to Congress a description of the property to be transferred together with a certification that the transfer of the property would not violate this section or any other provision of law.

(f) LIMITATIONS ON TRANSFERS.—(1) The Secretary may not transfer to Federal, Tribal, State, or local law enforcement agencies the following under this section:

(A) Controlled firearms, ammunition, bayonets, grenade launchers, grenades (including stun and flash-bang), and explosives.

(B) Controlled vehicles, highly mobile multi-wheeled vehicles, mine-resistant ambush-protected vehicles, trucks, truck dump, truck utility, and truck carryall.

(C) Drones that are armored, weaponized, or both.

(D) Controlled aircraft that—

(i) are combat configured or combat coded; or

(ii) have no established commercial flight application.

(E) Silencers.

(F) Long-range acoustic devices.

(G) Items in the Federal Supply Class of banned items.

(2) The Secretary may not require, as a condition of a transfer under this section, that a Federal or State agency demonstrate the use of any small arms or ammunition.

(3) The limitations under this subsection shall also apply with respect to the transfer of previously transferred property of the Department of Defense from one Federal or State agency to another such agency.

(4)(A) The Secretary may waive the applicability of paragraph (1) to a vehicle described in subparagraph (B) of such paragraph (other than a mine-resistant ambush-protected vehicle), if the Secretary determines that such a waiver is necessary for disaster or rescue purposes or for another purpose where life and public safety are at risk, as demonstrated by the proposed recipient of the vehicle.

(B) If the Secretary issues a waiver under subparagraph (A), the Secretary shall—

(i) submit to Congress notice of the waiver, and post such notice on a public Internet website of the Department, by not later than 30 days after the date on which the waiver is issued; and

(ii) require, as a condition of the waiver, that the recipient of the vehicle for which the waiver is issued provides public notice of the waiver and the transfer, including the type of vehicle and the purpose for which it is transferred, in the jurisdiction where the recipient is located by not later than 30 days after the date on which the waiver is issued.

(5) The Secretary may provide for an exemption to the limitation under subparagraph (D) of paragraph (1) in the case of parts for aircraft described in such subparagraph that are transferred as part of regular maintenance of aircraft in an existing fleet.

(6) The Secretary shall require, as a condition of any transfer of property under this section, that the Federal or State agency that receives the property shall return the property to the Secretary if the agency—

(A) is investigated by the Department of Justice for any violation of civil liberties; or

(B) is otherwise found to have engaged in widespread abuses of civil liberties.

(g) CONDITIONS FOR EXTENSION OF PROGRAM.—Notwithstanding any other provision of law, amounts authorized to be appropriated or otherwise made available for any fiscal year may not be obligated or expended to carry out this section unless the Secretary submits to Congress certification that for the preceding fiscal year that—

(1) each Federal or State agency that has received controlled property transferred under this section has—

((A) demonstrated 100 percent accountability for all such property, in accordance with paragraph (2) or (3), as applicable; or

(B) been suspended from the program pursuant to paragraph (4);

(2) with respect to each non-Federal agency that has received controlled property under this section, the State coordinator responsible for each such agency has verified that the coordinator or an agent of the coordinator has conducted an in-person inventory of the property transferred to the agency and that 100 percent of such property was

accounted for during the inventory or that the agency has been suspended from the program pursuant to paragraph (4);

(3) with respect to each Federal agency that has received controlled property under this section, the Secretary of Defense or an agent of the Secretary has conducted an in-person inventory of the property transferred to the agency and that 100 percent of such property was accounted for during the inventory or that the agency has been suspended from the program pursuant to paragraph (4);

(4) the eligibility of any agency that has received controlled property under this section for which 100 percent of the property was not accounted for during an inventory described in paragraph (1) or (2), as applicable, to receive any property transferred under this section has been suspended; and

(5) each State coordinator has certified, for each non-Federal agency located in the State for which the State coordinator is responsible that—

(A) the agency has complied with all requirements under this section; or

(B) the eligibility of the agency to receive property transferred under this section has been suspended; and

(6) the Secretary of Defense has certified, for each Federal agency that has received property under this section that—

(A) the agency has complied with all requirements under this section; or

(B) the eligibility of the agency to receive property transferred under this section has been suspended.

(h) PROHIBITION ON OWNERSHIP OF CONTROLLED PROPERTY.—A Federal or State agency that receives controlled property under this section may not take ownership of the property.

(i) NOTICE TO CONGRESS OF PROPERTY DOWNGRADES.—Not later than 30 days before downgrading the classification of any item of personal property from controlled or Federal Supply Class, the Secretary shall submit to Congress notice of the proposed downgrade.

(j) NOTICE TO CONGRESS OF PROPERTY CANNIBALIZATION.—Before the Defense Logistics Agency authorizes the recipient of property transferred under this section to cannibalize the property, the Secretary shall submit to Congress notice of such authorization, including the name of the recipient requesting the authorization, the purpose of the proposed cannibalization, and the type of property proposed to be cannibalized.

(k) QUARTERLY REPORTS ON USE OF CONTROLLED EQUIPMENT.— Not later than 30 days after the last day of a fiscal quarter, the Secretary shall submit to Congress a report on any uses of controlled property transferred under this section during that fiscal quarter.

(l) REPORTS TO CONGRESS.—Not later than 30 days after the last day of a fiscal year, the Secretary shall submit to Congress a report on the following for the preceding fiscal year:

(1) The percentage of equipment lost by recipients of property transferred under this section, including specific information about the type of property lost, the monetary value of such property, and the recipient that lost the property.

(2) The transfer of any new (condition code A) property transferred under this section, including specific information about the type of property, the recipient of the property, the monetary value of each item of the property, and the total monetary value of all such property transferred during the fiscal year.

(e) (o) PUBLICLY ACCESSIBLE WEBSITE.—(1) The Secretary shall create and maintain a publicly available Internet website that provides information on the controlled property transferred under this section and the recipients of such property.

(2) The contents of the Internet website required under paragraph (1) shall include all publicly accessible unclassified information pertaining to the request, transfer, denial, and repossession of controlled property under this section, including—

(A) a current inventory of all controlled property transferred to Federal and State agencies under this section, listed by the name of the recipient and the year of the transfer;

(B) all pending requests for transfers of controlled property under this section, including the information submitted by the Federal and State agencies requesting such transfers; and

(C) all reports required to be submitted to the Secretary under this section by Federal and State agencies that receive controlled property under this section.

(f) (p) CONTROLLED PROPERTY.—In this section, the term "controlled property" means any item assigned a demilitarization code of B, C, D, E, G, or Q under Department of Defense Manual 4160.21–M, "Defense Materiel Disposition Manual," or any successor document.

Committee Correspondence

JERROLD NADLER, New York
CHAIRMAN

JIM JORDAN, Ohio
RANKING MINORITY MEMBER

U.S. House of Representatives
Committee on the Judiciary
Washington, DC 20515–6216
One Hundred Sixteenth Congress

June 18, 2020

The Honorable Adam Smith
Chairman
Committee on Armed Services
U.S. House of Representatives
2216 Rayburn House Office Building
Washington, DC 20515

Dear Chairman Smith:

I am writing to you concerning section 365 of H.R.7120, the "Justice in Policing Act of 2020."

I appreciate your willingness to work cooperatively on this legislation. I recognize that section 365 of the bill contains provisions that fall within the jurisdiction of the Committee on Armed Services. I acknowledge that your Committee will not formally consider H.R. 7120 and agree that the inaction of your Committee with respect to the bill does not waive any future jurisdictional claim over the matters contained in H.R. 7120 which fall within your Committee's Rule X jurisdiction.

I will ensure that our exchange of letters is included in the *Congressional Record* during floor consideration of the bill. I appreciate your cooperation regarding this legislation and look forward to continuing to work with you as this measure moves through the legislative process.

Sincerely,

Jerrold Nadler
Chairman

c: The Honorable Jim Jordan, Ranking Member, Committee on the Judiciary
The Honorable Thomas J. Wickham, Jr., Parliamentarian
The Honorable Mac Thornberry, Ranking Member, Committee on Armed Services

COMMITTEE ON ARMED SERVICES

U.S. House of Representatives

Washington, DC 20515–6035

ONE HUNDRED SIXTEENTH CONGRESS

June 19, 2020

The Honorable Jerrold Nadler
Chairman
Committee on the Judiciary
U.S. House of Representatives
2138 Rayburn House Office Building
Washington, D.C. 20515

Dear Chairman Nadler:

I am writing to you concerning H.R. 7120, the "Justice in Policing Act of 2020." There are certain provisions in this legislation that fall within the Rule X jurisdiction of the Armed Services Committee.

In the interest of permitting your Committee to proceed expeditiously to floor consideration of this important bill, we will not formally consider H. R. 7120. We do so with the understanding that by waiving consideration of the bill, the Committee on Armed Services does not waive any future jurisdictional claims over the subject matters contained in the bill which fall within its Rule X jurisdiction.

Please ensure that our exchange of letters is included in the *Congressional Record* during floor consideration of the bill. Thank you for the cooperative spirit in which you have worked regarding this matter and others between our respective Committees.

Sincerely,

Adam Smith
Chairman

AS:jj

MINORITY VIEWS

Following the murder of George Floyd while in the custody of the Minneapolis Police Department, Americans across the political spectrum have called for a bipartisan response to address police misconduct. On June 8, 2020, House Democrats introduced H.R. 7120, the Justice in Policing

Act of 2020, sponsored by Representative Karen Bass.[177] Committee Democrats drafted its 135-page bill and a subsequent substitute amendment to the bill without any attempt at serious consultation with Republicans on this Committee. In doing so, Chairman Nadler and the Democrat Majority chose to prioritize political messaging over crafting consensus-based, effective legislation.

Chairman Nadler and Committee Democrats have affirmatively chosen not to work cooperatively with Republicans on this legislation. Prior to the introduction of H.R. 7120, Republicans reached out to Democrats to inquire if they would be willing to share legislative text for review by Committee Members. Democrats rejected that request. Republicans asked if Democrats would be willing to share a summary or section-by-section analysis of the bill. Democrats responded that all materials were under embargo until the bill was introduced. Likewise, Democrats allowed no consultation with Republicans in the drafting of Chairman Nadler's amendment in the nature of a substitute.

Chairman Nadler and the Democrat Majority's refusal to work collaboratively with Republicans—or even to share basic information about the legislation—prevents the Committee from developing sound public policy. Although Republican Members agree that police reform is needed and even support some aspects of H.R. 7120, the proposals must be thoughtfully considered so as not to endanger the public or law enforcement officers by creating under-resourced and over-restricted police departments. Such a deliberative process did not occur with this bill. Because the Democrat Majority shut Republicans out of the process and rushed to pass this legislation, several of the provisions within H.R. 7210 have serious shortcomings.

---

[177] H.R. 7120, 116th Cong. (2020).

H.R. 7120 as Drafted Will Handicap Law-Abiding Law Enforcement Officers and Make American Communities Less Safe

Lowering the Mens Rea Standard—Section 101

Section 101 of the bill would change the mens rea standard when charging an officer with criminal misconduct from "willfulness" to "knowingly or recklessly." Currently, to be convicted of a crime, an officer must specifically intend to "deprive a person of a federal right made definite by decision or other rule of law." The lower standard of "knowingly or recklessly" would allow an officer to be convicted without having a specific intent to deprive a person of a federal right. While law enforcement officers who commit crimes must be held accountable for their actions, lowering the mens rea standard could have unintended adverse consequences to public safety. Law enforcement officers often find themselves in situations that require split second decisions under considerable stress. In those harrowing moments, hesitation and second-guessing can be dangerous—and perhaps deadly—for the officers and the public. This section will cause law enforcement officers to hesitate the next time they encounter these difficult decisions.

Removal of the Qualified Immunity Doctrine—Section 102

Section 102 of the bill would single out federal law enforcement officers, along with state and local law enforcement and correctional officers, for reduced protection under the qualified immunity doctrine. Under the judicially-created doctrine of qualified immunity, government actors, such as police officers, teachers, and social workers, are shielded from alleged constitutional or statutory violations as long as their actions "[do] not violate 'clearly established' statutory or constitutional rights of which a reasonable person would have known."[178] Thus, qualified immunity serves to protect government officials from civil liability for

---

[178] *Harlow* v. *Fitzgerald*, 457 U.S. 800, 801 (1982).

their misconduct in certain instances while on the job.[179] Under this bill, Democrats eliminate qualified immunity for law enforcement officers, while persevering the existing standard for all other state and local officials, many of whom have less complex and dangerous jobs than law enforcement officers.

The removal of qualified immunity for law enforcement officers will have a detrimental effect on local communities. The Supreme Court has noted that "[q]ualified immunity gives government officials breathing room to make reasonable but mistaken judgments about open legal questions."[180] One commentator has also noted that the doctrine seeks to "strike a balance" because "you don't want to have a legal system or an officer who is going to shirk from doing their duty."[181] If the qualified immunity doctrine is no longer available to law enforcement officers, law enforcement agencies could have more difficulty in attracting and retaining qualified and talented people as law enforcement officers. The net result would be more dangerous communities and neighborhoods.

Establishment of a National Police Misconduct Registry—Section 201

Section 201 of the bill requires the Attorney General to establish a public registry maintained by the Department of Justice (DOJ) that contains complaints against federal, state, and local police officers (including complaints that have not yet been adjudicated), discipline records, termination records, records of lawsuits and settlements, and officer certifications. While Committee Republicans are supportive of transparency and holding bad officers accountable for their misconduct, the composition of the public registry under section 201 is problematic. A national public registry that includes unadjudicated complaints, or complaints that were determined to be unfounded, raises serious due

---

179 CHARLES DOYLE, CONG. RESEARCH SERV., WSLG1825, POLICE LIABILITY FOR LESS THAN EXCESSIVE FORCE (2017).

180 Ashcroft v. al-Kidd, 563 U.S. 731, 743 (2011).

181 Devin Dwyer, *"Qualified immunity" for police getting fresh look by Supreme Court after George Floyd death*, ABC NEWS (Jun. 4, 2020), https://abcnews.go.com/Politics/police-immunity-rule-fresh-supreme-court-george-floyd/story?id=71044230.

process concerns for the law-abiding law enforcement officers subjected to unadjudicated or unfounded complaints.

Limiting Federal Programs That Provide Military Equipment to Law Enforcement—Section 365

Section 365 seeks to drastically limit the Department of Defense's (DOD) 1033 program. This program, created through section 1033 of the National Defense Authorization Act of 1997, allows law enforcement agencies at all levels of government to receive surplus equipment such as bulletproof vests, helmets, and armored vehicles. This equipment—some of which may be financially unobtainable for local law enforcement agencies—protects law enforcement officers and the communities they serve during dangerous situations.[182] Equipment transferred under these programs has also been used to rescue victims in emergency situations such as natural disasters.[183] Recognizing the value in this program, President Trump signed an executive order in 2017 that restored the program after it had been scaled back under the Obama Administration.[184] As a result of section 365, state and local law enforcement agencies, and especially those that exist in jurisdictions with budget shortfalls, will be less equipped to serve their communities in emergencies.

Republican Amendments Rejected by the Democrat Majority Would Have Improved the Legislation

During the Committee's business meeting to consider H.R. 7120, Republicans offered a dozen amendments to improve the base bill. Chairman Nadler and the Democrat Majority declined to accept— or even serious entertain—a single amendment offered by Republicans. Democrats

---

182 Adam Goldman, *Trump Reverses Restrictions on Military Hardware for Police*, N.Y. TIMES (Aug. 28, 2017), https://www.nytimes.com/2017/08/28/us/politics/trump-police-military-surplus-equipment.html.

183 Kari Blakinger, *Military surplus program saved lives during Harvey, Houston-area law enforcement say*, HOUSTON CHRONICLE, October 22, 2017.

184 Adam Goldman, *Trump Reverses Restrictions on Military Hardware for Police*, N.Y. TIMES (Aug. 28, 2017), https://www.nytimes.com/2017/08/28/us/politics/trump-police-military-surplus-equipment.html.

missed a unique opportunity in the wake of national calls for bipartisan reform to actually work across the aisle and pass meaningful legislation.

Improving Police Accountability

Republicans offered amendments to improve police accountability. Although the bill requires state and local law enforcement agencies to expand their use of recording equipment in their day-to-day operations, Democrats rejected an amendment offered by Representative Armstrong to require federal law enforcement agencies record all interviews in connection to the investigation of a federal offense. Similarly, although Democrats asserted that the bill is designed to increase accountability for police officers who commit misconduct, Democrats rejected an amendment from Representative Cline that would have prevented union collective bargaining agreements from standing in the way of holding bad cops accountable.

Strengthening Penalties for Lynching

Included among the amendments that the Democrat Majority refused to support was an amendment from Representative Gohmert that provided meaningfulness to the Justice for Victims of Lynching Act, including in H.R. 7120 as Title IV. A crime as heinous as lynching deserves to be punished with a greater penalty than merely up to 10 years imprisonment. The amendment offered by Representative Gohmert would have augmented the allowable sentence to any term of years, including life and death. After Chairman Nadler announced his opposition to the amendment on the basis of it including the death penalty, Representative Gohmert offered to remove the death penalty language. Chairman Nadler and the Democrat Majority nonetheless rejected the amendment.

Ensuring Adequate Border Security

Representative Gaetz offered an amendment to ensure that those agencies engaged in border securities activities would still have access to excess DOD property through the 1033 program. These agencies are fighting against violent cartels, human traffickers, and smugglers on a daily basis. Democrats rejected this amendment on a party line vote.

All Americans want safe communities. All Americans want effective, transparent, and accountable policing. The Justice in Policing Act—conceived, introduced, and marked-up on a purely partisan basis—regrettably falls short of securing those goals.

Chairman Nadler and Committee Democrats had an opportunity to work collaboratively with Republicans to produce comprehensive, well-designed legislation to improve policing in America. President Trump has issued a bold executive order on police reform and House and Senate Republicans have introduced carefully considered legislation, the Justice Act, in each chamber. However, in a failure of leadership to meet the historic moment, Chairman Nadler chose not to solicit or seriously consider any Republican proposals. The result is a partisan piece of legislation with virtually no hope of becoming law.

The Committee process in reporting H.R. 7120 to the House floor demonstrates that Democrats would rather have an election-year talking point than a bipartisan bill that offers true advances in police reform. It is apparent that Democrats drafted this bill more to satisfy their far-left base who support efforts to defund, dismantle and disband the police than to secure Republican support. In an election year, Chairman Nadler and House Democrats chose partisanship over policy-making, and politics over police reform. Americans deserve better.

Jim Jordan.
Ranking Member.

In: Police Reform ...
Editor: Robert B. Smith

ISBN: 978-1-53618-504-1

Chapter 2

COMPARING POLICE REFORM BILLS: THE JUSTICE IN POLICING ACT AND THE JUSTICE ACT*

Joanna R. Lampe

On May 25, 2020, George Floyd died in the custody of the Minneapolis police after an officer pressed his knee into Floyd's neck while restraining him. That incident, others like it, and subsequent nationwide protests have sparked heightened interest in the federal government's ability to prevent and remedy police misconduct, especially the use of excessive force against people of color. The events of May and June 2020 have prompted action by the Executive Branch and legislative proposals in both houses of Congress. On June 16, 2020, President Donald Trump issued an Executive Order on Safe Policing for Safe Communities. On June 8, 2020, Members of the House of Representatives, led by the Congressional Black Caucus, introduced the George Floyd Justice in Policing Act of 2020 (Justice in Policing Act), and on June 17, 2020, Senate Republicans unveiled the Just

* This is an edited, reformatted and augmented version of Congressional Research Service Publication No. IN10812, dated updated July 6, 2020.

and Unifying Solutions To Invigorate Communities Everywhere Act of 2020 (JUSTICE Act). A previous Legal Sidebar briefly summarized the Executive Order and both bills, along with other recent reform proposals. This Legal Sidebar provides a comparison of the Justice in Policing Act and the JUSTICE Act. While this Sidebar does not purport to detail every provision of the two bills exhaustively, it analyzes key similarities and differences that are most relevant when evaluating the two proposals. The Sidebar first outlines subject matters that both bills cover, detailing similarities and differences between each bill on those subjects. It concludes by discussing provisions unique to each bill. This Sidebar was updated on July 6, 2020, and reflects amendments to each bill up to that date.

SUBJECTS COVERED BY BOTH BILLS

This section outlines subjects addressed by both the Justice in Policing Act and the JUSTICE Act. In addition to addressing some of the same topics, the two bills are broadly similar in that many of their provisions regulating state and local law enforcement would rely on Congress's power under the Spending Clause to require states or state and local law enforcement agencies that accept federal funding to implement certain policies as a condition of the grant. The primary sources of federal funding to which the bills would attach conditions are grants under the Byrne JAG program and the COPS grant program. In general, whenever either bill would impose an obligation on state or local governments who accept federal funds, funding recipients who fail to comply with such obligations would become ineligible for some or all funding from the specified sources. However, various provisions of both bills would directly regulate federal and even state and local law enforcement officers.

Limitations on Chokeholds and Other Uses of Force

Both the Justice in Policing Act and the JUSTICE Act include provisions designed to limit the use of chokeholds by federal, state, and local law enforcement, though the two statutes differ in their breadth and approach.

- Section 363 of the Justice in Policing Act would specifically govern chokeholds or carotid holds, defined as "the application of any pressure to the throat or windpipe, the use of maneuvers that restrict blood or oxygen flow to the brain, or carotid artery restraints that prevent or hinder breathing or reduce intake of air." That section of the bill would require states or localities that receive certain federal funding to enact laws banning *all* uses of chokeholds and carotid holds by law enforcement officers. As discussed further below, Section 363 would also amend 18 U.S.C. § 242 to criminalize the use of these maneuvers based on race.
- Section 364 of the Justice in Policing Act, entitled the PEACE Act, would prohibit federal law enforcement officers from using chokeholds or carotid holds unless the conditions for deadly force (discussed further below) are met.
- The JUSTICE Act would apply to chokeholds, defined as "a physical maneuver that restricts an individual's ability to breathe for the purposes of incapacitation." Section 105 of the JUSTICE Act would require states and local governments that receive certain federal funding to develop law enforcement agency policies "prohibit[ing] the use of chokeholds except when deadly force is authorized." That section would also require the Attorney General to develop such a policy at the federal level for federal law enforcement agencies.
- With respect to the use of force more broadly, the PEACE ACT, Section 364 of the Justice in Policing Act, would allow federal law enforcement officers to use:

- o deadly force (defined as "that force which a reasonable person would consider likely to cause death or serious bodily harm," specifically including chokeholds and carotid holds, the use of a gun, or multiple discharges of a taser) only as a last resort to prevent imminent death or serious bodily injury when there is no substantial risk of injury to a third person and reasonable alternatives to the use of deadly force have been exhausted;
- o "less lethal" force (defined as "any degree of force that is not likely to cause death or serious bodily injury") only if such force is "necessary and proportional" to effect an arrest supported by probable cause, and reasonable alternatives to the use of less lethal force have been exhausted.

- The PEACE Act would require federal officers to identify themselves and issue certain verbal warnings to a suspect prior to the use of any force, when feasible. Failure to abide by applicable standards concerning the use of force would limit the ability of a federal law enforcement officer charged with murder or manslaughter to argue that a killing was justified. The section also directs the Attorney General to issue guidance and provide training to federal law enforcement officials on use of force more generally. Finally, this section would condition certain federal grants to states, municipalities, and Indian Tribes on recipients' enacting laws to establish comparable use of force standards.
- The JUSTICE Act does not contain a comparable provision restricting the use of deadly or less-lethal force more broadly but, as discussed below, would require reporting of incidents involving law enforcement uses of force.

No-Knock Warrants

Both bills seek to address concerns related to the use of no-knock warrants, but the Justice in Policing Act would impose or encourage direct legal limits on the practice, while the JUSTICE Act would instead seek to gather data on the use of no-knock warrants.

- Section 362 of the Justice in Policing Act would ban no-knock warrants in drug cases at the federal level. The section would also condition certain federal funding upon states and localities enacting laws prohibiting the use of no-knock warrants in similar drug cases.
- The JUSTICE Act does not contain a comparable provision banning no-knock warrants but, as discussed below, would require reporting on their use.

Body Cameras

Both bills would seek to increase the use of body-worn cameras by state and local law enforcement officers. The Justice in Policing Act would additionally require the use of body cameras and in-vehicle video recording by federal law enforcement officers.

- Title III, Subtitle C of the Justice in Policing Act would require certain federal law enforcement officers to wear body cameras and use such cameras in responding to any call for service, or at the initiation of any "law enforcement or investigative stop. . . between a Federal law enforcement officer and a member of the public." The bill contains certain exceptions, such as when an immediate threat to the officer's life or safety makes activating the camera impossible or dangerous, or when recording is discontinued at the request of a person seeking to remain anonymous. Agencies would be required to retain camera footage for at least six months and allow inspection by certain interested parties. Officers who fail to comply with the bill's requirements could be subject to disciplinary proceedings, and lack of footage could result in evidentiary presumptions against the government in civil and criminal cases. This subtitle would also require installation and use of video recording equipment in all federal patrol vehicles.

- Part II of Subtitle C of the Justice in Policing Act, the Police CAMERA Act of 2020, would provide federal grants to expand the use of body cameras by state, local, and tribal law enforcement officers, subject to certain requirements related to safety, privacy, data retention, and reporting.
- Title II of the JUSTICE Act would provide grants to state, local, and tribal government agencies to support the use of body-worn cameras by law enforcement officials. Funding recipients would be required to provide "assurances" that they have specified policies and procedures in place, including requiring certain training and imposing discipline on officers who fail to use cameras as required.
- Unlike the Justice in Policing Act, the JUSTICE Act would *not* require the use of body cameras or cameras in patrol vehicles by federal law enforcement officers.

Law Enforcement Misconduct and Disciplinary Records

Both bills contain provisions designed to enhance transparency concerning records of misconduct by law enforcement officers.

- Sections 201 and 202 of the Justice in Policing Act would create a National Police Misconduct Registry maintained by the Department of Justice (DOJ). The publicly available registry would contain information including complaints (particularly those involving use of force or racial profiling), discipline records, and termination records for all federal, state, and local law enforcement officers. The bill would require states that receive certain federal funding to report such information on behalf of each law enforcement agency within the state. It would also require funding recipients to demonstrate that "all law enforcement officers of the State or other jurisdiction have completed all State certification requirements."

- Title III of the JUSTICE Act would require state and local governments that receive certain federal funding to "maintain a system for sharing disciplinary records of law enforcement officers" that meets certain specifications. The system would be accessible to other law enforcement agencies, and individual officers would have the ability to access their own records and submit related information. Before hiring any law enforcement officer, covered agencies would be required to search the system and review any records related to that officer.

Training, Best Practices, and Accreditation

Both bills seek to establish best practices for law enforcement officers and train officers in areas such as use of force and racial bias. Both bills would also create standards to accredit or otherwise identify law enforcement agencies that meet certain standards.

- Subtitle B of Title I of the Justice in Policing Act, the Law Enforcement Trust and Integrity Act of 2020, would require the Attorney General to develop uniform standards for accreditation of law enforcement agencies with respect to, among other areas, use of force procedures, stop and search procedures, training, and early warning systems. This subtitle would direct the Attorney General to make policies to encourage law enforcement agencies to pursue accreditation and to allocate DOJ discretionary funding only to states and municipalities that require agencies to gain and maintain accreditation. It would also authorize grants to community-based organizations to study and implement effective standards and programs for law enforcement agencies.
- Section 361 of the Justice in Policing Act would mandate training for federal law enforcement officers on racial profiling, implicit bias, and the duty to intervene when another officer is using excessive force. This section would also mandate that certain

federal grant recipients require state and local law enforcement officers within their jurisdictions to complete such training.

- Title VI of the JUSTICE Act would direct the Attorney General to develop training on alternatives to use of force, tactics for de-escalation, responding to behavioral health crises, and duty to intervene when another officer uses excessive force. This title would require the Attorney General to publish information about state and local law enforcement agencies that employ officers who have completed such training.
- Subtitle B of Title VIII of the JUSTICE Act would provide authorization and funding for the Director of the National Museum of African American History and Culture to develop and disseminate an educational curriculum for law enforcement personnel or candidates on the history of racism in the United States.

Reporting on Use of Force and Other Matters

Multiple provisions of both bills would facilitate federal data collection and oversight related to police reform.

- Section 117 of the Justice in Policing Act would establish a DOJ Task Force on Law Enforcement Oversight to coordinate the detection and referral of complaints regarding incidents of alleged law enforcement misconduct.
- Section 118 of the Justice in Policing Act would require federal law enforcement agencies, and state, local, and tribal law enforcement agencies that receive certain federal funding, to report on various practices including stops, searches, and uses of deadly force. Data on each covered practice would be broken down based on the race, ethnicity, age, and gender of the officers and members of the public involved in each incident.

- Title II, Subtitle B of the Justice in Policing Act, the PRIDE Act, would require recipients of certain federal funding to report to the Attorney General information about a broad range of incidents related to the use of force by and against law enforcement officers, including shootings, deaths in custody, and "any incident involving the death or arrest of a law enforcement officer." The reports would include various demographic information of the members of the public involved in such incidents. This subtitle would explicitly require reporting of incidents involving school resource officers. The bill would direct the Attorney General to issue a public report containing data collected under this section.
- Section 101 of the JUSTICE Act, the George Floyd and Walter Scott Notification Act, would require recipients of certain federal funding to report to the federal government information related to law enforcement uses of force involving death, serious injury, or use of a firearm; shootings of officers by civilians; and other incidents leading to the death or serious injury of an officer.
- Section 102 of the JUSTICE Act, the Breonna Taylor Notification Act, would require federal funding recipients to report to the federal government information related to law enforcement uses of no-knock warrants. This section would also direct the Attorney General to publish an annual report on the use of no-knock warrants in closed investigations by federal, state, and local law enforcement agencies.

Sexual Acts Under Color of Law

Both bills include provisions based on the Closing the Law Enforcement Consent Loophole Act of 2019.

- Title IV of the Justice in Policing Act and Title X of the JUSTICE Act use slightly different wording, but both would appear to impose criminal liability when a person "acting under color of law, knowingly engages in a sexual act" with an individual in federal custody. Aviolation of either provision would be punishable by a fine and/or up to fifteen years in prison.

- Title IV of the Justice in Policing Act would require recipients of certain federal funds to enact laws making it a criminal offense "for any person acting under color of law of the State or unit of local government to engage in a sexual act with an individual" in custody.
- Title X of the JUSTICE Act would authorize the Attorney General to make grants to states, municipalities, and Indian Tribes that enact similar laws.

Law Enforcement Demographics

Both bills contain provisions designed to promote hiring of law enforcement officers who live in or demographically represent the communities they serve.

- Section 366 of the Justice in Policing Act would, among other things, authorize the use of certain federal funds to recruit law enforcement officers who live in or are willing to relocate to communities "where there are poor or fragmented relationships between police and residents of the community, or where there are high incidents of crime."
- Section 801 of the JUSTICE Act would authorize the use of certain federal grant funding "for a law enforcement agency that has a substantially different racial and ethnic demographic makeup than the community served by the agency, to hire recruiters and enroll law enforcement officer candidates in law enforcement academies to become career law enforcement officers who have racial and ethnic demographic characteristics similar to the community."

PROVISIONS UNIQUE TO THE JUSTICE IN POLICING ACT

Criminal Liability For Civil Rights Violations

As discussed in more detail in this Sidebar, a provision of the federal criminal code, 18 U.S.C. § 242 (Section 242), makes it a crime for a government actor such as a law enforcement officer to willfully deprive a person of rights under the Constitution or federal law, or to impose different punishments based on a person's race.

- Section 101 of the Justice in Policing Act would amend Section 242 to change the mental state required for conviction from "willfully" to the less stringent "knowingly or recklessly.'' This section would also remove the possibility of a death sentence for violating Section 242.
- Section 363 of the Act would amend Section 242 to provide that "the application of any pressure to the throat or windpipe, use of maneuvers that restrict blood or oxygen flow to the brain, or carotid artery restraints which prevent or hinder breathing or reduce intake of air" is a punishment that may not be imposed based on race.

Qualified Immunity

As discussed in this Sidebar, the judicially created doctrine of qualified immunity provides that government officials performing discretionary functions generally may not be sued for such actions unless they violate "clearly established" law.

- Section 102 of the Justice in Policing Act would limit qualified immunity for state and local law enforcement officers in suits under 42 U.S.C. § 1983, and for federal law enforcement officers "in any action under any source of law," providing that it is not a defense to liability if a defendant believed in good faith that his or her conduct was lawful or that the rights the defendant allegedly infringed were not clearly established.

Civil Rights Investigations

As discussed in this Sidebar, DOJ has the authority under 34 U.S.C. § 12601 (Section 12601) to investigate any "pattern or practice" of constitutional violations by law enforcement agencies and sue to remedy such violations.

- Section 103 of the Justice in Policing Act would seek to enhance federal investigations into patterns or practices of law enforcement misconduct by granting subpoena power to DOJ under Section 12601 and authorizing state attorneys general to bring suit based on violations of that provision. This section would also provide federal grant funding to enhance state and local investigations into potential patterns and practices of constitutional violations. In addition, this section would prohibit recipients of certain federal funds from providing such funds to local law enforcement agencies that enter into contracts, including collective bargaining agreements, that "would prevent the Attorney General from seeking or enforcing equitable or declaratory relief against a law enforcement agency engaging in a pattern or practice of unconstitutional misconduct" or conflict with any consent decree.

Use of Force Investigations

States and state and local law enforcement agencies may also investigate potential law enforcement misconduct. However, some commentators worry that close relationships between law enforcement officers and prosecutors may hinder investigations and prosecutions of law enforcement misconduct.

- Section 104 of the Justice in Policing Act would provide federal grant funding to enhance independent investigations into uses of deadly force by state, local, and tribal law enforcement officers.

Racial Profiling

Title III, Subtitle A of the Justice in Policing Act, the End Racial and Religious Profiling Act, would seek to prevent and remedy racial profiling by law enforcement.

- Part I of this subtitle would prohibit racial profiling by federal, state, local, and tribal law enforcement. The bill would define racial profiling as "a law enforcement agent or agency relying, to any degree, on actual or perceived race, ethnicity, national origin, religion, gender, gender identity, or sexual orientation" in deciding the scope and substance of law enforcement activities. To enforce this prohibition, the act would authorize civil suits for declaratory or injunctive relief by the DOJ or affected individuals. It would suffice to show a violation of the bill if "spontaneous investigatory activities of law enforcement agents in a jurisdiction have had a disparate impact" on a covered group.
- Part II would require federal law enforcement agencies to establish policies to help eliminate racial profiling.
- The remainder of Title III, Subtitle A would provide funding for training of state and local police and data collection related to racial profiling, and require the Attorney General to make annual reports to Congress on racial profiling by law enforcement agencies.

Restrictions on transfer of military equipment. Under a federal program known as the 1033 Program, the federal government transfers excess military equipment to state and local law enforcement agencies.

- Section 365 of the Justice in Policing Act, the Stop Militarizing Law Enforcement Act, would limit the transfer of certain military-grade equipment (primarily weapons and vehicles designed for combat) to state and local law enforcement.

PROVISIONS UNIQUE TO THE JUSTICE ACT

New Criminal Offense

The JUSTICE Act would create a new criminal offense related to law enforcement oversight and reform.

- Section 106 of the JUSTICE Act would create a new criminal offense of "knowingly and willfully falsify[ing] a report . . . in furtherance of the deprivation of any rights, privileges, or immunities secured or protected by the Constitution or laws of the United States where death or serious bodily injury . . . occurs." The penalty for violating this provision would be a fine and/or imprisonment for up to twenty years.

Anti-Lynching Provisions

The JUSTICE Act incorporates an anti-lynching provision drawn from the Justice for Victims of Lynching Act.

- Title IV of the JUSTICE Act, entitled the Justice for Victims of Lynching Act, would create a new section of the federal criminal code entitled "Lynching." The provision would criminalize conspiring to violate certain federal civil rights or hate crime statutes (18 U.S.C. §§ 245, 247, or 249 or 42 U.S.C. § 3631). Violations would be punishable by a fine and/or up to ten years in prison (or longer if authorized by the underlying statute that the defendant conspired to violate).

- The version of the Justice in Policing Act introduced in the House on June 8, 2020 included an anti-lynching provision substantively identical to the one in the JUSTICE Act. That provision, referred to as both the Justice for Victims of Lynching Act and the Emmett Till Anti-Lynching Act, was not included in the version of the Justice in Policing Act that passed the house on June 25, 2020.

Exploratory Commissions

The JUSTICE Act would create two commissions to investigate issues and propose reforms in areas related to law enforcement oversight.

- Title V would create a Commission on the Social Status of Black Men and Boys to "conduct a systematic study of the conditions affecting Black men and boys, including homicide rates, arrest and incarceration rates, poverty, violence, fatherhood, mentorship, drug abuse, death rates, disparate income and wealth levels, school performance in all grade levels including postsecondary education and college, and health issues." Composed of 19 members, including Members of Congress and individuals appointed by Congress, the President, and certain executive branch officials, the Commission would document trends in these areas and propose measures to address any issues it recorded.
- Title VII would establish a temporary National Criminal Justice Commission to "undertake a comprehensive review of the criminal justice system," disseminate findings, and propose reforms. The President and the leader of the Senate would each appoint a co-

chair of the 14-person Commission, and each co-chair would appoint six additional members, in consultation with certain Members of Congress.

- Title IX would direct the National Criminal Justice Commission to develop best practices related to law enforcement oversight. It would also direct the Commission to conduct studies on state and local use of force review boards; officer training on issues related to mental health, homelessness, and addiction; and improving accountability for DOJ grants.

In: Police Reform …
Editor: Robert B. Smith
ISBN: 978-1-53618-504-1

Chapter 3

CONGRESS AND POLICE REFORM: CURRENT LAW AND RECENT PROPOSALS*

Joanna R. Lampe

In May and June 2020, protests erupted nationwide after the publication of video footage of a Minneapolis police officer pressing his knee into the neck of George Floyd, leading to his death. That incident and its aftermath have sparked heightened interest in Congress's ability to implement reforms of state and local law enforcement.

As a companion to this Sidebar outlines in greater detail, congressional power to regulate state and local law enforcement is not without limits. The Constitution grants the federal government only certain enumerated authorities, with the Tenth Amendment reserving all other powers for the states. The regulation of state and municipal law enforcement is an area that the Constitution generally entrusts to the states. However, Congress possesses some authority to legislate on that subject, primarily through statutes designed to enforce the protections of the Fourteenth Amendment

* This is an edited, reformatted and augmented version of Congressional Research Service Publication No. LSB10486, updated June 25, 2020.

and legislation requiring states to take specified action in exchange for federal funds disbursed under the Spending Clause. This Sidebar provides an overview of existing federal authorities intended to prevent and redress constitutional violations by state and local public safety officials. It then presents some recent proposals that would change federal regulation of state and local law enforcement. The Sidebar concludes with a list of additional CRS resources related to law enforcement reform.

FEDERAL REGULATION OF STATE AND LOCAL LAW ENFORCEMENT

Existing federal remedies for constitutional violations by state and local law enforcement include civil and criminal enforcement by the U.S. Department of Justice (DOJ) and private suits by individuals deprived of their rights by someone acting "under color of" state law. In addition, the federal government encourages states to enact certain policies related to law enforcement by placing conditions on federal funding. Federal agencies also independently investigate and gather data on law enforcement activities.

Federal Criminal Law

A provision of the federal criminal code, 18 U.S.C. § 242 (Section 242), makes it a crime for (among other things) a person acting "under color of any law, statute, ordinance, regulation, or custom" to "willfully subject [ ] any person . . . to the deprivation of any rights, privileges, or immunities secured or protected by the Constitution or laws of the United States[.]" Section 242 also prohibits a person acting under color of law from subjecting any person to "different punishments, pains, or penalties, on account of such person being an alien, or by reason of his color, or race, than are prescribed for the punishment of citizens[.]" A simple violation of the statute is punishable by a fine and/or up to a year in prison. If bodily injury results, the offender may be fined and/or imprisoned for up to ten years. If death results or other aggravating factors are present, Section 242 provides for a fine and/or imprisonment for ten years to life or a death sentence (though the Constitution forbids imposition of the death penalty for non-homicide offenses). A related provision, 18 U.S.C. § 241 (Section 241), makes it a crime for "two or more persons [to] conspire to injure, oppress, threaten, or intimidate any person . . . in the free exercise or enjoyment of any right or privilege secured to him by the Constitution or laws of the United States[.]" Violations of Section 241 are punishable by up to ten years in prison or, if certain aggravating factors are present, up to life in prison or death.

The Supreme Court has held that "officers of the State . . . performing official duties," including public safety officials, act "under color of . . . law" for purposes of Section 242. As DOJ has explained, law enforcement officers may violate Section 242 through "excessive force, sexual assault, intentional false arrests, theft, or the intentional fabrication of evidence resulting in a loss of liberty to another." DOJ enforces Sections 241 and 242 by bringing criminal charges against officers accused of violating those statutes. People who believe their rights have been infringed may report such violations to DOJ, but Sections 241 and 242 provide no private right of enforcement. Notably, if DOJ elects to pursue criminal charges under Section 242, it faces a high standard of proof: in *Screws v. United States*, the Supreme Court held that to show a violation of a prior statute whose wording mirrored that of Section 242, the prosecution must prove the defendant had "a specific intent to deprive a person of a federal right made definite by decision or other rule of law." The Supreme Court extended this holding to Section 241 cases in *United States v. Guest.* In practice, the specific intent requirement requires the prosecution to prove that a local official intended to violate a federal right, as opposed to simply intending to, for example, assault a victim. This results in what some view as a significant hurdle to bringing Section 241 and 242 claims.

DOJ Civil Enforcement

Another section of the U.S. Code, 34 U.S.C. § 12601 (formerly codified at 42 U.S.C. § 14141) renders it "unlawful for any governmental authority, or any agent thereof, . . . to engage in a pattern or practice of conduct by law enforcement officers or by officials . . . that deprives persons of rights, privileges, or immunities secured or protected by the Constitution or laws of the United States." According to DOJ, potential violations of this provision include "excessive force, discriminatory harassment, false arrests, coercive sexual conduct, and unlawful stops, searches or arrests." DOJ enforces this provision by filing civil complaints against allegedly offending law enforcement agencies. The statute does not create a private right of action (i.e., a right for individuals harmed by violations to sue). Moreover, because the law applies only to a "pattern or practice of conduct," it cannot remedy isolated instances of misconduct. Finally, the statute does not provide for monetary penalties. If DOJ successfully sues under the provision, it may "obtain appropriate equitable and declaratory relief to eliminate the pattern or practice."

Private Civil Rights Litigation

Federal law also allows individuals to seek civil redress for violations of their legal rights. The applicable statute, 42 U.S.C. § 1983 (Section 1983), provides in relevant part:

> Every person who, under color of any statute, ordinance, regulation, custom, or usage, of any State . . . subjects, or causes to be subjected, any citizen of the United States or other person within the jurisdiction thereof to the deprivation of any rights, privileges, or immunities secured by the Constitution and laws, shall be liable to the party injured[.]

Unlike the foregoing statutory provisions, Section 1983 creates a private right of action, meaning that anyone suffering a covered deprivation of rights may sue the persons responsible. Moreover, unlike Sections 241 and 242, courts have interpreted Section 1983 *not* to contain a specific intent requirement. A prevailing Section 1983 plaintiff may be entitled to injunctive relief, attorney's fees, and/or money damages. Recovery may include both compensatory damages (designed to make the plaintiff whole and compensate for the legal injury) and punitive damages (designed to punish the defendant and deter future, similar misconduct).

Similar to Section 242, Section 1983 applies to persons acting "under color of" state law. State and local public safety officers generally act under color of state law for purposes of Section 1983: as the Supreme Court has stated, "a public employee acts under color of state law while acting in his official capacity or while exercising his responsibilities pursuant to state law." However, law enforcement liability under Section 1983 is subject to a significant judicially created limitation: based on concerns that frequent litigation could interfere with the work of law enforcement officers, the Supreme Court has held that law enforcement officers benefit from *qualified immunity* from suit. The Supreme Court announced the modern qualified immunity test in *Harlow v. Fitzgerald*, holding that "government officials performing discretionary functions, generally are shielded from liability for civil damages" if they do not "violate clearly established statutory or constitutional rights of which a reasonable person would have known."

The Supreme Court has explained that qualified immunity is "an immunity from suit rather than a mere defense to liability; and like an absolute immunity, it is effectively lost if a case is erroneously permitted to go to trial." As a result, courts generally consider qualified immunity early in a Section 1983 case, and a defendant whose qualified immunity defense is denied is entitled to an immediate interlocutory appeal. A court evaluating a claim of qualified immunity considers two questions: (1) whether, viewed in the light most favorable to the plaintiff, "the facts alleged show the officer's conduct violated a constitutional right"; and (2) "whether the law clearly established that the officer's conduct was unlawful in the circumstances of the case." While that two-step analysis was once considered mandatory, in the 2009 case *Pearson v. Callahan*, the Supreme Court held that judges could "exercise their sound discretion in deciding which of the two prongs of the qualified immunity analysis should be addressed first. " In a series of recent cases involving police use of force, the Roberts Court has reversed lower court denials of qualified immunity, stating that "clearly established law" must not be defined at a high level of generality and instead needs to be particularized to the facts of the case, which can amount to a high bar for plaintiffs to overcome.

The Supreme Court articulated another limitation on Section 1983 suits in *Monell v. Department of Social Services*. In that case, the Court held that a municipality is a "person" subject to suit under Section 1983. However, the Court further held that a local government cannot be sued "for an injury inflicted solely by its employees or agents" under the theory of *respondeat superior* (the legal doctrine that an employer may be liable to suit for wrongful acts of its employees). Rather, under *Monell*, a Section 1983 plaintiff must show that an injury stems from a "policy or custom" of the municipality. This requires a showing that "through its deliberate conduct, the municipality was the 'moving force' behind the injury alleged," and that the municipality acted with "deliberate indifference to the risk that a violation of a particular constitutional or statutory right will follow." This exacting standard has led one commentator to assert that municipal liability "is practically a dead letter."

Grant Conditions and Federal Oversight

The federal government provides financial support to state and local law enforcement in the form of grants, and may require states to enact certain policies to qualify for such funding. As one example, the Edward Byrne Memorial Justice Assistance Grant (Byrne JAG) Program provides federal support for state and local criminal justice programs. Among other conditions, states that receive Byrne JAG funding must certify compliance with the Death in Custody Reporting Act (DCRA). Enacted in 2014 the DCRA requires states to report to the Attorney General certain information regarding the deaths of individuals in the custody of law enforcement agencies. Byrne JAG grants have also have been used to train officers on use of force and de-escalation of conflict. In addition to guiding state and local law enforcement policy through grant funding, federal government agencies independently collect data related to the use of force by state and local law enforcement.

June 2020 Executive Order

On June 16, 2020, President Donald Trump issued an Executive Order on Safe Policing for Safe Communities. In perhaps its most consequential provision, the Executive Order directs the Attorney General to establish best practices for law enforcement agencies and condition federal grants on compliance with those standards. Specifically, the Executive Order directs the Attorney General to certify independent credentialing bodies that can assess agencies' policies in areas such as use of force, de-escalation, and identifying officers who may require intervention. Of particular note, credentialing bodies will need to "confirm" that state and local use-of-force policies prohibit the use of chokeholds. The Executive Order directs the Attorney General to allocate DOJ discretionary grant funding only to state and local law enforcement agencies that have sought or are in the process of seeking such credentials.

In addition, the Executive Order directs the Attorney General to create a database to track and publish data related to instances of excessive use of force by law enforcement, requiring law enforcement agencies that receive discretionary grant funding to submit information to the database. The Executive Order also requires the Attorney General to develop and propose legislation to improve law enforcement practices and build community engagement, and to identify and develop opportunities to train law enforcement officers with respect to encounters with individuals suffering from impaired mental health, homelessness, and addiction. Importantly, the Executive Order provides that many of its requirements must be implemented "as appropriate and consistent with applicable law." As a result, provisions that seek to change existing grant conditions may be tempered by recent court rulings expressing skepticism of the executive branch's ability to unilaterally change conditions related to federal grants, such as those provided under the Byrne JAG program.

Proposals for Law Enforcement Reform in Congress

Even before the high-profile events of May and June 2020, commentators and legislators had suggested numerous avenues for congressional reform and oversight of state and local law enforcement, and recent events have prompted additional proposals in this area. This section provides a sample of these proposals, including bills that would target specific issues related to police reform as well as comprehensive proposals that would alter federal regulation of law enforcement on many fronts.

Qualified Immunity

Qualified immunity has been the subject of significant debate in recent years. A May 2020 report by Reuters found that "since 2005, the [federal appellate] courts have shown an increasing tendency to grant immunity in excessive force cases." Critics of qualified immunity assert that the test the Supreme Court announced in *Pearson v. Callahan* improperly hinders Section 1983 claims. Not only is it difficult for plaintiffs to overcome a claim of qualified immunity, these commentators assert, but furthermore courts often consider *only* whether a defendant violated clearly established law, without reaching the question of whether the defendant violated the plaintiff's rights—albeit in circumstances courts have not yet assessed. Legal commentators have argued that this limited inquiry prevents the development of clearly established law that could govern future Section 1983 cases. Some commentators also assert that the current doctrine of qualified immunity fails to protect law enforcement officers from suit. Others defend the doctrine or favor limited judicial reforms, asserting the need to afford police officers some level of deference when making split-second decisions about the use of force, for example to subdue a fleeing or resisting suspect. The doctrine of qualified immunity arises from the Supreme Court's interpretation of Section 1983. Thus, either the Court or Congress could modify the doctrine, and some legal scholars have called on both branches to address the issue. The Court has considered multiple petitions for certiorari raising challenges to qualified immunity, and Justice Thomas and Justice Sotomayor have both expressed concerns about the doctrine. On the legislative side, the Ending Qualified Immunity Act introduced in June 2020 would wholly "remove the defense of qualified immunity." Another proposal aimed at removing barriers to Section 1983 liability is the Reforming Qualified Immunity Act. Unlike current law, which grants officials qualified immunity if the constitutional right alleged to have been violated is not "clearly established," this proposal would place the burden on Section 1983 defendants to affirmatively show with some particularity that the conduct at issue was authorized by law. Specifically, the proposal would seek to remove the existing doctrine of qualified immunity and instead provide that an individual defendant "shall not be liable" if the defendant reasonably believed that his or her conduct was lawful *and* either (1) the conduct at issue was "specifically authorized or required" by federal or state law, or (2) a federal or state court had issued a final decision holding that "the specific conduct alleged to be unlawful was consistent with the Constitution of the United States and Federal laws." The Reforming Qualified Immunity Act would also revise the rule articulated in *Monell* by providing that "a municipality or other unit of local government shall be liable for a violation [of Section 1983] by an agent or employee of the municipality or other unit of local government acting within the scope of his or her employment," in effect applying the doctrine of *respondeat superior* to such governmental entities.

Criminal Liability

While changes to the doctrine of qualified immunity could alter *civil* liability for law enforcement officers, other proposals would aim to expand *criminal* liability for civil rights violations by officers. For example, the Eric Garner Excessive Use of Force Prevention Act of 2019 would amend Section 242 to provide explicitly that "the application of any pressure to the throat or windpipe which may prevent or hinder breathing or reduce intake of air is a punishment" that may not be imposed on a racially disparate basis. The Police Accountability Act of 2020 would provide a federal criminal penalty for assault or homicide committed by certain state or local law enforcement officers. Some commentators also advocate removing the specific intent requirement for Sections 241 and 242 announced in *Screws* and *Guest*.

Limitations on Military-Grade Equipment

Under a federal program known as the 1033 Program, the federal government transfers certain excess military equipment to state and local law enforcement agencies. Some commentators contend that this type of equipment contributes to militarization of police forces without increasing public safety and increases the risk of incidents of excessive force. The 1033 Program is authorized by statute, so Congress has the power to alter or discontinue the program. There are a number of specific proposals on this front.

For instance, on May 31, 2020, Sen. Brian Schatz announced his intention to introduce legislation that would end the 1033 Program. Another proposal related to the 1033 Program, the Stop Militarizing Law Enforcement Act, would maintain the program but impose additional limitations and reporting requirements.

Grants and Conditions on Federal Funds

Numerous proposals currently before Congress would invoke the Spending Clause in an effort to regulate state and local law enforcement activities. Some proposals would fund voluntary state and local measures, such as use of force and bias awareness training or body cameras. Other proposals would require states to enact certain policies in exchange for federal grants. For instance, the Police Training and Independent Review Act of 2019 would fund training on cultural diversity and de-escalation tactics while requiring participating states to "enact laws requiring the independent investigation and prosecution of the use of deadly force by law enforcement officers." The Preventing Tragedies Between Police and Communities Act of 2019 would oblige Byrne JAG grant recipients to mandate training on ways to reduce the use of force. The Police Exercising Absolute Care With Everyone Act of 2019 (PEACE Act) would require Byrne JAG grantees to enact laws limiting the use of lethal and less than lethal force by law enforcement. The Next Step Act of 2019 would, among other things, direct Byrne JAG grant recipients to submit quarterly reports to the Attorney General on officers' use of force.

Comprehensive Reform Efforts

Congress is currently considering two comprehensive police reform bills: the Justice in Policing Act of 2020 and the JUSTICE Act. This section summarizes key provisions of the two bills, and has been updated to reflect amendments up to June 24, 2020. Another Legal Sidebar compares key provisions of the two proposals in more detail.

The Justice in Policing Act of 2020

On June 8, 2020, Members of Congress led by the Congressional Black Caucus presented the Justice in Policing Act of 2020. According to the reported version of the bill from June 19, 2020, the legislation would build on some of the foregoing proposals to reform multiple facets of federal, state, and local law enforcement, including, but not limited to, the following:

- Section 101 of the bill would amend Section 242 to change the mental state required for conviction from "willfully" to "knowingly or recklessly." It would also remove the possibility of a death sentence for violating Section 242.

- Section 102 would limit qualified immunity for state and local law enforcement officers in suits under Section 1983, and for federal law enforcement officers "in any action under any source of law," providing that it is not a defense to liability if an officer believed in good faith that his or her conduct was lawful or that the rights the officer allegedly infringed were not clearly established.
- Sections 103 and 104 would seek to enhance investigations into incidents involving law enforcement uses of force or a pattern or practice of law enforcement misconduct by, among things, granting subpoena power to DOJ under 34 U.S.C. § 12601 and authorizing state attorneys general to bring suit based on violations of that provision.
- Multiple provisions of the Act would facilitate federal data collection related to police reform. For instance, Section 118 and Title II, Subtitle B of the Act would require federal funding recipients to report incidents involving uses of force by law enforcement, and Section 201 would create a federal law enforcement misconduct registry.
- Section 362 would ban no-knock warrants in drug cases at the federal level. The section would also condition certain federal funding upon states and localities prohibiting the use of no-knock warrants in similar drug cases.
- Section 363 would require states and municipalities that receive certain federal funding to enact laws banning the use of chokeholds by law enforcement officers.
- Section 364, the PEACE Act, would allow federal law enforcement officers to use deadly force only as a last resort to prevent imminent death or serious bodily injury when certain conditions are met and impose limits on the use of "less lethal" force. This provision would also condition federal grants on state and local law enforcement agencies' establishing the same use of force standard.

- Section 365, the Stop Militarizing Law Enforcement Act, would limit the transfer of certain military-grade equipment (primarily weapons and vehicles designed for combat) to state and local law enforcement.
- Title III, Subtitle A of the Act would seek to prevent and remedy racial profiling by law enforcement, including by authorizing civil suits by DOJ and affected individuals. The Title would also establish various programs and policies to help eliminate racial profiling, such as by funding training programs for state and local police.
- Title III, Subtitle C would require the use of body cameras by certain federal law enforcement officers and fund expanded use of body cameras by state and local officers.
- Title IV, the Justice for Victims of Lynching Act, would create a new criminal prohibition on lynching, defined as conspiracy to violate certain federal hate crime statutes.

The JUSTICE Act

On June 17, 2020, Senate Republicans unveiled the Just and Unifying Solutions to Invigorate Communities Everywhere Act of 2020 (JUSTICE Act). The JUSTICE Act would enact various reforms related to law enforcement, including but not limited to the following:

- Under Title I, Section 101 of the bill, the George Floyd and Walter Scott Notification Act, and Section 102, the Breonna Taylor Notification Act, would respectively require recipients of certain federal funding to report to the federal government information related to incidents involving law enforcement uses of force and no-knock warrants.
- Section 105 would require recipients of certain federal funding to develop law enforcement agency policies "prohibit[ing] the use of chokeholds except when deadly force is authorized." This section

would also require the Attorney General to develop such a policy at the federal level.

- Section 106 would create a new criminal offense of "knowingly and willfully falsify[ing] a report . . . in furtherance of the deprivation of any rights, privileges, or immunities secured or protected by the Constitution or laws of the United States where death or serious bodily injury . . . occurs." The penalty for violating this provision would be a fine and/or imprisonment for up to twenty years.
- Title II of the bill would provide grants to covered government agencies to support the use of body-worn cameras by law enforcement officials.
- Title III would require law enforcement agencies that receive certain federal funding to retain various disciplinary records and to search the records of prior employers before hiring a law enforcement officer.
- Title IV, the Justice for Victims of Lynching Act, like the corresponding section of the Justice in Policing Act, would create a new criminal prohibition on lynching, defined as conspiracy to violate certain federal hate crime statutes.
- Title V would create a Commission on the Social Status of Black Men and Boys to "conduct a systematic study of the conditions affecting Black men and boys."
- Title VI would direct the Attorney General to develop training on alternatives to use of force, de-escalation tactics, responding to behavioral health crises, and duty to intervene when another officer uses excessive force.
- Titles VII and IX would establish a temporary National Criminal Justice Commission and require the Commission to create best practices and conduct certain studies related to law enforcement oversight.
- Title VIII would provide for development of an educational curriculum for law enforcement personnel or candidates on the history of racism in the United States.

- Title X would impose criminal liability when a person "acting under color of law, knowingly engages in a sexual act" with a person in federal custody. Violation of this provision would be punishable by a fine and/or up to fifteen years in prison. This provision would also authorize grants to states, municipalities, and Indian Tribes that enact similar laws.

In: Police Reform …
Editor: Robert B. Smith
ISBN: 978-1-53618-504-1

Chapter 4

CONGRESS AND LAW ENFORCEMENT REFORM: CONSTITUTIONAL AUTHORITY*

Whitney K. Novak

Nationwide protests in response to the publication of video footage of a Minneapolis police officer pressing his knee into the neck of George Floyd leading to his death have generated renewed interest in the issue of reforming the policing practices of state and local officials. As discussed in more detail in this companion sidebar, several *existing* federal laws seek to prevent and redress constitutional violations by state and local law enforcement officials. However, because the Constitution generally grants states the authority to regulate issues of local concern—which includes policing and criminal law—Congress is limited in its ability to legislate on matters related to state and local law enforcement—limits that may inform any *new* laws Congress seeks to enact on this evolving issue. This Sidebar begins with an overview of Congress's authority to enact legislation and the limits on those powers. It then discusses in more detail two of the

---

* This is an edited, reformatted and augmented version of Congressional Research Service Publication No. LSB10487, dated June 4, 2020.

enumerated powers—congressional powers that are found within the Constitution—that may be most relevant when Congress legislates on matters relating to state and local law enforcement.

LIMITS TO CONGRESSIONAL AUTHORITY

The Constitution establishes a "system of dual sovereignty between the States and the Federal Government." Under the Tenth Amendment, "[t]he powers not delegated to the United States by the Constitution, nor prohibited by it to the States, are reserved to the States respectively, or to the people." Thus, states generally have broad authority to enact legislation, including to regulate the states and its localities' law enforcement approaches. In contrast, Congress may only enact legislation under a specific power that is enumerated in the Constitution and cannot use its power to intrude impermissibly on the sovereign powers of the states. In this vein, the Supreme Court has recognized that there are certain subjects that are largely of a local concern where states "historically have been sovereign," such as issues related to the family, crime, and education.

Because of these principles, the Supreme Court has recognized various limitations on Congress's power to legislate in areas that fall within a state's purview, observing that congressional power is "subject to outer limits," and that Congress must take care not to "effectually obliterate the distinction between what is national and what is local." In addition, under the anti-commandeering doctrine, Congress is prohibited from passing laws requiring states or localities to adopt or enforce federal policies. Although these principles constrain Congress's power, Congress can rely on its enumerated powers to regulate in areas it could not otherwise reach. The spending power and section 5 of the Fourteenth Amendment are two of the most relevant authorities that Congress has used in the past to address local law enforcement issues.

Spending Power and Regulating Law Enforcement Activities

The Spending Clause empowers Congress to "lay and collect Taxes, Duties, Imposts, and Excises, to pay the Debts and provide for the common Defence and general Welfare of the United States." The Supreme Court has held that incident to the spending power, Congress may further its policy objectives by attaching conditions on the receipt of federal funds. These conditions often involve compliance with statutory or administrative directives and can apply to any entity receiving federal funds, including states and localities. In *South Dakota v. Dole*, for example, the Supreme Court upheld as a valid exercise of Congress's spending power a statute that conditioned the grant of federal highway funds to any state upon that state prohibiting the legal purchase or possession of alcohol by individuals less than 21 years old.

There are, however, four limitations on Congress's authority to attach conditions to federal funds. First, a funding condition must be "in pursuit of the general welfare." However, courts generally afford Congress substantial deference in determining what expenditures are "intended to serve general public purposes." Second, if Congress intends to place conditions on federal funds, it must do so "unambiguously" so that states can knowingly choose whether or not to accept the funds. Third, conditions on federal funding must be related or "germane" to "the federal interest in particular national projects or programs." Fourth, other constitutional provisions may bar the conditions placed on the grant of federal funds. For instance, Congress may not condition a monetary grant on "discriminatory state action or the infliction of cruel and unusual punishment." Relatedly, conditions on federal funding are unconstitutional when they become coercive to the point that "pressure turns into compulsion" or commandeering. For example, in *National Federation of Independent Business (NFIB) v. Sebelius*, the Supreme Court held that a provision in the Affordable Care Act that withheld all Medicaid grants from any state that refused to accept expanded Medicaid funding was unconstitutionally coercive because it threatened to terminate "significant independent grants" that were already provided to the states.

Courts have rarely used these spending power limitations to invalidate conditions placed on the receipt of federal funds. *NFIB* remains the only instance in the modern era of the Supreme Court invalidating an exercise of the congressional spending power. Post-*NFIB* Spending Clause challenges have largely been unsuccessful in the lower courts.

Using its spending power, Congress has enacted legislation to influence the activities of state and local law enforcement. Federal regulation of state and local law enforcement primarily comes in the form of grant programs that provide money to local governments and police forces. For example, the Community Oriented Policing Services (COPS) program authorizes the Department of Justice to distribute grants to support community policing. Recipients can use these grants for hiring officers, procuring equipment, or establishing partnerships between local law enforcement agencies and local school districts. Andthe Edward Byrne Memorial Justice Assistance Grant (Byrne JAG) program provides federal financial support for state and local criminal justice programs. Funding for these grant programs are subject to various conditions that may further federal interests in regulating law enforcement activities. For instance, grants under the COPS program prohibit the grantee from subjecting any person to discrimination on the basis of race, color, or national origin (among other protected classes) in connection with any programs or activities funded in whole or in part with federal funds. Funds under the JAG program are conditioned on, among other things, compliance with the Death in Custody Reporting Act (DCRA), which requires states to report information regarding the deaths of individuals in law enforcement custody.

Section 5 of the Fourteenth Amendment and Regulating Law Enforcement Activities

The Fourteenth Amendment, in relevant part, provides that no state shall "deprive any person of life, liberty, or property, without due process of law" or "deny to any person within its jurisdiction the equal protection of the laws." And the Supreme Court has interpreted the substantive component of the Due Process Clause as incorporating against state actors nearly all the rights found in the Bill of Rights, including those that pertain to criminal procedure and regulate the conduct of the police. In turn, Section 5 of the Fourteenth Amendment grants Congress the power to enforce the Amendment through "appropriate legislation." Section 5's "positive grant of legislative power" authorizes Congress to both deter and remedy constitutional violations; and in doing so, Congress may prohibit otherwise constitutional conduct that intrudes into "legislative spheres of autonomy previously reserved to the States." The section 5 enforcement power (and the parallel enforcement powers found in the Thirteenth and Fifteenth Amendments) has been used to, for example, ban the use of literacy tests in state and national elections and abolish "all badges and incidents of slavery" by banning racial discrimination in the acquisition of real and personal property. Congress has also used its section 5 power to provide remedies for the deprivation of constitutional rights. For example, 42 U.S.C. § 1983 (Section 1983) provides a private cause of action for individuals claiming that their constitutional rights were violated by state actors acting pursuant to state law. And 18 U.S.C. § 242 (Section 242)—also passed using the section 5 power— imposes criminal liability on state actors who deprive individuals of their constitutional rights.

While Congress's section 5 enforcement power is broad, it is not unlimited. Section 5 allows Congress to directly enforce constitutional rights through laws like Section 1983 and Section 242, however, the power does not allow Congress to supplement those rights through prophylactic legislation that regulates state and local matters without evidence of a history and pattern of past constitutional violations by the state. And, according to the Supreme Court, when Congress exercises its section 5 authority, its response must be congruent and proportional to a demonstrated harm. Congress may justify the need for section 5 legislation by establishing a legislative record that shows "evidence . . . of a constitutional wrong." For example, in holding that Congress exceeded its section 5 authority in enacting the Religious Freedom Restoration Act (RFRA)—which, in relevant part, supplanted normal First Amendment standards to impose a heightened standard of review for state government actions that substantially burdened a person's religious exercise—the Supreme Court determined that Congress had failed to establish a widespread pattern of religious discrimination by the states. As a result, RFRA could not be justified as a remedial measure designed to prevent unconstitutional conduct and was outside of Congress's power over the states. As a result, the Court struck down the law in so far as it applied to the states.

As a consequence of this case law, the scope of Congress's section 5 power hinges in part on the scope of the constitutional right that a given law aims to protect. With respect to regulating state and local police forces, one constitutional right that may be particularly relevant to Congress's use of its section 5 power is the Fourth Amendment, which prohibits unreasonable searches and seizures by the government. The Fourth Amendment applies to many situations involving law enforcement including when police stop an individual on the street for questioning, when police conduct traffic stops, or when police make an arrest. Police violate the Fourth Amendment, for example, if they use excessive force during an investigatory stop or arrest. According to the Supreme Court, the force used by law enforcement during an investigatory stop or arrest violates the constitution when it is unreasonable considering the facts and circumstances of the case. This analysis requires a careful balancing of "the nature and quality of the intrusion on the individual's Fourth Amendment interests against the importance of the governmental interests alleged to justify the intrusion." For example, the Supreme Court has held that police use of deadly force against a fleeing suspect who poses no immediate safety threat is unreasonable in violation of the Fourth Amendment. Determining whether an act of force is excessive in violation of the constitution, however, requires a fact specific analysis—a certain act may be reasonable under some facts while in a different case, the same act may amount to excessive force. For example, some courts have ruled that police use of a chokehold is objectively unreasonable when used against individuals who are already under restraint and not a danger to others. In other circumstances, courts have upheld police use of a chokehold as reasonable in instances where an individual was unrestrained and continued to pose a threat of serious harm.

CONSIDERATIONS FOR CONGRESS

Although Congress is limited in its ability to regulate local policing, the constitution does provide authority for some congressional reform and oversight into matters of state and local law enforcement. Some Members of Congress have expressed interest in proposing legislation to address police reforms in the wake of the response to George Floyd's death. Several bills on the issue have already been introduced in the 116th Congress. These include those that utilize Congress's Spending Clause authority to impose new conditions on existing grant programs to states and localities, such as H.R. 120, the Police CAMERA Act of 2019; H.R. 5777, the Police Accountability Act of 2020; H.R. 4359, the Police Exercising Absolute Care With Everyone Act of 2019, H.R. 2927; the Preventing Tragedies Between Police Communities Act of 2019; and H.R. 125, the Police Training and Independent Review Act of 2019. Other proposals, such as H.R. 4408—the Eric Garner Excessive Use of Force Prevention Act of 2019—would utilize Congress's section 5 authority to amend 18 U.S.C. § 242 to criminalize the use of chokeholds. While a companion to this Sidebar provides a look at some of these proposals, the limitations to Congress's constitutional authority to regulate state and local police forces may be a consideration when evaluating these and other reforms.

In: Police Reform …
Editor: Robert B. Smith
ISBN: 978-1-53618-504-1

Chapter 5

POLICING REFORM LEGISLATION: CONDITIONS ON FUNDING AND NEW AUTHORIZATIONS*

Nathan James

ABSTRACT

The death of George Floyd in Minneapolis, MN, while he was in the custody of law enforcement, combined with several other recent high-profile deaths of African Americans at the hands of the police, have generated congressional interest in legislation to reform state and local policing practices, and to require law enforcement agencies to collect more data on law enforcement actions and activities and share these data with the public.

Two pieces of legislation—the George Floyd Justice in Policing Act of 2020 (H.R. 7120), and the Just and Unifying Solutions to Invigorate Communities Everywhere Act of 2020 (JUSTICE Act; S. 3985)—were introduced in June 2020. Both bills are omnibus measures that would address a variety of policing reform topics and approaches. These include

* This is an edited, reformatted and augmented version of Congressional Research Service Publication No. R46431, dated June 25, 2020.

attempting to reform state and local policing practices through two means: placing conditions on existing Department of Justice (DOJ) grant programs, such as the Edward Byrne Memorial Justice Assistance Grant (JAG) or Community Oriented Policing Services (COPS) programs; and authorizing new grant programs.

Some examples of conditions H.R. 7120 and S. 3985 would place on existing DOJ grant programs include the following:

- H.R. 7120 would authorize grants to states and tribal governments to assist with implementing statutes that provide for the independent investigation or prosecution of law enforcement officers who allegedly use deadly force. The bill would authorize $750 million each fiscal year from FY2020 to FY2022.
- H.R. 7120 would prohibit federal law enforcement officers from seeking a no-knock warrant in drug cases. State and local governments would not be eligible for COPS funding unless they have a law that similarly prohibits the use of no-knock warrants in drug cases.
- S. 3985 would require state and local governments to submit data to the Federal Bureau of Investigation's (FBI's) Use of Force Data Collection program. State and local governments that do not submit data to the FBI would be subject to a 20% penalty on their JAG allocation for the first year of noncompliance and up to a 25% penalty for each subsequent year of noncompliance.
- S. 3985 would establish incentives for state and local law enforcement agencies to limit the use of chokeholds. State and local governments would be ineligible for JAG or COPS funding unless they have a policy that prohibits the use of chokeholds by state and local law enforcement officers, respectively, except when deadly force is authorized.

Some examples of new grant programs that would be authorized by H.R. 7120 and S. 3985 include the following:

- H.R. 7120 would authorize grants to states and tribal governments to assist with implementing statutes that provide for the independent prosecution of law enforcement officers who use deadly force. The bill would authorize $750 million each fiscal year from FY2020 to FY2022.
- H.R. 7120 would authorize grants to states to conduct pattern and practice investigations. The bill would authorize $100 million each fiscal year from FY2020 to FY2022.
- S. 3985 would authorize DOJ to make grants to assist state and local governments with collecting data on use of force and no-

knock warrants. The bill would also appropriate $112 million for these grants, to remain available until expended.

S. 3985 would require DOJ to make grants to states for the purpose of providing training to law enforcement officers on alternatives to use of force, on de-escalation tactics, or on techniques and strategies for responding to a behavioral health crisis. The bill would appropriate $50 million each fiscal year for these grants, to remain available until expended, from FY2021 to FY2025.

The death of George Floyd in Minneapolis, MN, while in the custody of law enforcement, along with several other high-profile deaths of African Americans at the hands of the police (including Eric Garner in Staten Island, NY; Philando Castile in Falcon Heights, MN; and Breonna Taylor in Louisville, KY), have served as the catalyst for protests against police violence in cities across the country. These deaths and the resulting protests have spurred interest in policing reform legislation in Congress.

On June 8, 2020, Representative Karen Bass introduced the George Floyd Justice in Policing Act of 2020 (H.R. 7120). Ten days later, Senator Tim Scott introduced the Just and Unifying Solutions to Invigorate Communities Everywhere Act of 2020 (JUSTICE Act; S. 3985). Both pieces of legislation are omnibus measures that would address a variety of policing reform topics, such as requiring law enforcement agencies to submit data to the federal government on the use of force or no-knock warrants; increasing the use of body-worn camera (BWCs); providing for the external, independent prosecution of law enforcement officers' use of deadly force; banning chokeholds; and providing implicit-bias and de-escalation training to law enforcement officers. Both pieces of legislation would use Congress's power of the purse to reform state and local policing practices through two means: (1) placing conditions on existing Department of Justice (DOJ) grant programs, such as the Edward Byrne Memorial Justice Assistance Grant (JAG) or Community Oriented Policing Services (COPS) programs, to incentivize state and local governments to adopt certain policing reforms; and (2) authorizing new programs to assist state, local, and tribal governments with adopting such reforms.

This report provides an overview of the new conditions that would be placed on existing grant programs and the authorizations for new grant programs contained in both pieces of legislation. The report does not discuss provisions of either bill that do not establish new requirements for state and local governments or authorize new funding (e.g., proposals to make lynching a federal crime or to make the use of chokeholds a federal civil rights violation).

Do the New Requirements and Grants in H.R. 7120 and S. 3985 Apply to Indian Tribes?

In general, it appears that the requirements and grant programs under H.R. 7120 would apply to Indian tribes. In some cases, tribal governments are specifically identified in the text of the bill. In other cases, requirements or grant programs apply to "units of local government," and in the bill this term has the same meaning as it does in 34 U.S.C. Section 10251, which includes Indian tribes with law enforcement responsibilities. It is not always clear if the requirements that would be established by S. 3985 would apply to Indian tribes. For example, Section 105(b) of S. 3985 would amend the authorization for the Community Oriented Policing Services (COPS) program to make state and units of local government ineligible for funding under the program unless they have a policy that bans the use of chokeholds. Under the COPS authorization (34 U.S.C. §10381(a)), units of local government and tribal governments are identified as separate entities for the purposes of eligibility for grants. Section 105(b) would also make states and units of local government ineligible for funding under the Edward Byrne Memorial Justice Assistance Grant (JAG) program unless they have the same prohibition in place. Under 34 U.S.C. Section 10251(a)(3), the definition of a "unit of local government" includes "an Indian Tribe that performs law enforcement functions, as determined by the Secretary of the Interior," so in this case the condition appears to apply to Indian tribes.

To avoid speculating about congressional intent, in *Table 1* and *Table 2* of this report identification of entities as being either subject to a requirement or eligible for a grant program is based on the language used in that specific section. Therefore, tribal governments are only identified when they are specifically mentioned in the bill language.

Conditions on Department of Justice Grant Programs in H.R. 7120 and S. 3985

Both H.R. 7120 and S. 3985 would attach new requirements and conditions to funding under the JAG or COPS programs to provide an incentive for state and local law enforcement agencies to submit data on policing actions and activities and to adopt reforms to their policing practices.[1] The proposed conditions generally take two forms: making state and local governments ineligible for funding under these programs unless they submit required data or adopt a particular reform, or authorizing DOJ to reduce funding under these programs if state and local governments do not comply. *Table 1* provides an overview of these conditions.

Table 1. Proposed Requirements and Conditions on DOJ Grant Programs in H.R. 7120 and S. 3985

Proposed Requirement	**Condition**
H.R. 7120, the George Floyd Justice in Policing Act of 2020	
Section 114(a) would require applicants under the JAG program to study and implement effective management, training, recruiting, hiring, and oversight standards and programs to promote effective community and problem solving strategies for law enforcement agencies.	JAG applicants would be required to use not less than 5% of their allocation for this purpose.
Section 118 would require federal, state, tribal, and local law enforcement agencies to report data to DOJ on stops for traffic violations, pedestrian stops, frisks and body searches, and the use of deadly force by a law enforcement officer.	States that do not comply would be ineligible to receive funding under JAG or any other law enforcement assistance program (such as the COPS program) unless the state has ensured, to DOJ's satisfaction, that it and each local law enforcement agency within it is in substantial compliance with the

[1] For more information on the JAG program see CRS In Focus IF10691, *The Edward Byrne Memorial Justice Assistance Grant (JAG) Program*. For more information on the COPS program, see CRS In Focus IF10922, *Community Oriented Policing Services (COPS) Program*.

Table 1. (Continued)

Proposed Requirement	Condition
	requirements of the section.
Section 201 would require states to submit disciplinary records to the National Police Misconduct Registry, which would be	Submitting records would be a condition of receiving JAG funds. States would be required to submit records at the
established by the bill. DOJ would have to establish the registry within 180 days of the enactment of the bill.	beginning of the first fiscal year that is one year after the enactment of the bill, and every fiscal year thereafter. States would be required to submit specified records every 180 days.
Section 202 would require states and units of local government, other than Indian tribes, to submit records to DOJ showing that their officers are certified to work as law enforcement officers in the state. State and local governments would also be required to submit evidence to DOJ that they have a certification and decertification for purposes of employment as a law enforcement officer in that state or unit of local government that is consistent with the rules that DOJ would be required to publish.	States and units of local government would be ineligible for funding under the JAG program unless they submit the required records. These records would be treated in the same manner as other records states are required to submit to the National Police Misconduct Registry. This requirement would go into effect at the beginning of the fiscal year that is one year after the date of enactment of the bill.
Section 223 would require states and Indian tribes to submit reports to DOJ on the use of force by, and against, law enforcement officers, including incidents where a law enforcement officer uses deadly force against a civilian, incidents where a law enforcement officer shoots a civilian, incidents where a civilian shoots a law enforcement officer, incidents involving the death or arrest of a law enforcement officer, and any other incidents involving use of force by or against a law enforcement officer that is not included in one of the above instances; deaths in custody; and arrests	States or Indian tribes that do not submit the required reports would be subject to a penalty of up to 10% of their JAG award. This requirement would go into effect at the beginning of the fiscal year that is one year after the date of enactment of the bill.

Proposed Requirement	**Condition**
and bookings. States and tribal governments would be required to establish a system and a set of policies to ensure that all use of force incidents are reported by local and tribal law enforcement officers.	
Section 331 would require that state and local governments or state and local law enforcement agencies have policies and procedures designed to eliminate racial profiling and show that they have eliminated any existing practices that permit or encourage racial profiling. These policies would be required to include training on racial profiling, and collection of data on racial profiling required under Section 341 of the bill.	State and local governments or state or local law enforcement agencies that apply for funding under the JAG and COPS programs would be required to certify that they have these policies in place. This requirement would go into effect 12 months after the date of enactment of the bill.
Section 332 would require that DOJ, within six months of enactment of the bill, issue regulations for the operation of administrative complaint procedures and independent audit programs to ensure that such programs and procedures provide an appropriate response to allegations of racial profiling by law enforcement agents or agencies.	If DOJ determines that a recipient of a JAG or COPS grant is not in compliance with the requirements of Section 331 or the regulations issued by DOJ under Section 332, DOJ would be required to withhold, in whole or in part, a grantee's funds under the JAG and COPS programs until the recipient complies.
Section 334 would require applicants under the JAG program to develop and implement best practices to eliminate racial profiling.	JAG applicants would be required to use not less than 10% of their allocation under the program for this purpose.
Section 361 would require DOJ to establish a training program for law enforcement officers on racial profiling, implicit bias, and procedural justice; establish a clear duty for federal law enforcement officers to intervene in cases where another law enforcement officer is using excessive force against a civilian; and establish a training program that covers the duty to intervene.	State and units of local government would not be eligible for JAG funding unless they require their law enforcement officers to undergo the training DOJ establishes under Section 361. This requirement would go into effect at the beginning of the fiscal year that is one year after the date of enactment of the bill.

Table 1. (Continued)

Proposed Requirement	Condition
Section 362 would prohibit federal law enforcement officers from seeking a no-knock warrant in drug cases.	State and units of local government would not be eligible for COPS funding unless they have a law that prohibits the use of no-knock warrants in drug cases. This requirement would go into effect at the
	beginning of the fiscal year that is one year after the date of enactment of the bill.
Section 363 would seek to ban the use of chokeholds or carotid holds by state and local law enforcement officers.	State and units of local government would not be eligible for JAG or COPS funding unless they have a law that prohibits the use of chokeholds or carotid holds by state and local law enforcement officers. This requirement would go into effect at the beginning of the fiscal year that is one year after the date of enactment of the bill.
Section 364 would establish new standards for the use of force by federal law enforcement officers so that the use of less-than-lethal force is necessary and proportionate to effect an arrest. When deadly force must be used, other alternatives to the use of force have been exhausted and the use of deadly force is a measure of last resort and used only to prevent imminent serious bodily injury to the officer or another person and where its use poses no risk to a third party. Federal law enforcement officers would also be required to give a suspect a verbal warning that the officer will use force if the suspect resists arrest or flees and give the suspect a chance to surrender.	States and units of local government, other than an Indian tribe, would not be eligible to receive funds under the JAG program unless they have a law that is consistent with the standards that would be established by Section 364. States and units of local government would be eligible to receive withheld JAG funds (for up to five prior fiscal years) if they enact a law consistent with the standards of Section 364 and demonstrate substantial efforts to enforce the law. This requirement would go into effect at the beginning of the fiscal year that is one year after the date of enactment of the bill.
Section 382 would require applicants under the JAG program to establish body-worn camera (BWC) programs.	JAG applicants would be required to use not less than 5% of their allocation for this purpose.
S. 3985, the JUSTICE Act	
Section 101 would require state and local	State and local governments that do not

Proposed Requirement	**Condition**
governments to submit data to the Federal Bureau of Investigation's (FBI's) Use of Force Data Collection program.[a]	submit data to the FBI's Use of Force Data Collection program would be subject to a 20% penalty on their JAG allocation for the first year of noncompliance and up to a 25% penalty for each subsequent year of noncompliance. This requirement would go into effect at the beginning of the fiscal year after the date of enactment of the bill.
Section 102 would require state and local governments to submit an annual report to DOJ on the use of no- knock warrants by law enforcement agencies. States would be required to submit the first report no later than January 31 of the first year after the enactment of the bill, and each year thereafter.	State and local governments that do not submit the required annual report would be subject to a 20% penalty on their JAG allocation for the first year of noncompliance and up to a 25% penalty for each subsequent year of noncompliance. This penalty would take effect after the third year after the date of enactment of the bill.
Section 105 would establish incentives for state and local law enforcement agencies to limit the use of chokeholds by officers.	State and local governments would not be eligible for JAG or COPS funding unless they have a policy that prohibits the use of chokeholds by state and local law enforcement officers except when deadly force is authorized. This requirement would go into effect at the beginning of the fiscal year after the date of enactment of the bill.
Section 202 would establish penalties for states and "other entities" that do not have policies in place for the discipline of a law enforcement officer who does not ensure that a federally funded BWC is engaged, functional, and properly secured at all times during which the camera is required to be worn.	Potential penalties would apply to grants awarded under the BWC program that would be authorized by Section 201 (see Table 2) of the bill and any other program that provides funding for purchasing BWCs. State and local governments that do not have the required policy in effect would be subject to a 20% penalty under these programs for the first year of noncompliance and up to a 25% penalty for each subsequent year of noncompli- ance.
Section 301 would require states and units of local government that receive funding under Part E of Title I of the Omnibus Crime Control and Safe Streets	States and units of local government that do not meet the disciplinary records requirements would be ineligible for JAG funding.[b]

Table 1. (Continued)

Proposed Requirement	Condition
Act (Bureau of Justice Assistance Grants) to maintain a system for sharing disciplinary records of law enforcement officers.	

Source: CRS analysis of H.R. 7120 and S. 3985.

[a] For more information on the FBI's Use of Force Data Collection program, see https://www.fbi.gov/services/ cjis/ucr/use-of-force.

[b] S. 3985 would also make state and local governments ineligible for grants under Chapter B, Subpart 2, Part E, Title I of the Omnibus Crime Control and Safe Streets Act, but these grants are not regularly funded by Congress.

AUTHORIZED AND APPROPRIATED FUNDING IN H.R. 7120 AND S. 3985

Both H.R. 7120 and S. 3985 would authorize new grant programs to help promote policing reforms, for purposes such as conducting external, independent investigations or prosecutions of law enforcement officers who allegedly use deadly force, helping law enforcement agencies purchase BWCs, or assisting state and local law enforcement agencies with collecting data that would be required under each bill. In addition to authorizing new grant programs, both bills would authorize funding for DOJ to provide training and technical assistance to state and local governments on how to implement the requirements of the legislation, and S. 3985 would authorize funding for a National Criminal Justice Commission. A key difference between the two bills is that H.R. 7120 would authorize appropriations for several new programs, while S. 3985 would both authorize new programs and appropriate funding for them. The new authorizations and appropriations that would be provided by the bills are outlined in *Table 2*.

Table 2. New Authorizations in H.R. 7120 and S. 3985

Program	**Authorization/Appropriation**
H.R. 7120, the George Floyd Justice in Policing Act of 2020	
Section 103(b) would authorize grants for states to conduct pattern and practice investigations.	The bill would authorize $100 million each fiscal year from FY2021 to FY2023.
Section 104 would authorize grants to states and tribal governments to assist with implementing statutes that provide for the independent investigation or prosecution of law enforcement officers who allegedly use deadly force.	The bill would authorize $750 million each fiscal year from FY2021 to FY2023.
Section 114(b) would authorize grants to community- based organizations to promote effective community and problem solving strategies for law enforcement agencies, or effective strategies and solutions for public safety, including strategies that do not rely on responses from law enforcement agencies.	The bill would authorize $25 million for FY2021.
Section 116 would authorize additional funding for DOJ's pattern and practice and civil rights investigations as well as the Community Relations Service (CRS).	The bill would authorize $25 million for FY2021 for pattern and practice and civil rights investigations and $3 million for CRS.
Section 117 would create a task force at DOJ to coordinate the process of detection and referral of complaints regarding incidents of alleged law enforcement misconduct.	The bill would authorize $5 million each fiscal year.
Section 224 would authorize DOJ to make training and technical assistance grants to assist tribal and local law enforcement agencies that employ fewer than 100 officers with meeting the use of force data reporting requirements under Section 223 or creating a system that tracks use of force complaints against officers. Section 225 would require DOJ to audit states to determine whether they are complying with use of force data	The bill would authorize such sums as necessary for these purposes.

Table 2. (Continued)

Program	Authorization/Appropriation
submission requirements.	
Section 333 would authorize a demonstration grant program for DOJ to fund data collection programs on the hit rates (i.e., when contraband is found) for stops and searches by law enforcement agencies. DOJ can award up to five grants	The bill would authorize $5 million for a two-year period for the program and $500,000 for the evaluation.
to law enforcement agencies that serve communities where there is a significant concentration of racial or ethnic minorities and that are not already collecting data voluntarily. DOJ would be required to enter into a contract with an institution of higher education to analyze the data collected through the funded program.	
Section 335 would authorize funding for DOJ to carry out the requirements related to programs to end racial profiling by state and local law enforcement in Part III, Subtitle A, Title III of the bill.	The bill would authorize such sums as necessary for these purposes.
S. 3985, the JUSTICE Act	
Section 104 would authorize DOJ to make grants to assist state and units of local government with collecting data on use of force (Section 101) and no- knock warrants (Section 102).	The bill would appropriate $112 million to remain available until expended.
Section 201 would authorize DOJ to make grants to state, local, and tribal governments to help law enforcement agencies establish BWC programs.	The bill would appropriate $100 million each fiscal year, to remain available until expended, for FY2021 to FY2025.
Section 301 would authorize DOJ to make grants to states to help states and their units of local government develop systems for sharing disciplinary records of law enforcement officers.	The bill would appropriate $100 million to remain available until expended.
Section 601(b) would require DOJ to develop a training program for law enforcement officers on alternatives to the	The bill would appropriate $20 million each fiscal year, to remain available until expended, for FY2021 to FY2025 for

Program	Authorization/Appropriation
use of force, on de-escalation techniques, and on strategies for safely responding to people suffering from mental health crises. DOJ would be required to develop a process for certifying programs that offer this training. DOJ would also be required to provide regional "train the trainer" programs through the end of FY2023.	these purposes.
Section 601(c) would require DOJ to make grants to states for the purpose of providing training to law enforcement officers on alternatives to use of force, on de-escalation tactics, or on techniques and strategies for responding to a behavioral health crisis.	The bill would appropriate $50 million each fiscal year, to remain available until expended, for FY2021 to FY2025.
Section 602 would require DOJ to develop training for law enforcement agencies and officers on the development, implementation, fulfillment, and enforcement of the duty of a law enforcement officer to intervene when another law enforcement officer is engaged in excessive use of force. DOJ would be required to develop a process for certifying programs that offer the training. DOJ would also be required to provide regional "train the trainer" programs until the end of FY2023. This section would authorize DOJ to make grants to state and local law enforcement agencies to pay for officers to attend duty-to-intervene training.	The bill would appropriate $100 million each fiscal year, to remain available until expended, for FY2021 to FY2025.
Title VII of would establish a National Criminal Justice Commission, which would be tasked with undertaking a comprehensive review of the criminal justice system, submitting recommendations to the President and Congress regarding federal criminal	The bill would appropriate $7 million each fiscal year for FY2021 and FY2022 to fund the commission's operations.

Table 2. (Continued)

Program	Authorization/Appropriation
justice reform, and disseminating its findings and supplemental guidance to all levels of government.	
Section 802(a) would extend the authorization of appropriations for the JAG program. Section 802(b) would extend the authorization of appropriations for the COPS program.	The bill would extend the authorization of appropriations at $800 million each fiscal year for FY2021 to FY2025. The bill would extend the authorization of appropriations at $400 million each fiscal year for FY2021 to FY2025.
Section 812 would require the Director of the National Museum of African American History and Culture to develop and disseminate a program to train federal, state, and local law enforcement officers or recruits on the history of racism in the United States. The director would also be required to conduct education programs for law enforcement officers and recruits that focuses on racial reconciliation, with the goals of understanding the history of racism in the United States, improving relationships between law enforcement and the communities they serve, and training law enforcement officers who can effectively train their peers on these topics.	The bill would appropriate $2 million each fiscal year, to remain available until expended, for FY2021 to FY2025 for this training.
Section 1002 would authorize DOJ to make grants to states that have laws that make it a criminal offense for any person acting under color of law of the state to engage in a sexual act (as defined at 18 U.S.C. § 2246) with an individual who has been arrested by, is detained by, or is in custody of any law enforcement officer; and prohibits a person charged with such an offense from asserting the consent of the other individual as a defense. Grants must be used for the same purposes as	The bill would appropriate $5 million each fiscal year, to remain available until expended, for FY2021 to FY2025.

Program	Authorization/Appropriation
formula grants under the STOP Violence Against Women and the Sexual Assault Services programs.[a]	

Source: CRS analysis of H.R. 7120 and S. 3985.

[a] For more information on the STOP Violence Against Women and the Sexual Assault Services programs, see CRS Report R45410, The Violence Against Women Act (VAWA): Historical Overview, Funding, and Reauthorization.

In: Police Reform …
Editor: Robert B. Smith
ISBN: 978-1-53618-504-1

Chapter 6

POLICING THE POLICE: QUALIFIED IMMUNITY AND CONSIDERATIONS FOR CONGRESS*

Whitney K. Novak

In the wake of unrest arising from George Floyd's death on May 25, 2020, after a Minneapolis police officer pressed a knee into his neck, broader questions have arisen with regard to how existing law regulates the conduct of local police officers. While these issues are explored more broadly in these separate Sidebars, one particular issue of recent judicial and legislative focus has been the doctrine of qualified immunity. Qualified immunity is a judicially created doctrine shielding public officials who are performing discretionary functions from civil liability. The doctrine plays a particularly prominent role in defense of civil rights lawsuits against federal law enforcement officials under the *Bivens* doctrine and against state and local police under 42 U.S.C. § 1983 (Section 1983). With regard to its role in civil lawsuits concerning violations of

* This is an edited, reformatted and augmented version of Congressional Research Service Publication No. LSB10492, updated June 25, 2020.

constitutional norms regulating the police, defenders of the doctrine have suggested that qualified immunity plays an important role in affording police officers some level of deference when making split-second decisions about whether to, for example, use force to subdue a fleeing or resisting suspect. Critics of the doctrine have questioned its legal origins and have argued that its practice has provided too much deference to the police at the expense of accountability and the erosion of criminal suspects' constitutional rights. With increasing focus on whether Congress should legislate to abrogate or otherwise modify the doctrine, this Sidebar explores the legal basis for qualified immunity, how it has operated in practice, and current debate over the efficacy of the doctrine. The Sidebar concludes by discussing considerations for Congress regarding qualified immunity.

WHAT IS QUALIFIED IMMUNITY?

Qualified immunity is a judicially created legal doctrine that shields government officials performing discretionary duties from civil liability in cases involving the deprivation of statutory or constitutional rights. Government officials are entitled to qualified immunity so long as their actions do not violate "clearly established statutory or constitutional rights of which a reasonable person would have known." The Supreme Court has observed that qualified immunity balances two important interests—"the need to hold public officials accountable when they exercise power irresponsibly and the need to shield officials from harassment, distraction, and liability when they perform their duties reasonably." The immunity's broad protection is intended for "all but the plainly incompetent or those who knowingly violate the law" and to give government officials "breathing room" to make reasonable mistakes of fact and law.

According to the Supreme Court, the "driving force" behind qualified immunity was to ensure that "insubstantial claims" against government officials were resolved at the outset of the lawsuit. Qualified immunity, when applied, provides immunity not only from civil damages, but from having to defend liability altogether.

Courts apply a two-part analysis when determining whether an official is entitled to qualified immunity: (1) whether the facts alleged by the plaintiff amount to a constitutional violation, and (2) if so, whether the constitutional right was "clearly established" at the time of the misconduct. Recent Supreme Court precedent provides flexibility in applying this standard, granting courts the discretion to decide which prong to first address in light of the circumstances of the facts of the case at hand. Whether a right is clearly established depends on whether "the contours of a right are sufficiently clear" so that every "reasonable official would have understood that what he is doing violates that right." When conducting this analysis, courts look to see whether it is "beyond debate" that existing legal precedent establishes the illegality of the conduct."

Qualified immunity is available for local and state government officials such as, for example, law enforcement officers, teachers, or social workers. Federal officials who face liability in cases brought under the *Bivens* doctrine—which allows for individuals to recover for the deprivation of constitutional rights against federal officials in a few, limited circumstances—may also claim qualified immunity.

Historical Development of Qualified Immunity

The Supreme Court developed qualified immunity as part of its interpretation of the Civil Rights Act of 1871 (also known as the Ku Klux Klan Act) and its codified cause of action at Section 1983. That statute provides a cause of action for "the deprivation of any rights, privileges, or immunities secured by the Constitution and laws" by any person acting "under color of any statute, ordinance, regulation, custom, or usage, of any State or Territory." As applied to the conduct of police officers, Section 1983 provides a legal remedy for individuals claiming that their constitutional rights, such as the right to be free from excessive force under the Fourth Amendment, were violated by state or local police acting pursuant to state or local law. According to the Supreme Court, Section 1983 is a "vital component . . . for vindicating cherished constitutional guarantees," as the law has been viewed much like common law tort actions which deter against wrongful actions. (While Section 1983 facially applies only to those acting under state law, the Court functionally expanded its application when it recognized an implied damages claim for Fourth Amendment violations by federal law enforcement officers in Bivens v. Six Unknown Federal Narcotics Agents.)

While the modern qualified immunity test was first set forth in the Supreme Court's 1982 decision Harlow v. Fitzgerald, the concept of qualified immunity as a "good faith defense" has origins in common law. The Court first extended a "good faith defense" to police officers in a Section 1983 case in its 1967 decision Pierson v. Ray. There, the Court held that Section 1983 "should be read against the background of tort liability that makes a man responsible for the natural consequences of his actions," and therefore, common law defenses such as good faith were applicable to actions brought under Section 1983. The Court determined that although they were not expressly included in Section 1983, there was no evidence in the legislative record that Congress intended to abolish common law immunities.

Fifteen years later in Harlow, the Court—while again recognizing that the common law afforded government officials some level of immunity to "shield them from undue interference with their duties and from potentially disabling threats of liability"—distinguished qualified immunity from absolute immunity. Absolute immunity provides a complete immunity from civil liability and is usually extended to, for example, the President of the United States, legislators, judges, and prosecutors acting in their official duties. Absolute immunity, according to the Court, provides high-level officials a "greater protection than those with less complex discretionary responsibilities," however; for other government officials, qualified immunity is still necessary, in the Court's view, to balance "the importance of a damages remedy to protect the rights of citizens" with "the need to protect officials who are required to exercise their discretion and the related public interest in encouraging the vigorous exercise of official authority." Thus, the Court established the modern objective test, granting qualified immunity to those government officials whose conduct "does not violate clearly established statutory or constitutional rights of which a reasonable person would have known."

In the years since Harlow, the Supreme Court has continued to refine and expand the reach of the doctrine. For example, one legal scholar examined eighteen qualified immunity cases that the Supreme Court heard from 2000 until 2016, all considering whether a particular constitutional right was clearly established. In sixteen of those cases, many of which involved police use of excessive force in violation of the Fourth Amendment, the Court found that the government officials were entitled to qualified immunity because they did not act in violation of clearly established law. In deciding what constitutes clearly established law, the Court has focused on the "generality at which the relevant legal rule is to be identified." Recently, the Court has emphasized that the clearly established right must be defined with specificity, such that even minor differences between the case at hand and the case in which the relevant legal right claimed to be violated was first established, can immunize the defendant police officer. For example, in the 2019 case City of Escondido, California v. Emmons, the Court reviewed a claim brought by a man who alleged police used excessive force in arresting him. Following past incidents of domestic abuse by a husband against his wife, police in Escondido, California, responded to a domestic disturbance call at the residence of the couple. After failing to make contact with anyone inside the home, a man—who later turned out to be the wife's father—eventually opened the door and passively brushed past the police. An officer took the man to the ground and handcuffed him, allegedly injuring him in the process. In holding the officer was entitled to qualified immunity, the Court explained that the appropriate inquiry is not whether the officer violated the man's clearly established right to generally be free from excessive force, but whether clearly established law "prohibited the officers from stopping and taking down a man in these circumstances." In so holding, the Court rejected the lower court's attempts to analogize this case to another that generally involved the use of excessive force in response to passive resistance by a criminal suspect. Instead, the Court, citing other recent precedent, stressed the need to "identify a case where an officer under similar circumstances was held to violate the Fourth Amendment."

The Debate over Qualified Immunity

As courts have expanded the protections of qualified immunity over the years, criticism of the doctrine has also increased. At least three major criticisms of the doctrine have emerged. First, some scholars have argued that qualified immunity has no basis in the common law—the body of law from where the Court determined the doctrine originated. In a recent concurrence, Justice Thomas advocated for reconsidering the Court's qualified immunity jurisprudence on these grounds, arguing that the modern doctrine bears little resemblance to the common law immunity and instead represents a "freewheeling policy choice" that the Court lacks the power to make and usurps the role of Congress.

Other criticisms of the doctrine focus more on its practical applications, with some arguing that qualified immunity no longer achieves its policy goals of protecting public officials from the expense and distraction of litigation, and from the danger that the fear of being sued will prevent officials from performing their duties or from entering public service altogether. For example, Justice Breyer has argued that indemnification by police departments of their employees may alleviate employees' concerns about facing liability upon accepting employment. And according to one study, police officers are "virtually always indemnified,"—meaning even if they are found liable for their own individual conduct, the city or county covers any monetary damages.

And there is some concern that the level of specificity required has made it increasingly difficult for plaintiffs to show that the law was clearly established—which some scholars have argued may jeopardize the purpose of Section 1983 as a tool for allowing individuals to recover for constitutional violations.

Justice Sotomayor, in dissenting in several cases in which the Court found officers were entitled to qualified immunity, expressed her disfavor with the modern approach, fearing its application essentially provides an absolute shield for law enforcement officers and "renders the protections of the Fourth Amendment hollow." And some statistics may support this hypothesis. According to one recent study, appellate courts have shown an increasing tendency to grant qualified immunity, particularly in excessive force cases. From 2005 to 2007, for example, 44 percent of courts favored police in excessive force cases. That number jumped to 57 percent in excessive force cases decided from 2017 to 2019.

The modern application of qualified immunity, however, is not without its proponents. Throughout its qualified immunity jurisprudence involving the police, a majority of the Supreme Court has emphasized the important role the doctrine plays in allowing law enforcement the flexibility to make judgment calls in rapidly evolving situations. According to one defender of the doctrine, members of law enforcement find it "comforting" to know the doctrine protects all but "the plainly incompetent or those who knowingly violate the law." And although a majority of jurisdictions may indemnify police officers, some do not— leaving officers at risk of personal financial liability. Other scholars have defended qualified immunity on stare decisis grounds (i.e., the doctrine that promotes maintaining long settled interpretations of the law— especially statutes—absent a special justification), while questioning both the historical and practical arguments lodged against the doctrine. And some studies, while perhaps also undermining the need for the doctrine, may also refute the concern that qualified immunity is a significant barrier to recovery under Section 1983. For example, according to one study, "qualified immunity is rarely the formal reason that civil rights damages actions against law enforcement end."

Considerations for Congress

As the debate over qualified immunity continues, there is discussion over which branch of government should be responsible for reforming the doctrine. Because qualified immunity is judicially created, the Supreme

Court may, as it has in the past, choose to revise the doctrine. As mentioned above, some justices—for varying reasons—believe the modern application of qualified immunity should be reexamined. And some observers suggest that the Court may be preparing to reconsider the doctrine. The Court is currently considering multiple petitions for certiorari in cases that involve challenges to qualified immunity. Other scholars, however, express skepticism that the Roberts Court will reverse course on its expansion of the doctrine, pointing out that the Court is generally reluctant to overturn its interpretation of statutes. Another group of scholars suggest that even if it does not completely repeal the doctrine, the Court may choose to revisit its prior precedent to "better align" qualified immunity with its originally intended role. The Court, however, recently rejected a number of petitions to review cases involving qualified immunity.

Even without action from the Court, there may be a potential role for Congress in revising qualified immunity. Because qualified immunity is a product of statutory interpretation, Congress has wide authority to amend, expand, or even abolish the doctrine. For example, H.R. 7085—the Ending Qualified Immunity Act—would amend Section 1983 by abolishing both the "good faith" defense and the defense that the law was not clearly established at the time of the alleged misconduct. A similar proposal—limited to cases brought against certain state and local police officers and federal investigative or law enforcement officers, as defined in 28 U.S.C. § 2680(h)—is found in the Justice in Policing Act of 2020. These proposals would effectively eliminate the judicially created doctrine applied in modern Section 1983 litigation and in any actions against federal law enforcement officers.

Another proposal aimed at removing barriers to Section 1983 liability is the Reforming Qualified Immunity Act. Unlike current law, which grants officials qualified immunity if the constitutional right alleged to have been violated is not "clearly established," this proposal would place the burden on Section 1983 defendants to affirmatively show with some particularity that the conduct at issue has been authorized by law. Specifically, the proposal would seek to remove the existing doctrine of qualified immunity and instead provide that an individual defendant "shall not be liable" if the defendant reasonably believed that his or her conduct was lawful and either (1) the conduct at issue was "specifically authorized or required" by federal or state law, or (2) a federal or state court had issued a final decision holding that "the specific conduct alleged to be unlawful was consistent with the Constitution of the United States and Federal laws."

Questions could remain, however, as to whether eliminating the doctrine in Section 1983 cases or beyond properly calibrates the competing interests that drove the Supreme Court to recognize qualified immunity in the first place. There may also be questions about whether eliminating qualified immunity for *state* law enforcement agents (or some subset of state actors) under Section 1983—as several proposals would do— would create an anomaly where the doctrine would still exist for *federal* law enforcement agents under *Bivens.* And eliminating qualified immunity entirely—as other legislation proposes—would appear to have effects beyond state and local police officers, as the doctrine extends to all government employees who make discretionary decisions in their work.

As an alternative, Congress could instead choose to scale back qualified immunity to more limited circumstances. For example, Congress could limit the reach of the doctrine to only certain government actors (as the Justice in Policing Act of 2020 does) or limit the doctrine's application in cases where certain rights are at stake, such as Fourth Amendment excessive force claims. Or, similar to the Reforming Qualified Immunity Act, Congress may choose to impose a new statutory test to apply to state and local actors sued in their individual capacities. Congress could also abrogate recent Supreme Court jurisprudence requiring a high level of specificity for a finding of "clearly established" law.

And beyond the doctrine of qualified immunity, Congress could, as some have suggested, explore reforming or eliminating the separate immunity rules set forth in *Monell v. Department of Social Services.* In that case, the Supreme Court held that while a municipality is a "person" subject to suit under Section 1983, a local government cannot be sued "for an injury inflicted solely by its employees or agents" under the theory of *respondeat superior* (the legal doctrine that an employer may be liable to suit for wrongful acts of its employees). Some have suggested that the

Reforming Qualified Immunity Act would revise the *Monell* rule by providing that "a municipality or other unit of local government shall be liable for a violation [of Section 1983] by an agent or employee of the municipality or other unit of local government acting within the scope of his or her employment," in effect applying the doctrine of *respondeat superior* to such governmental entities.

In: Police Reform …
Editor: Robert B. Smith
ISBN: 978-1-53618-504-1

Chapter 7

POLICE ACCOUNTABILITY MEASURES*

Nathan James

A series of high-profile deaths of people of color at the hands of law enforcement personnel have generated interest among policymakers about what steps could be taken to promote police accountability. In the wake of these high- profile deaths, policymakers have shown increased interest in considering legislation that would promote police accountability for the use of excessive force. The 21st Century Policing Task Force (Task Force), established by Executive Order 13684 in 2015 in response to a number of serious incidents between law enforcement and members of the communities they serve, recommended a series of actions that would help law enforcement agencies establish a culture of transparency and accountability in order to build public trust and legitimacy. This In Focus provides an overview of some frequently proposed measures, many of which were recommended by the Task Force, that policymakers could consider if they move forward with legislation to promote accountability in policing.

---

* This is an edited, reformatted and augmented version of Congressional Research Service Publication No. IF11572, dated June 11, 2020.

DATA ON USE OF FORCE

Collecting and analyzing data on the use of force by police officers may enhance transparency, improve police- community relations, and promote accountability. The Department of Justice (DOJ) is currently collecting data on arrest-related deaths through implementation of the Death in Custody Reporting Act of 2013 (DCRA, P.L. 113-242). The act requires states to submit data to DOJ regarding the death of any person who is detained; under arrest; in the process of being arrested; en route to be incarcerated; or incarcerated at a municipal or county jail, a state prison, a state-run boot camp prison, a boot camp prison that is contracted out by the state, any state or local contract facility, or any other local or state correctional facility (including juvenile facilities). States face up to a 10% reduction in their funding under the Edward Byrne Memorial Justice Assistance Grant (JAG) program if they do not participate in this effort.

The Federal Bureau of Investigation (FBI) is also collecting data on use of force incidents that result in the death or serious bodily injury of a person or when a police officer discharges a firearm at or in the direction of a person. The FBI launched the program on January 1, 2019, but has yet to release any data collected through it. While the FBI is working with other national law enforcement organizations to encourage law enforcement agencies to submit data, participation in the program is voluntary.

The Office of the Inspector General (OIG) for DOJ believes that data collected under these two programs are duplicative. The OIG has also raised concerns that the methodology used by DOJ to collect DCRA data might undercount arrest-related deaths because it relies on states to collect and report these data and they might not be aware of all applicable deaths that occur in the state.

Independent Investigations of the Use of Excessive Force

Concerns about whether law enforcement agencies and local prosecutors can properly investigate allegations of the use of excessive force by their own officers have generated calls for mechanisms for independent investigations of these cases. The Task Force recommended that law enforcement agencies have use of force policies that include a mandate for the independent investigation of allegations of use of force by police officers that result in death, police- involved shootings resulting in injury or death, and in- custody deaths. The Task Force recommended that jurisdictions either create a multi-agency investigatory body comprised of state and local investigators or establish laws or policies for referring investigations to neighboring jurisdictions or to the next highest levels of government as a means of promoting independent investigations of police use of force.

A former member of the Los Angeles Inspector General's Office, in a April 2015 commentary for the Harvard Law Review, argued for legislatures to establish independent agencies that would investigate allegations of the use of excessive force. He argues that for these agencies to be effective, they must have the ability to investigate potential criminal wrongdoing by police officers and to make recommendations that are then evaluated by special prosecutors. He says these agencies should be open and transparent, and independent of other law enforcement agencies, but have unrestricted access to police officers and agency records. He also argues that the agencies must be adequately funded, have the power to issue subpoenas and conduct search warrants, and have well-defined jurisdictions and mandates.

Early Warning Systems

Early warning systems (EWSs) are management tools for identifying police officers with possible behavioral problems before they "slip through the cracks." EWSs have three key components: (1) identifying officers whose behavior appears problematic; (2) intervening, through counseling or training, to correct the problematic behavior; and (3) following up with the officer who is the subject of an intervention. EWSs are not meant to punish officers for misconduct, but rather to allow for proactive management and administrative interventions—such as training, counseling by supervisors, or referral to professional counselors—before serious problems arise. According to DOJ, EWSs are common features of consent decrees that the department enters into with law enforcement agencies to reform their policing practices.

Officers in need of possible intervention are identified using different criteria, including use of force reports, citizen complaints, high-speed pursuit reports, preventable damage to agency vehicles, and involvement in civil litigation. The numbers of events and time frames used to identify officers in need of intervention (e.g., three use of force reports in 12 months) vary from system to system.

In many cases, a performance review or counseling session serves as the first level of intervention. Officers can be required to attend specialized training courses. EWSs also indicate to supervisors that their actions are subject to scrutiny and that they have a responsibility to monitor their officers' behavior. However, some have argued that EWSs are only effective if agencies have a culture of accountability. Generating lists of potential problem officers and conducting interventions with them would arguably be for naught if officers are not held accountable for continued misconduct.

National Decertification Index

Media accounts of police officers who have been fired from a law enforcement position in one city due to misconduct only to find work as a police officer in another city have raised interest in what can be done to prevent what some call "wandering officers." Utilizing the National Decertification Index (NDI) might be one avenue to address this issue. NDI is a database operated by the International Association of Directors of Law Enforcement Standards and Training (IADLEST) that contains information on police officers who have had their certifications to serve as a police officer revoked. NDI data are submitted by a state's Peace Officer Standards and Training (POST) Commission or a similar body. NDI is a "pointer system" and does not contain information about a specific officer or the actions leading to decertification. NDI only refers the querying agency to the holder of the appropriate record.

Officer decertification standards vary by state. In some states, officers can only be decertified if they are convicted of a felony, whereas in other states officers can be decertified for misconduct that does not constitute a crime (e.g., using alcohol while on duty). Also, participation in NDI is voluntary: federal law does not require POST commissions to submit data on decertified officers or hiring agencies to search it before making hiring decisions. The Task Force recommended expanding NDI so it could serve as a national registry of decertified officers. The Task Force noted, "currently the criteria for reporting an action on an officer is determined by each POST independently, as is the granting of read-only access to hiring departments to use as part of their pre-hire screening process. Expanding this system to ensure national and standardized reporting would assist in ensuring that officers who have lost their certification for misconduct are not easily hired in other jurisdictions."

Body-Worn Cameras

Body-worn cameras (BWCs) are mobile cameras that allow law enforcement officers to record what they see and hear.

They can be attached to a helmet, a pair of glasses, or an officer's shirt or badge. BWCs are viewed as a potential remedy for resolving issues of community trust and as a way to increase police accountability. The Bureau of Justice Statistics reported that in 2016, nearly half (47.4%) of police departments and sheriffs' offices had acquired BWCs and a similar proportion (44.7%) had some BWCs in service.

A 2019 meta-analysis reviewed the findings of 70 studies of BWC programs. The researchers noted that while early studies suggested that BWCs decreased the use of force by police officers, more-recent studies have found mixed results, though this could be the result of differences in agencies' policies about when officers have to use their cameras (e.g., BWCs might have less effects on the use of force if officers have discretion about when they can turn off their cameras). Research suggests that BWCs reduce complaints against officers, but questions remain "as to whether and to what degree these changes reflect citizens' reporting behaviors or improvements in officers' behavior or their interactions with citizens."

From FY2016 to FY2020, Congress appropriated $112.5 million for a grant program under DOJ to help law enforcement agencies purchase BWCs. While Congress has provided funding to help law enforcement agencies purchase BWCs, there is not a formal authorization for this grant program.

Civilian Review Boards

Civilian Review Boards review complaints against officers and issue recommendations on disciplinary actions. The U.S. Commission on Civil Rights, in its 2018 report on the use of force by police, observes that "many policing experts advocate for these boards, believing that they can help foster police accountability through their independent authority to investigate and audit departments facing allegations of abuse, including unconstitutional use of force, unauthorized detentions or arrests, or racial profiling." Research generally indicates that effective civilian review boards have the following elements:

- the authority to investigate or review complaints from the public on unconstitutional actions by the police;
- the ability to conduct regular, independent investigations and audits of internal complaints against officers and a department's disciplinary process;
- the power to require witnesses to appear and compel cooperation from police departments and individual officers;
- the authority to require police agencies to provide information on action taken in individual cases, with reasons for inaction;
- the authority to review and make recommendations on policy and training; and
- the provision of detailed public reports on the board's investigations and actions.

In: Police Reform …
Editor: Robert B. Smith

ISBN: 978-1-53618-504-1

Chapter 8

PROGRAMS TO COLLECT DATA ON LAW ENFORCEMENT ACTIVITIES: OVERVIEW AND ISSUES*

Nathan James and Kristin Finklea

ABSTRACT

The death of George Floyd in Minneapolis, MN, while he was in the custody of law enforcement, and several other recent high-profile deaths of African Americans at the hands of police, have generated interest in legislation to reform policing practices. Two major pieces of legislation that contain police reform proposals are before Congress: H.R. 7120, the George Floyd Justice in Policing Act of 2020—passed by the House on June 25, 2020—and S. 3985, the Just and Unifying Solutions to Invigorate Communities Everywhere (JUSTICE) Act.

Each bill would establish programs to collect data on a variety of policing activities, such as the use of force, racial profiling, the use of no-knock warrants, and in-custody deaths. In some cases, state and local law enforcement agencies would report these data directly to the Department

* This is an edited, reformatted and augmented version of Congressional Research Service Publication No. R46443, dated July 6, 2020.

of Justice (DOJ). In other instances, states would be required to establish systems for collecting required data and reporting them to DOJ. Both pieces of legislation would provide incentives for state and local governments to report data by attaching conditions to the Edward Byrne Memorial Justice Assistance Grant (JAG) or the Community Oriented Policing Services (COPS) programs.

DOJ currently operates programs to collect and report data on the use of force by police officers and in -custody deaths. For instance, the Federal Bureau of Investigation (FBI) collects data on use-of-force incidents that result in the death or serious bodily injury of a person, as well as when a police officer discharges a firearm at or in the direction of a person. DOJ also collects data on deaths of people who are temporarily detained, under arrest, in the process of being arrested, en route to be incarcerated, or incarcerated at a municipal or county jail, a state prison, a state-run boot camp prison, a boot camp prison that is contracted out by the state, any state or local contract facility, or any other local or state correctional facility (including juvenile facilities), per the requirement of the Death in Custody Reporting Act of 2013 (P.L. 113-242).

The data collection programs proposed by the House and Senate bills might raise the following questions that policymakers could consider:

- Could these programs require state and local governments to submit duplicative data to DOJ, and might the requirement to submit overlapping data to different components of DOJ decrease the quality of the data due to "reporting fatigue"?
- Is the purpose of collecting data on racial profiling to further knowledge about how the police might use an individual's race or ethnicity in decisions about enforcing the law, or is it to serve as a potential deterrent to racial profiling?
- Could the requirement for states to collect data from local law enforcement agencies and then submit these data to DOJ—while possibly lessening the administrative burden on DOJ—result in less accurate and incomplete data? A local law enforcement agency may be more likely to recognize a reportable excessive use-of-force incident by one of its officers than a state official. State officials may be faced with the choice of accepting submissions at face value or putting in place a mechanism for auditing the data submitted to them by local law enforcement (similar to what the FBI uses to audit data submitted to the Uniform Crime Reporting Program).
- Could attaching conditions to JAG and COPS funding as a means of incentivizing state and local governments to report data prohibit agencies such as the FBI and the Bureau of Justice Statistics (BJS)—both of which have experience with managing large data collection programs—from collecting data for the programs? The entity that collects these data would be responsible for certifying that grant

recipients are meeting the reporting requirements, but Office of Budget and Management guidance requires statistical agencies to operate separately from policymaking activities.

Does the threat of reducing a local government's JAG funding provide enough incentive for it to comply with data reporting requirements, especially if the costs of complying would exceed the amount of funding the local government would lose for noncompliance? JAG funding, though a large grant program at DOJ, most likely accounts for a relatively small portion of any local government's policing budget.

INTRODUCTION

The death of George Floyd in Minneapolis, MN, while in the custody of law enforcement, along with several other high-profile deaths of African Americans at the hands of the police (including Michael Brown in Ferguson, MO, Eric Garner in Staten Island, NY, Philando Castile in Falcon Heights, MN, and Breonna Taylor in Louisville, KY), have served as catalysts for anti-police brutality protests in cities across the country. These deaths and the resulting protests have spurred congressional interest in policing reform legislation.

Two major pieces of legislation that contain police reform proposals are before Congress: H.R. 7120, the George Floyd Justice in Policing Act of 2020—passed by the House on June 25, 2020—and S. 3985, the Just and Unifying Solutions to Invigorate Communities Everywhere (JUSTICE) Act. Both bills would address a variety of topics—such as promoting better training for law enforcement officers, making the use of chokeholds a federal crime, prohibiting racial profiling, and changing how law enforcement officers use force. Both bill also would require state and local governments to submit to the federal government more data on police activities.

The 21st Century Policing Task Force, which President Obama established through executive order in the wake of the events in Ferguson,

MO,[1] was charged with identifying best practices and offering recommendations on how policing practices can promote effective crime reduction while building public trust. In testimony before the task force, the Division of Policing of the American Society of Criminology noted that "the United States presently employs a broad array of social and economic indicators in order to gauge the overall 'health' of the nation, it has a much more limited set of indicators concerning the behavior of the police and the quality of law enforcement."[2] The task force stated that more research and data collection are needed to know "what works and what does not work, which policing practices are effective and which ones have unintended consequences."[3] In its final report, the task force encouraged law enforcement agencies to adopt a culture of transparency by, among other things, making available to the public data on stops, summonses, arrests, reported crimes, and other law enforcement activities.[4] The task force also recommended that law enforcement agencies' use-of-force policies include a requirement for data on officer-involved shootings and in-custody deaths to be reported to the federal government.[5]

This report discusses the programs to collect data on state and local law enforcement activities that would be authorized by H.R. 7120 and S. 3985. It also provides an overview of existing Department of Justice (DOJ) programs to collect data on the use of force by law enforcement officers and in-custody deaths. The report concludes with a review of selected issues policymakers might consider when debating policing reform.

---

1 Executive Order 13684, "Establishment of the President's Task Force on 21 st Century Policing," 79 *Federal Register* 76865, December 23, 2014.

2 President's Task Force on 21st Century Policing, Final Report of the President's Task Force on 21 st Century Policing, U.S. Department of Justice, Office of Community Oriented Policing Services Office, May 2015, p. 19 (hereinafter President's Task Force on 21st Century Policing Final Report, 2015).

3 President's Task Force on 21st Century Policing Final Report, 2015, pp. 19-20.

4 President's Task Force on 21st Century Policing Final Report, 2015, p. 13.

5 President's Task Force on 21st Century Policing Final Report, 2015, p. 21.

LEGISLATIVE PROPOSALS TO COLLECT DATA ON LAW ENFORCEMENT ACTIVITIES

Since the events in Ferguson, MO, in 2014, there have been numerous legislative proposals that would have established programs to collect data on law enforcement activities. Although DOJ collects data on certain federal law enforcement activities, comprehensive data regarding state and local practices are unavailable. This section of the report provides an overview of data collection programs that would be created by H.R. 7120 and S. 3985.[6]

H.R. 7120, the George Floyd Justice in Policing Act

H.R. 7120, the George Floyd Justice in Policing Act, would direct data collection on a variety of policing practices, including law enforcement use of force and racial profiling.

Data on Law Enforcement Practices

H.R. 7120 would require federal, state, tribal, and local law enforcement agencies to report data to DOJ on traffic violation stops, pedestrian stops, frisks and body searches, and the use of deadly force by a law enforcement officer. Reporting agencies would be required to include in these data the race, ethnicity, age, and gender of the officers and members of the public involved. In incidents involving the use of deadly force, agencies would also be required to provide

- a description of when and where law enforcement officers used deadly force and whether it resulted in death;

---

[6] This report does not include a discussion of proposals in the two bills to expand law enforcement's access to records related to officer misconduct because these efforts are qualitatively different than the data collection proposals discussed in this report. For more information on proposals on access to information related to officer misconduct, see CRS In Focus IF11585, *Proposals for Systems of Records on "Wandering Officers"*.

- a description of deadly force directed against an officer and whether it resulted in injury or death; and
- the law enforcement agency's justification for use of deadly force, if the agency determines it was justified.

States would be required to ensure to DOJ's satisfaction that the state and each local law enforcement agency in the state are in substantial compliance with the data reporting requirements. In the case of noncompliance, a state would not be allowed to receive funding under the Edward Byrne Memorial Justice Assistance Grant (JAG) program,[7] the Community Oriented Policing Services (COPS) program,[8] or any other DOJ law enforcement assistance program.

Data on Use of Force

H.R. 7120 would require states and Indian tribes receiving JAG funds to report to DOJ data on the use of force by any local or tribal law enforcement officers. States and tribes would be required to submit reports on

- incidents where a local or tribal law enforcement officer uses deadly force against a civilian;
- incidents where a civilian shoots a local or tribal law enforcement officer;
- incidents involving the death or arrest of a local or tribal law enforcement officer;
- any other incidents involving use of force by or against a local or tribal law enforcement officer that are not included in one of the above instances;
- deaths in custody; and
- use of force in arrests and bookings.

---

[7] For more information on the JAG program, see CRS In Focus IF10691, *The Edward Byrne Memorial Justice Assistance Grant (JAG) Program*.

[8] For more information on the COPSprogram, see CRS In Focus IF10922, *Community Oriented Policing Services (COPS) Program*.

A report for each incident would be required to include the following information:

- the national origin, sex, race, ethnicity, age, disability, English language proficiency, and housing status of each civilian against whom a local or tribal law enforcement officer used force;
- the date, time, and location of the incident—including whether it was on school grounds—the zip code, and whether the jurisdiction in which the incident occurred allows for the open carry or concealed carry of a firearm;
- whether the civilian was armed, and if so, what type of weapon the civilian had;
- the type of force used against the officer, the civilian, or both, including the types of weapons used;
- the reason force was used;
- a description of any injuries sustained as a result of the incident;
- the number of civilians involved in the incident; and
- a brief description of the circumstances surrounding the incident, including the type of force used by all involved persons; the legitimate police objective necessitating the use of force; resistance encountered by each law enforcement officer involved in the incident; efforts by officers to de-escalate the situation and minimize the level of force used; and, if applicable, why efforts were not made to de-escalate the situation or minimize the use of force.

States and Indian tribes would be required to develop their own systems to ensure that all local and tribal law enforcement officers are reporting all applicable incidents, but would not be required to submit reports under this program for incidents that are reportable under the Death in Custody Reporting Act (see "Deaths in Custody Reporting Program").

States and Indian tribes would be required to use open source data (e.g., media accounts) to verify information on incidents they report to DOJ. States and Indian tribes would be required to update the information they submit to DOJ to include any reportable incidents they discover through a search of open sources. Failure to search open source data would be considered noncompliance with the program's conditions. States and Indian tribes that do not comply with the program's requirements would be subject to a penalty of up to 10% of their JAG award. DOJ would be required to publish an annual report using the data collected under this program.

Data on Racial Profiling

H.R. 7120 would require DOJ, in consultation with stakeholders, to issue regulations regarding the collection of data to eliminate racial profiling by federal, state, and local law enforcement agencies. The regulations would need to provide for data collection on all routine or spontaneous investigatory activities[9] and for these data to

- be disaggregated by race, ethnicity, national origin, gender, disability, and religion;
- include the date, time, and location of such investigatory activities; and
- include detail sufficient to permit an analysis of whether a law enforcement agency is engaging in racial profiling.

These data would be submitted to DOJ's Civil Rights Division and the Bureau of Justice Statistics (BJS), and agencies would be prohibited from including any personally identifiable information in submitted data. BJS would be required to analyze the data for disparities in the percentage of drivers or pedestrians stopped relative to the proportion of the population

---

[9] H.R. 7120 would define *routine or spontaneous investigatory activities* as interviews; traffic stops; pedestrian stops; frisks and other types of body searches; consensual or nonconsensual searches of the persons, property, or possessions (including vehicles) of individuals using any form of public or private transportation, including motorists and pedestrians; data collection and analysis, assessments, and predicated investigations; inspections and interviews of entrants into the United States that are more extensive than those customarily carried out; immigration -related workplace investigations; and such other types of law enforcement encounters compiled for or by the Federal Bureau of Investigation (FBI) or Bureau of Justice Statistics (BJS).

passing through the neighborhood; hit rates (i.e., contraband was found during a search); and the frequency of searches performed on drivers who are people of color relative to white drivers.

BJS would be required to make a report of its findings available to Congress and the public. State, tribal, and local governments that apply for JAG or COPS funding would be required to certify that they have policies that require data collection in accordance with the regulations issued by DOJ.

S. 3985, the JUSTICE Act

S. 3985, the JUSTICE Act, among other things, would incentivize reporting to an existing data collection program on law enforcement use of force and would direct data collection on no-knock warrants.

Mandatory Participation in the Federal Bureau of Investigation's Use-of-Force Data Collection Program

S. 3985, the JUSTICE Act would require state, local, and tribal governments to submit data to the Federal Bureau of Investigation's (FBI) Use-of-Force Data Collection program (see "Use-of- Force Data Collection").

State and local governments that do not submit data to the FBI's Use-of-Force Data Collection program would be subject to a 20% penalty on their JAG allocation for the first year of noncompliance and up to a 25% penalty for each subsequent year of noncompliance.

Data on No-Knock Warrants

S. 3985 would require state and local governments to submit reports to DOJ on the use of no- knock warrants. They would be required to submit the following data on each instance where a law enforcement agency serves a no-knock warrant:

- the reason for which the warrant was issued, including each violation of law listed on the warrant;
- whether, in the course of carrying out the warrant, force was used that resulted in property damage, serious bodily injury, or death or whether any law enforcement officer, suspect, or bystander was injured or killed;
- the sex, race, ethnicity, and age of each person found at the location for which the no-knock warrant was issued;
- whether the location searched matched the location described in the warrant; and
- whether the warrant included the specific information required under the Fourth Amendment and any applicable federal, state, or local law related to the use of no-knock warrants.

States would be required to ensure that all units of local government in the state are submitting data on no-knock warrants. State and local governments that do not submit the required data would be subject to a 20% penalty on their JAG allocation for the first year of noncompliance and up to a 25% penalty for each subsequent year of noncompliance.

DOJ would be required to publish a report that includes the data submitted by federal, state, and local law enforcement agencies, along with information on the crime rate in local jurisdictions that submit data on no-knock warrants. Data on no-knock warrants related to investigations that are open as of the date the applicable data report is due would not be included.

CURRENT DEPARTMENT OF JUSTICE EFFORTS TO COLLECT DATA ON LAW ENFORCEMENT ACTIVITIES

DOJ currently has programs that seek to collect data on the use of force by the police. These programs include the FBI's Use-of-Force Data Collection program, which collects data on certain instances of the use of force by law enforcement officers, and data collected pursuant to the Death in Custody Reporting Act of 2013 (P.L. 113-242), which collects data on deaths that occur when someone is in the custody of law enforcement or corrections agencies.

Use-of-Force Data Collection Program

The FBI launched its Use-of-Force Data Collection program on January 1, 2019. The FBI notes,

> law enforcement use of force has long been a topic of national discussion, but a number of high-profile cases involving law enforcement use of force have heightened awareness of these incidents in recent years. However, the opportunity to analyze information related to use-of-force incidents and to have an informed dialogue is hindered by the lack of nationwide statistics. To address the topic, representatives from major law enforcement organizations are working in collaboration with the FBI to develop the National Use-of- Force Data Collection.[10]

The program's stated goal is "not to offer insight into single use-of-force incidents but to provide an aggregate view of the incidents reported and the circumstances, subjects, and officers involved."[11] The data collected are not intended to be used to assess whether the officers involved in use-of-force incidents acted lawfully or within the bounds of department policy.

The FBI's program collects data on use-of-force incidents that result in the death or serious bodily injury[12] of a person or any incident when a law enforcement officer discharges a firearm at or in the direction of a person.

---

[10] U.S. Department of Justice, FBI, "National Use-of-Force Data Collection," at https://www.fbi.gov/services/cjis/ucr/ use-of-force (hereinafter FBI's Use of Force Data website).

[11] FBI's Use of Force Data website.

[12] The FBI defines *serious bodily injury* as "bodily injury that involves a substantial risk of death, unconsciousness, protracted and obvious disfigurement, or protracted loss or impairment of the function of a bodily member, organ, or mental faculty." FBI's Use of Force Data website.

For each incident, the FBI collects data on the circumstances surrounding the incident (e.g., date and time, number of officers who applied force, and reason for the initial contact between the officer and the subject); subject information (e.g., demographic information, injuries sustained, type of force used, and whether the subject was armed); and officer information (e.g., demographic information, whether the officer discharged a firearm, and whether the officer was injured).[13] Federal, state, tribal, and local law enforcement agencies are responsible for submitting use-of-force data to the FBI. Although participation is voluntary, law enforcement agencies are encouraged to participate. The FBI works with major law enforcement organizations and the FBI's Criminal Justice Information Services' Advisory Policy Board to develop support for participation.[14]

Beginning in 2019, law enforcement agencies could submit use-of-force data to the FBI, and the FBI indicated that data would be released "on a regular basis of no less than two times a year."[15] However, the FBI has not yet released any use of force data. According to the FBI, approximately 40% of law enforcement agencies are submitting data, and the first tranche of data is expected to be available in summer 2020.[16]

Deaths in Custody Reporting Program

On behalf of DOJ, BJS started collecting data on arrest-related deaths in 2000, pursuant to the Death in Custody Reporting Act of 2000 (DCRA 2000; P.L. 106-297). The act required recipients of Violent Offender Incarceration/Truth-in-Sentencing Incentive grants[17] to submit data to DOJ

---

[13] More information on the specific data the FBI collects on each use-of-force incident can be found on the FBI's Use of Force Data website.

[14] The Advisory Policy Board is responsible for reviewing policy and technical and operational issues related to Criminal Justice Information Services Division programs. It is comprised of 35 representatives from criminal justice agencies and national security agencies and organizations throughout the United States.

[15] FBI's Use of Force Data website.

[16] Tom Jackman, "FBI Launched Database on Police Use of Force Last Year, but Only 40 Percent of Police Participated," *Washington Post*, June 17, 2020.

[17] The Violent Crime Control and Law Enforcement Act of 1994 (P.L. 103-322) authorized funding for grants to states for building or expanding correctional facilities. To be

on the death of any person who is in the process of being arrested, en route to be incarcerated, or incarcerated at a municipal or county jail, state prison, or other local or state correctional facility (including juvenile facilities). The provisions of this act expired in 2006.[18]

Congress reauthorized the act by passing the Death in Custody Reporting Act of 2013 (DCRA 2013). The act requires states to submit data to DOJ regarding the death of any person who is detained, under arrest, in the process of being arrested, en route to be incarcerated, or incarcerated at a municipal or county jail, a state prison, a state-run boot camp prison, a boot camp prison that is contracted out by the state, any state or local contract facility, or any other local or state correctional facility (including juvenile facilities). States face up to a 10% reduction in their funding under the JAG program if they do not provide the data. The act extends the reporting requirement to federal agencies.

BJS established the Deaths in Custody Reporting Program (DCRP) as a way to collect the data required by DCRA 2000, and it continued to collect data after the initial authorization expired in 2006. BJS collected data on deaths that occurred in correctional institutions and arrest-related deaths (ARDs)—though BJS acknowledged problems with ARD data before suspending that data collection effort in 2014. In a report on ARDs for 2003-2009, BJS noted that "arrest-related deaths are under-reported" and that the data are "more representative of the nature of arrest- related deaths than the volume at which they occur."[19] An assessment of data collected by BJS from 2003 to 2009 and in 2011 indicated that the DCRP had captured about half of ARDs in this time frame.[20]

---

eligible for funding under the program , a state had to demonstrate it had either increased the number of violent offenders who were arrested and sentenced to incarceration, along with increasing the average length of violent offenders' sentences, or that the state had implemented truth-in- sentencing laws that would require violent offenders to serve at least 85% of their sentences.

[18] H.Rept. 113-285.

[19] Andrea M. Burch, *Arrest-Related Deaths, 2003-2009—Statistical Tables*, U.S. Department of Justice, Office of Justice Programs (OJP), BJS, NCJ 235385, November 2011, p. 1 (hereinafter BJS, *Arrest-Related Deaths, 2003-2009*).

[20] U.S. Department of Justice, Office of the Inspector General (OIG), *Review of the Department of Justice's Implementation of the Death in Custody Reporting Act of 2013* , December 2018, p. 3, at https://oig.justice.gov/reports/ 2018/e1901.pdf (hereinafter OIG's report on DOJ's implementation of the Death in Custody Reporting Act).

BJS has since replaced the DCRP with the Mortality in Correctional Institutions (MCI) program, which collects data on deaths that occur while inmates are in the custody of local jails, state prisons (including inmates housed in private prisons), or the Bureau of Prisons. BJS notes that MCI collects "many, but not all, of the elements outlined in [DCRA 2013], but because MCI is collected for statistical purposes only, it cannot be used for DCRA enforcement."[21]

Starting with FY2019 JAG awards, states are required to submit DCRA2013 data to the Bureau of Justice Assistance (BJA) where it can be used for DCRA enforcement, not to BJS where it is used for statistical purposes. States are responsible for establishing their own policies and procedures to ensure they collect and submit complete data.[22] DCRA2013 does not require DOJ to publish data submitted by states pursuant to the act, and BJA has noted that it will maintain the information internally—though the data may be subject to Freedom of Information Act requests.[23]

DOJ's Office of the Inspector General (OIG) notes that data collected by BJA pursuant to DCRA 2013 is duplicative of data collected by BJS through the MCI program. Both agencies collect data on deaths in state and local correctional institutions through their respective programs. BJS plans to continue to collect data through the MCI program because it "compliments BJS's overall correctional research."[24]

---

[21] U.S. Department of Justice, OJP, BJS, "Mortality In Correctional Institutions (MCI) (Formerly Deaths In Custody Reporting Program (DCRP))," at https://www.bjs.gov/index.cfm?ty=tp&tid=19.

[22] U.S. Department of Justice, OJP, Bureau of Justice Assistance (BJA), *Death in Custody Reporting Act, Performance Measurement Tool, Frequently Asked Questions*, February 2020, p. 2, at https://bja.ojp.gov/sites/g/files/xyckuh186/ files/media/document/DCRA-FAQ_508.pdf (hereinafter BJA's Death in Custody Reporting Act, Performance Measurement Tool FAQ).

[23] BJA's Death in Custody Reporting Act, Performance Measurement Tool FAQ, p. 3.

[24] OIG's report on DOJ's implementation of the Deat h in Custody Reporting Act, p. 14.

SELECTED ISSUES

H.R. 7120 and S. 3985 would expand the amount of data the federal government collects on certain law enforcement activities. DOJ's experiences with implementing the requirements of the Death in Custody Reporting Act and the Sex Offender Registration and Notification Act (SORNA; P.L. 109-248)[25] may provide insight into some of the issues policymakers might consider when evaluating legislation to provide incentives for state and local governments to submit data to DOJ on law enforcement activities.

Potential Overlap Between Data Collection Programs in H.R. 7120 and S. 3985

In a 2018 report, DOJ's OIG raised concerns that DOJ collects duplicative data on the use of force by law enforcement officers and in-custody deaths.[26] Both the FBI's Use-of-Force Data Collection program and BJA's data collection pursuant to DCRA 2013 include data on deaths resulting from the use of force by police officers. In addition, data BJA collects pursuant to DCRA 2013 are duplicative of data collected by BJS through the MCI program; both collect data on deaths in state and local correctional institutions as of FY2019. The OIG noted that "duplicative reporting requirements can confuse respondents and increase the risk of respondent fatigue, which can diminish data quality."[27]

Some of the proposed data collection programs in the House and Senate bills might partially duplicate existing DOJ data collection programs. H.R. 7120, for example, would require states to submit use-of-force data. These

---

[25] The Sex Offender Registration and Notification Act (SORNA; P.L. 109-248) provides a " comprehensive set of minimum standards for sex offender registration and notification in the United States." U.S. Department of Justice, OJP, Office of Sex Offender Sentencing, Monitoring, Apprehending, Registering, and Tracking, " SORNA, Sex Offender Registration and Notification Act," at https://smart.ojp.gov/sorna.

[26] OIG's report on DOJ's implementation of the Death in Custody Reporting Act.

[27] OIG's report on DOJ's implementation of the Death in Custody Reporting Act, p. 14.

data would be similar to data collected by state and local governments for purposes of being submitted to the FBI's Use-of-Force Data Collection program. If H.R. 7120 were enacted, it is possible that local law enforcement agencies would be submitting data on officer-involved shootings to a state agency so the state agency could report those data to DOJ while also submitting similar data on officer-involved shootings to the FBI for its existing Use-of-Force Data Collection program. Local law enforcement agencies would have to submit somewhat different data to the state than what they send to the FBI, potentially complicating these data collection and reporting efforts.

Under H.R. 7120, local law enforcement agencies would be required to submit to the state data that includes the following: whether an individual in an officer-involved shooting had a disability; the individual's English proficiency; and whether the shooting occurred in a jurisdiction that allows open or concealed carry of a firearm. Local law enforcement agencies currently are not asked to submit these data to the FBI. However, local law enforcement agencies who participate in the FBI's Use-of-Force Data Collection program are required to submit data to the FBI that would not be included in any use-of-force data collection program that would be created by H.R. 7120. For example, participating law enforcement agencies must submit data to the FBI indicating whether the shooting occurred during an ambush situation, whether the officer approached the suspect, and the years of service for the officer(s) involved in the shooting.

There might also be concern that in each of these two bills, state and local governments would be required to submit some of the same data to two different programs. For example, under H.R. 7120, the proposal for state, tribal, and local law enforcement agencies to collect data on law enforcement practices would require law enforcement agencies to submit data to DOJ on the race and ethnicity of people stopped by law enforcement officers for traffic violations, pedestrian stops, and frisks and body searches, along with the race and ethnicity of the officers involved in the stops. These data could overlap with data that state and local governments would be required to submit to DOJ's Civil Rights Division and BJS under H.R. 7120's proposed racial profiling data collection program (see "Data on

Racial Profiling," above), which would also require state, tribal, and local law enforcement agencies to submit data on traffic stops, pedestrian stops, and frisks and body searches disaggregated by race and ethnicity. The bill's racial profiling data collection requirements, however, would require law enforcement agencies to collect data on a wider variety of law enforcement actions (e.g.,interviews).

Similarly, under S. 3985, the proposal for law enforcement agencies to submit data to DOJ on the use of no-knock warrants (see "Data on No-Knock Warrants," above) might also contain some information that would be submitted to the FBI's existing Use-of-Force Data Collection program, particularly in instances where the use of no-knock warrants might involve serious bodily injury or death. However, the FBI's Use-of-Force Data Collection program does not collect specific information on instances when no-knock warrants are involved, and S. 3985's proposed data collection efforts on no-knock warrants would not capture all cases involving law enforcement use of force.

Scope of Racial Profiling Data in H.R. 7120

H.R. 7120 would require that DOJ issue regulations to collect data on potential racial profiling by law enforcement agencies around the country (see "Data on Racial Profiling," above).[28] Racial profiling data may include race, ethnicity, national origin, gender, disability, and religion, as well as sufficient information to determine if agencies are engaging in profiling.

Congress may consider debating which data should and should not be collected and submitted to DOJ for this program. For instance, H.R. 7120, would require submitted data to include the demographic information of individuals in police-involved incidents but would protect the identities of those individuals. Congress may also consider debating what might be accomplished by collecting these racial profiling data.

---

[28] S. 3985 does not address the collection of data on racial profiling.

- *Understanding the Scope of Racial Profiling.* If all law enforcement agencies are consistent in submitting these data to DOJ, this could help provide insight into the scope of racial profiling around the country, indicate whether there are certain areas or agencies that appear to conduct more racial profiling than others, and inform opportunities for change. At a local level, these data could help agencies understand if individual officers are engaging in profiling.
- *Collecting Racial Profiling Data as a Potential Deterrent.* Some may question whether the collection of racial profiling data could act as a deterrent for agencies to engage in racial profiling. Under H.R. 7120, DOJ's report on racial profiling would be submitted to Congress and be made available the public. Policymakers and researchers may question whether the availability of this information could influence state and local practices.

Structures for Collecting Data in H.R. 7120 and S. 3985

Both H.R. 7120 and S. 3985 would establish methods for state and local governments to submit required data to DOJ. In some cases, state and local governments would be required to report data directly to DOJ. In other cases, states would be required to collect data from the law enforcement agencies in the state and submit them to DOJ. DOJ's experience with collecting data on ARDs under its DCRP may illustrate some of the potential issues DOJ might experience if states are required to collect data from local governments.

As discussed in the "Deaths in Custody Reporting Program" section, BJS collected data on ARDs pursuant to DCRA 2000 but eventually stopped collecting these data because deaths were underreported. Under the DCRP, BJS relied on state criminal justice agencies to voluntarily report these data on behalf of all law enforcement agencies in the state.[29] DOJ's OIG noted that DOJ found during its implementation of DCRA 2013 that requiring

[29] OIG's report on DOJ's implementation of the Death in Custody Reporting Act, p. 3.

states to collect data on and report ARDs can be a challenge because the effort requires states to report data they might not possess.[30] DOJ officials and state-level statistical analysis centers have noted that BJS's experience with the ARD program suggests that state-level reporting might not produce complete data because (1) state-level agencies are generally less aware of and less knowledgeable about deaths that occurred in their states than are the local jurisdictions where the deaths occurred, and (2) many state governments cannot compel subordinate levels of government to report crime data without state laws requiring such reporting.[31]

The issues with BJS's ARD program might raise questions about how DOJ would determine whether a local or state government is submitting all required data. Under H.R. 7120 and S. 3985, DOJ would be required to reduce a state or local government's JAG allocation if they were not in compliance with the conditions of the proposed legislation. However, unless DOJ or states periodically audit the data that local law enforcement agencies submit, it is difficult to know if participating law enforcement agencies are reporting all required data. Were these bills to become enacted, DOJ might consider having a mechanism that would certify that state and local governments were complying with the conditions of the legislation. For example, if state and local governments were to demonstrate that they have a system in place to collect and report the data required under the proposals, and then they were to either submit these data or affirm that they have no applicable incidents to report, DOJ might find such a mechanism useful. Some observers criticize the FBI's Hate Crimes Statistics program for similar reasons regarding uncertainty around the completeness of data collected by DOJ—more than 80% of law enforcement agencies report to this program that they have zero hate crimes in their jurisdictions for the year.[32]

---

[30] OIG's report on DOJ's implementation of the Death in Custody Reporting Act, p. 17.

[31] OIG's report on DOJ's implementation of the Death in Custody Reporting Act, p. 17.

[32] For more information on the FBI's Hate Crime Statistics program, including information on zero -reporting agencies, see CRS Report R46318, *Federal Data on Hate Crimes in the United States.*

Agency Responsible for Overseeing Data Collection in H.R.7120 and S.3985

Both BJS and the FBI work with state and local entities to collect and report crime and policing data. BJS is DOJ's statistical agency and one of 13 principal statistical agencies in the federal government.[33] BJS works with state and local agencies to collect criminal justice data, including from state and local law enforcement agencies, through its Law Enforcement Management and Administrative Statistics program and its Census of State and Local Law Enforcement Agencies. The FBI works with law enforcement agencies to collect crime data through its Uniform Crime Reporting Program. Both agencies would appear to be natural fits to manage the data collection programs that could be authorized by H.R. 7120 and S. 3985. Both proposals, however, would require state and local governments to submit the required data or face a penalty if they do not comply with the requirements. Therefore, BJA, which administers the JAG program, might be further considered for collecting these data because BJA would have to determine whether state and local governments are complying with the data submission requirements.

DOJ's OIG reported that in 2016, BJS participated in an effort initiated by a task force of state and local law enforcement organizations to develop and implement what would eventually become the FBI's Use-of-Force Data Collection program.[34] BJS recognized that there were similarities and overlap between the DCRP and the FBI's program, and BJS asked the FBI to manage a combined data collection effort. The task force ended up rejecting BJS's proposal, in part because they did not want the FBI making decisions about whether states were meeting the requirements of DCRA 2013. Members of the task force told the OIG that

> because state and local law enforcement believed that the [Justice] Department may use DCRA data to punish law enforcement agencies, the task force decided that it should limit [the FBI's] data collection to only those

[33] OIG's report on DOJ's implementation of the Death in Custody Reporting Act , p. 2.
[34] OIG's report on DOJ's implementation of the Death in Custody Reporting Act, p. 10.

specific elements needed for researchers to better understand events and behaviors that led to officer use of force.[35]

DOJ's Office of Justice Programs (OJP) decided that BJS would not serve as the data collection agent for the DCRP because Office of Budget and Management guidance requires statistical agencies to operate separately from policymaking activities.[36] OJP considers administration of the DCRP to be a policymaking activity because of the authority under DCRA2013 for DOJ to withhold up to 10% of a state's JAG funds if they do not submit the required data.[37] OJP also decided not to have BJS serve as the data collection agent for the program because

> it would be inadvisable for BJS to collect state DCRA data on behalf of another entity that would perform the compliance assessment because even such limited involvement could undermine BJS's position as an objective statistical collection agency and could cause survey respondents to withhold future data.[38]

OJP made BJA the data collection agent because BJA administers the JAG program and can engage in policymaking.

Congress could consider requiring DOJ to establish new programs to collect data on law enforcement activities such as the use of force, traffic stops, and no-knock warrants, and not condition JAG funding on submitting data to these programs. Removing the policymaking consideration from data submission could allow BJS or the FBI to manage these programs. However, some are concerned that the data might not be reported unless state and local governments are given a financial incentive to do so. The FBI's experience with the Use-of-Force Data Collection program and the Uniform Crime Reporting Program provide two examples relevant to this discussion. The FBI started accepting data from law enforcement agencies for its Use-of-Force Data Collection program at the

---

[35] OIG's report on DOJ's implementation of the Death in Custody Reporting Act, p. 10.
[36] OIG's report on DOJ's implementation of the Death in Custody Reporting Act, p. 11.
[37] OIG's report on DOJ's implementation of the Death in Custody Reporting Act, p. 11.
[38] OIG's report on DOJ's implementation of the Death in Custody Reporting Act, p. 11.

beginning of 2019; thus far, 40% of the law enforcement agencies are submitting use-of-force data to the FBI. In contrast, the Uniform Crime Reporting Summary Reporting System, which collects data on the number of homicides, rapes, robberies, aggravated assaults, burglaries, larcenies, motor vehicle thefts, and arsons reported to the police has wide participation even though law enforcement agencies are not required to submit these data to the FBI.[39] The FBI has been trying to replace the Summary Reporting System with the National Incident Based Reporting System (NIBRS), which has collected detailed data on a wider variety of crimes since 1988. Participation in NIBRS is voluntary; in 2018, 44% of law enforcement agencies reported NIBRS-compliant data to the FBI.[40]

Conditions on JAG Funds in H.R. 7120 and S. 3985

Both H.R. 7120 and S. 3985 would require, in many cases, state and local governments to submit data to DOJ. If states do not comply with the reporting condition, they could face a penalty under the program, such as a reduction in their annual allocation. Depending on the costs of compliance (e.g., whether state and local governments would have to spend money to upgrade their information technology infrastructure or would have to increase staff to process data), there might be a question about whether the JAG program provides enough funding to encourage compliance.

The Urban Institute notes that "nearly all spending on both police and corrections was funded by state and local governments because federal grants account for a very small share of both expenditures."[41] Data on state and local finances show that in 2017, state governments spent $15.426

---

[39] In 2018, 18,585 law enforcement agencies serving jurisdictions that included 327,167, 434 people reported summary data to the FBI. FBI, Uniform Crime Reporting Program, Crime in the United States, 2018, "About CIUS," at https://ucr.fbi.gov/crime-in-the-u.s/2018/crime-in-the-u.s.-2018/topic-pages/about -cius (hereinafter FBI, Crime in the United States, 2018).

[40] FBI, Crime in the United States, 2018.

[41] Urban Institute, State and Local Finance Initiative, "Police and Corrections Expenditures," at https://www.urban.org/policy-centers/cross-center-initiatives/state-and-local-finance-initiative/state-and-local-backgrounders/police-and-corrections-expenditures.

billion on police services, and local governments spent $99.078 billion.[42] In comparison, for FY2019, BJA awarded a total of $175 million to states and $78 million to local governments under the JAG program. In addition, although every state receives an allocation under the JAG program, not all units of local government receive a direct allocation. In general, direct JAG awards are made to a state's largest jurisdictions. For FY2019, BJA awarded a total of 873 grants to units of local government. Many local governments' allocations are less than $10,000, which is the threshold below which funds are included in the state's allocation rather than allocated directly; and the state is required to award these funds to the units of local government or to a state enforcement agency that provides law enforcement services for these jurisdictions.

For these smaller jurisdictions, there might be a question about whether any of the proposed penalties under the JAG program would provide enough of an incentive for them to adopt the proposed data reporting requirements. For example, a local government whose JAG allocation is $20,000 would lose $5,000 if the penalty is 25%, which may not be more than it costs to comply with the reporting requirements. Also, depending on the text of the legislation that Congress considers, there might be a question about whether any potential penalties would apply to funds awarded to "less than $10,000 jurisdictions" because they would not apply directly to BJA for funding—hence, they would not be considered *applicants* and instead may be considered *recipients* of JAG funds.

Policymakers may look to instances of states not complying with a condition Congress placed on the JAG program because states determined that the costs of complying were greater than what they would lose if they took the penalty. For example, SORNA mandated a 10% reduction in JAG funding for any jurisdictions that failed to substantially implement SORNA. The National Conference of State Legislatures found that many states did not comply with SORNA's requirements because they "discovered it would be cheaper to take the financial hit than implement the policy."[43]

---

[42] Data taken from https://state-local-finance-data.taxpolicycenter.org/pages.cfm.

[43] Dylan Scott, " States Find SORNA Non-Compliance Cheaper," *Governing*, November 7, 2011.

States noted that compliance was "labor intensive," and it was "cheaper not to comply."[44] As of 2019, the Office of Sex Offender Sentencing, Monitoring, Apprehending, Registering, and Tracking reports that 18 states are fully in compliance with SORNA.[45]

The potential for many jurisdictions to face a relatively small penalty under the JAG program might raise a question about whether Congress could incentivize participation by offering these jurisdictions grants to help them comply with data reporting requirements. It is possible that for many of these smaller jurisdictions, the costs of compliance—which could include hiring new staff to manage data, upgrading information technology infrastructure, and training officers on data collection requirements—could require a significant increase in their operating budgets.

Were the federal government to offset some of those expenses, it could have a positive effect on participation. The two policing reform bills have provisions that could address this issue. H.R. 7120 would authorize DOJ to make training and technical assistance grants to assist tribal and local law enforcement agencies that employ fewer than 100 officers with meeting the use-of-force data reporting requirements that would be established by the bill or to create a system that tracks use-of-force complaints against officers. S. 3985 would create a grant program to assist state and units local government with collecting data on the use of force and no-knock warrants.

---

[44] Ibid.

[45] U.S. Department of Justice, OJP, Office of Sex Offender Sentencing, Monitoring, Apprehending, Registering, and Tracking, *Sex Offender Registration and Notification Act (SORNA) State and Territory Implementation Progress Check*, June 10, 2019, at https://smart.ojp.gov/sites/g/files/xyckuh231/files/media/document/sorna-progress-check.pdf.

In: Police Reform …
Editor: Robert B. Smith
ISBN: 978-1-53618-504-1

Chapter 9

FEDERAL POLICE OVERSIGHT: CRIMINAL CIVIL RIGHTS VIOLATIONS UNDER 18 U.S.C. § 242*

Joanna R. Lampe

INTRODUCTION

The May 2020 death of George Floyd in police custody and subsequent nationwide protests against the use of force by law enforcement have sparked heightened interest in Congress's ability to prevent and remedy civil rights abuses by public safety officers. Among other existing legal remedies, a provision of the federal criminal code, 18 U.S.C. § 242 (Section 242) makes it a crime for government officials, including law enforcement officers, to subject any person to a deprivation of federally protected rights or impose different punishments based on a person's race. This chapter provides an overview of Section 242 before discussing

* This is an edited, reformatted and augmented version of Congressional Research Service Publication No. LSB10495, dated June 15, 2020.

proposals to amend the law, as well as certain legal considerations related to those proposals.

History and Text of Section 242

Section 242 originates from section 2 of the Civil Rights Act of 1866. Congress amended and broadened the statute in 1874 pursuant to its constitutional authority to enforce the protections of the Fourteenth Amendment through "appropriate legislation." Although Congress has amended the statute several times since then and changed its location in the U.S. Code, the law's core prohibition has changed little since the nineteenth century. As currently in force, Section 242 imposes criminal penalties on any person acting "under color of any law, statute, ordinance, regulation, or custom" who

> willfully subjects any person . . . to [1] the deprivation of any rights, privileges, or immunities secured or protected by the Constitution or laws of the United States, or to [2] different punishments, pains, or penalties, on account of such person being an alien, or by reason of his color, or race, than are prescribed for the punishment of citizens[.]

A simple violation of the statute is punishable by a fine and/or up to a year in prison. If bodily injury results, the offender may be fined and/or imprisoned for up to ten years. If death results or other aggravating factors are present, Section 242 provides for a fine and/or imprisonment for ten years to life or a death sentence (though the Constitution forbids death sentences for non-homicide offenses).

A related provision of federal criminal law, 18 U.S.C. § 241 (Section 241), makes it a crime for "two or more persons [to] conspire to injure, oppress, threaten, or intimidate any person . . . in the free exercise or enjoyment of any right or privilege secured to him by the Constitution or laws of the United States[.]"

Violations of Section 241 are punishable by up to ten years in prison or, if certain aggravating factors are present, up to life in prison or death.

Enforcement and Judicial Interpretation of Section 242

The U.S. Department of Justice (DOJ) enforces Section 242 by bringing criminal charges against individuals accused of violating the statute. People who believe their rights have been infringed may report such violations to DOJ, but Section 242 provides no private right of enforcement, meaning that victims of official misconduct cannot sue under the statute. (Avictim of conduct that violates Section 242 may be able to bring a separate civil suit under 42 U.S.C. § 1983 (Section 1983) or, for federal officers, under the *Bivens* doctrine, though qualified immunity may limit officials' liability.) To secure a criminal conviction under Section 242, DOJ must establish three elements: (1) the defendant acted "under color of" law; (2) the defendant acted "willfully"; and (3) the defendant deprived the victim of rights under the Constitution or federal law *or* subjected the victim to different punishments on account of the victim's race, color, or alien status. The following subsections examine each of those elements in greater detail.

Acting Under Color of Law

Section 242 applies only to persons acting "under color of" law, meaning "under 'pretense' of law." That statutory phrase originates from the Reconstruction era, and variations of it appear in multiple federal hate crime and civil rights statutes. Essentially, a person acts under color of law when they act with either actual or apparent federal, state, or local government authority. Officers and employees of the government generally fall within this category: the Supreme Court has held that "officers of the State . . . performing official duties," including public safety officers, act under color of law for purposes of Section 242. State officials act under color of law if they *derive their perceived authority* from state or local law, even if their conduct was *not actually authorized* under state or local law.

For instance, in one leading case, a Georgia sheriff who arrested a black man on suspicion of theft and then beat him to death argued that he did not act under color of state law because the killing was illegal under Georgia law. The Supreme Court rejected that argument, explaining that "[a]cts of officers who undertake to perform their official duties are included whether they hew to the line of their authority or overstep it."

Off-duty law enforcement officers may be subject to Section 242 if they act or claim to act in their official capacity. Moreover, a person need not actually be a government employee or official to act under color of law. For example, in *United States v. Price*, the Supreme Court held that private individuals who conspired with law enforcement to murder three civil rights workers could be charged under Section 242. However, a person acting purely in a private capacity is not subject to the statute, even if the person is a government employee: the Supreme Court has stated that "acts of [law enforcement] officers in the ambit of their personal pursuits are plainly excluded."

Deprivation of Rights

A defendant may violate Section 242 by depriving a person of "any rights, privileges, or immunities secured or protected by" either the "laws of the United States" or the Constitution. With regard to the "laws of the United States," it is unclear if DOJ has brought Section 242 charges in recent history based solely on statutory violations. In the analogous context of civil claims under Section 1983, courts have shown reluctance to imply a *civil* remedy for statutory violations; the courts may be even less likely to impose *criminal* liability under statues that do not expressly provide for it. Moreover, the scope of statutory rights subject to Section 242 may be limited by the constitutional authority Congress relied on to enact the statute. As noted, Section 242 is a product of Congress's power under Section 5 of the Fourteenth Amendment, which allows Congress to enforce the Fourteenth Amendment's guarantees through "appropriate legislation." As a recent Legal Sidebar discusses in greater detail, Supreme Court precedent allows Congress to use its Section 5 authority to enact prophylactic legislation regulating state and local matters based on evidence of a history and pattern of past constitutional violations by the states, if such federal legislation is congruent and proportional to a demonstrated constitutional wrong. Absent such circumstances, however, it uncertain when Section 242 could be used to prosecute violations of "laws of the United States" that do not amount to violations of the Constitution.

In light of the foregoing, prosecutions under Section 242 generally allege a deprivation of constitutional rather than statutory rights. Charges under Section 242 may involve rights guaranteed by the Fourteenth Amendment, including provisions of the Bill of Rights that have been incorporated against the states. For example, DOJ has brought Section 242 charges based on infringement of the right to vote, imposition of cruel and unusual punishment, and various due process violations. And, of particular relevance to law enforcement reform, DOJ may bring Section 242 charges alleging the use of excessive force in violation of the Fourth Amendment's protections against unreasonable seizures.

Differential Punishment

In the alternative, a defendant may violate Section 242 by subjecting a person to different "punishments, pains, or penalties" "by reason of" the victim's color or race or "on account of" the victim's alien status. In practice, however, it appears DOJ rarely brings charges under this provision of Section 242. One reason for this seems to be the general difficulty of proving that a defendant had a particular subjective motivation—in this context, the motivation to impose a different punishment "by reason of" the victim's race or other covered characteristic. Furthermore, a DOJ official involved in Section 242 litigation in the 1940s stated: "When a community has consistently permitted its law enforcement officers to deny the protection of the laws to certain groups, the same methods will assuredly be used against members of other groups who happen to offend the officials." Thus, pervasive misconduct by law enforcement officers could undermine DOJ's case on this element. Another possible reason for the dearth of charges under the "punishments, pains, or penalties" provision of Section 242 is that conduct that violates that provision likely also violates the statute's deprivation of rights provision: the Equal Protection Clause prohibits the government from imposing different punishments because of a person's race.

Willfulness Requirement

By its text, Section 242 applies only to violations that are committed "willfully." The Supreme Court stringently construed the willfulness standard in the 1945 case *Screws v. United States* (the main opinion in *Screws* was joined by only four justices, but binding opinions of the Supreme Court have since adopted its analysis). In *Screws*, a defendant convicted of violating the statute now codified as Section 242 argued that the law was void for vagueness—that is, it violated the Fifth Amendment's Due Process Clause because it did not give potential defendants clear notice of the conduct it proscribed. The Supreme Court rejected that argument by interpreting "willfully" to require the government to show that a defendant acted with a "specific intent to deprive a person" of constitutional rights or with "open defiance or in reckless disregard of a constitutional requirement."

The *Screws* plurality recognized that its interpretation of Section 242 differed from the usual mental state standard in criminal cases. To obtain a conviction for a crime, the plurality explained, the prosecution usually must show that the defendant intentionally performed some action, and the action was prohibited by law; but prosecutors ordinarily need not show that the defendant knew the conduct at issue was illegal or specifically intended to violate the law. However, Section 242 imposes criminal liability for constitutional violations, and courts examining the "broad and fluid definitions of due process" may interpret the Constitution to protect rights not expressly enumerated in the Constitution or prior court decisions. In those circumstances, the plurality observed, "Those who enforced local law today might not know for many months (and meanwhile could not find out) whether what they did deprived some one of due process of law." In the view of the *Screws* plurality, such a construction would raise serious vagueness concerns:

> Under that test a local law enforcement officer violates [Section 242] and commits a federal offense for which he can be sent to the penitentiary if he does an act which some court later holds deprives a person of due process of law. And he is a criminal though his motive was pure and though his purpose was unrelated to the disregard of any constitutional guarantee.

To avoid that result, the plurality concluded that in a Section 242 case the prosecution must prove the defendant had "a specific intent to deprive a person of a federal right made definite by decision or other rule of law." Such a defendant cannot assert a lack of notice because he "is aware that what he does is precisely that which the statute forbids." However, the plurality explained, the defendant's "purpose need not be expressed; it may at times be reasonably inferred from all the circumstances attendant on the act."

Much of the analysis in *Screws* indicates that Section 242 requires proof that a government official intended to violate a specific federal right of which the officer either knew or had notice. For instance, the defendant in *Screws* was a sheriff who beat to death a man in his custody. The plurality concluded that it was not enough to show a "generally bad purpose" to assault the arrestee; rather "it was necessary for [the jury] to find that [the defendant] had the purpose to deprive the prisoner of a constitutional right, e.g., the right to be tried by a court rather than by ordeal." However, other portions of the *Screws* plurality opinion could suggest a less stringent mental state requirement. For instance, the plurality stated that "[t]he fact that the defendants may not have been thinking in constitutional terms is not material where their aim was . . . to deprive a citizen of a right and that right was protected by the Constitution." The plurality further opined that Section 242 defendants must "at least act in reckless disregard of constitutional prohibitions or guarantees"—indicating it might suffice for a defendant to ignore rather than deliberately violate a constitutional right.

Lower federal courts vary in how they apply the willfulness analysis in *Screws*. The U.S. Court of Appeals for the Fifth Circuit has held that "willfully" means "that the act was committed voluntarily and purposely with the specific intent to do something the law forbids. That is to say, with a bad purpose either to disobey or to disregard the law." By contrast, the U.S. Court of Appeals for the Third Circuit, while remarking that "*Screws* is not a model of clarity," upheld a jury instruction stating both that "an act is done willfully if it is done voluntarily and intentionally, and with a specific intent to do something the law forbids," and that the jury could "find that a defendant acted with the required specific intent even if you find that he had no real familiarity with the Constitution or with the particular constitutional right involved." Overall, however, the Supreme Court's interpretation of the willfulness requirement has resulted in what some view as a significant hurdle to bringing Section 242claims.

Considerations forCongress

Several recent proposals before Congress would amend Section 242, with some proposals seeking to alter the statute's mental state requirement and others seeking to criminalize certain practices by law enforcement officers. With respect to the mental state requirement, even before recent calls for police reform, some commentators advocated altering the specific intent requirement for Section 242 announced in *Screws*. Section 101 of the Justice in Policing Act of 2020 would do so, amending Section 242 by striking the requirement that an offense be committed "willfully" and instead requiring that it be committed "knowingly or with reckless disregard."

With respect to deterring specific police practices, several recent proposals would seek to limit the use of chokeholds and similar maneuvers. For example, the Eric Garner Excessive Use of Force Prevention Act of 2019 and a Senate counterpart introduced in June 2020 would amend Section 242 to provide explicitly that "the application of any pressure to the throat or windpipe which may prevent or hinder breathing or reduce intake of air is a punishment, pain, or penalty" that may not be imposed by reason of race.

Likewise, section 363 of the Justice in Policing Act would provide that "the application of any pressure to the throat or windpipe, use of maneuvers that restrict blood or oxygen flow to the brain, or carotid artery restraints which prevent or hinder breathing or reduce intake of air" constitutes a "punishment, pain, or penalty" under Section 242.

More broadly, the Justice in Policing Act would appropriate $25,000,000 for DOJ enforcement of Section 242 and a related statute, 34 U.S.C. § 12601, which allows DOJ to bring civil suits against law enforcement agencies that engage in a pattern or practice of unconstitutional behavior.

Amendments to Section 242 may raise new legal questions. For instance, if an amendment to the statute sought to alter the scope of "rights, privileges, or immunities secured or protected by the Constitution or laws of the United States," challenges could arise asserting that the amendment exceeded Congress's authority. Amendments such as those related to chokeholds discussed above—which would declare that specific conduct is a "punishment, pain, or penalty" that may not be applied "by reason of" race—may raise fewer constitutional concerns if viewed as simply creating an enforcement mechanism against a specific violation of a constitutional right. If legislation were understood to go beyond that and to attempt to create prophylactic measures to prevent violations of the Constitution, the Supreme Court has held that Congress would need to show the legislation was a congruent and proportional response to a history and pattern of past constitutional violations by the states.

In addition, an amendment to Section 242's mental state requirement might revive the questions about vagueness and notice that the Supreme Court addressed in *Screws*. It appears Congress may have some ability to act in this area—in construing the willfulness requirement, the *Screws* plurality suggested, "If Congress desires to give the Act wider scope, it may find ways of doing so." However, Congress may need to examine whether any revision of Section 242's mental state requirement provides potential defendants with clear notice of what conduct violates the statute.

In: Police Reform …
Editor: Robert B. Smith
ISBN: 978-1-53618-504-1

Chapter 10

REGULATING FEDERAL LAW ENFORCEMENT: CONSIDERATIONS FOR CONGRESS

Whitney K. Novak

INTRODUCTION

In the wake of unrest arising from the May 2020 death of George Floyd, broader questions have arisen regarding Congress's authority to regulate law enforcement officers. While federalism principles limit the extent to which Congress may pass laws directly affecting state and local police officers, Congress has broader authority to regulate *federal* law enforcement officers and agencies such as the Federal Bureau of Investigation (FBI), the Drug Enforcement Administration (DEA), or the Customs and Border Protection (CBP). This Sidebar explores the existing criminal, administrative, and civil remedies that impose liability on federal law enforcement officials for claims of excessive use of force, including those brought under the *Bivens* doctrine and the Federal Tort Claims Act

(FTCA). It then concludes by discussing considerations for Congress regarding further regulation of federal law enforcement officials.

Current Law Regulating Federal Law Enforcement

Existing federal laws provide a number of criminal, administrative, and civil remedies for holding law enforcement officers and agencies accountable for misconduct.

Federal Criminal Law

Perhaps the most stringent way to regulate the behavior of federal law enforcement officials is through criminal law. The chief criminal law regulating not only federal law enforcement officials, but state and locals ones as well, is 18 U.S.C. § 242 (Section 242)—described more in depth in this Sidebar. In relevant part, that statute makes it a crime for a person "acting under the color of law" to deprive someone of their constitutionally protected rights. "Under the color of law" means that an individual is acting "using power given to him or her by a governmental agency," and it is irrelevant whether the actor is "exceeding his or her rightful power." Moreover, the Supreme Court has explained that to successfully prosecute an alleged offender—such as a police officer—under Section 242, the Department of Justice (DOJ) must show that the defendant had "a specific intent to deprive a person of a federal right made definite by decision or other rule of law." According to the DOJ, which enforces Section 242, examples of misconduct prosecuted under the statute include "excessive force, sexual assault, intentional false arrests, theft, or the intentional fabrication of evidence resulting in a loss of liberty to another."

Use of Section 242 against federal law enforcement officials is not the primary use of the statute.

According to one study looking at Section 242 cases from last decade, 12.4% of all prosecutions studied targeted federal defendants. Section 242 covers federal officials, as well, and has been used in recent years to investigate border patrol agents, United States Park Police, and FBI agents for instance.

Violations of Section 242 are punishable by fine and/or up to a year in prison or, if certain aggravating factors are present, up to life in prison or death.

Administrative Remedies

Beyond criminal law, other federal statutes and guidelines provide more limited methods of remedying misconduct by federal law enforcement within the confines of a given agency. Internal policies may address how federal law enforcement agents conduct themselves during investigations, including provisions on when the use of force is appropriate. For example, the Attorney General's Guidelines for Domestic FBI Operations instructs that "acts of violence" are not authorized unless the FBI agent is engaging in the lawful use of force, such as in incidents of self-defense or "otherwise in the lawful discharge of their duties." Federal law enforcement agencies, similar to other federal agencies, have various legal avenues to address employees whose conduct departs from established norms, such as through censures, reprimands, suspensions, demotions, and removals.

Beyond the ordinary employee discipline process, federal law enforcement agencies may have other review processes to examine civil rights violations by federal agents. For example, Section 1001 of the USA PATRIOT Act directs the Office of the Inspector General (OIG) of the DOJ to "review information and receive complaints alleging abuses of civil rights and civil liberties" by DOJ employees, including employees of the FBI, DEA, Federal Bureau of Prisons (BOP), the Bureau of Alcohol, Tobacco, Firearms, and Explosives (ATF), and the U.S. Marshals Service (USMS). The DOJ has relied on this congressional directive to investigate allegations of civil rights violations against "ethnic and religious groups who would be vulnerable to abuse due to a possible backlash from the terrorist attacks of September 11, 2001." Under Section 1001, for example, the OIG has investigated allegations that BOP employees tortured a prisoner because of his Muslim religion. Pursuant to statutes like Section 1001 and more general authorities, Inspectors General have sometimes investigated allegations of illicit use of force by federal law enforcement agents and reported findings to the DOJ Civil Rights Division to review for possible prosecution or other administrative misconduct.

Civil Remedies Under Bivens and the FTCA

Beyond criminal and administrative remedies to address illicit use of force, some limited civil remedies also exist to police federal law enforcement conduct.

Bivens Claims

As discussed in this Sidebar, a key federal law designed to prevent and redress constitutional violations, such as the right to be free from excessive force under the Fourth Amendment, by *state and local* government actors is found in 42 U.S.C. § 1983 (Section 1983). That statute provides a civil cause of action to recover money damages for "the deprivation of any rights, privileges, or immunities secured by the Constitution and laws" by any person acting "under color of any statute, ordinance, regulation, custom, or usage, of any State or Territory." However, *federal* action is beyond the statute's reach.

Nonetheless, the Supreme Court has recognized an implied cause of action, similar to the remedy found in Section 1983, for individuals seeking money damages against individual federal law enforcement officers. In a 1971 decision, *Bivens v. Six Unknown Named Agent of Federal Bureau of Narcotics*, the Supreme Court established that in limited circumstances, "victims of a constitutional violation by a federal agent have a right to recover damages against the official in federal court despite the absence of any statute conferring such a right." In *Bivens*, the plaintiff filed a claim against a group of federal narcotics agents after they conducted what he alleged to be an unconstitutional search of his home in violation of the Fourth Amendment. The Court, in holding that the plaintiff could pursue money damages for his Fourth Amendment claim, reasoned that when federally protected rights have been "invaded," a plaintiff is entitled to a remedy—whether that remedy is statutorily or judicially created. Thus, the

Court implied a private cause of action for individuals seeking money damages for Fourth Amendment violations.

The Court implied a remedy for constitutional violations committed by federal actors in two other circumstances following *Bivens*. In a 1979 case, *Davis v. Passman*, the Court held that an administrative assistant, who sued a Congressman for gender discrimination, could pursue money damages for violating the equal protection principles embodied in the Fifth Amendment's Due Process Clause. And a year later in *Carlson v. Green,* the Court extended a *Bivens* remedy to a federal prisoner's estate seeking money damages against the Director of the Federal Bureau of Prisons for allegedly failing to provide adequate medical treatment in violation of the Eighth Amendment.

The Supreme Court, however, has not implied a new cause of action under *Bivens* in more than 30 years. For example, the Court declined to extend a *Bivens* remedy in a First Amendment suit against a federal employer, in several Eighth Amendment cases brought against private prison officials under contract with the Federal Bureau of Prisons, and in a Fifth Amendment case for federal government interference with a landowner's property rights. The Court continued its trend of limiting *Bivens* remedies in its 2017 decision *Ziglar v. Abassi*. In *Abassi*, the Court considered the availability of a *Bivens* remedy for a group of non-citizens—mostly of Arab or South Asian decent—who had been detained following the September 11, 2001 attacks. In declining to extend the doctrine, the Court noted that since *Bivens* was decided, the Court had "adopted a far more cautious course" in allowing recovery under judicially created causes of action, recognizing that it is a "significant step under separation-of-powers principles for a court to determine that it has the authority . . . to create and enforce a cause of action for damages against federal officials in order to remedy a constitutional violation." As a result, further expansion of the *Bivens* doctrine, according to the Court, is now considered a "disfavored judicial activity."

The *Abassi* Court provided a two-part test used to determine whether a *Bivens* remedy is available. First, the Court looks at whether the case presents a "new context"–that is, whether the case differs meaningfully from the three cases where a *Bivens* remedy has been established (i.e., *Bivens*, *Davis*, or *Carlson*). Second, if the case does present a new context, the Court considers whether there are "special factors" counseling against creating a remedy. Central to this analysis, according to the Court, are separation-of-powers principles, and the Court has declined to extend *Bivens* remedies in cases implicating issues more appropriate for the other branches, such as federal fiscal policy or international relations.

Applying this test earlier this year in *Hernandez v. Mesa*, the Court declined to extend a *Bivens* remedy in a case involving a United States Border Patrol agent who fatally shot a 15-year-old Mexican national who was on the Mexican side of the U.S.-Mexico border. In so holding, the Court determined that the case arose under a "new context" because it involved a cross-border shooting claim. Moreover, the special factors analysis precluded extension of a *Bivens* remedy because the necessity of a damages remedy for incidents arising on foreign soil implicated considerations involving foreign policy, counseling hesitation about extending *Bivens* to this context.

Despite these limitations on the *Bivens* doctrine, the Court has emphasized that *Bivens* itself is "well- settled law," and it continues to allow for claims against federal actors for money damages in the three limited contexts the Court has already recognized, including those against federal law enforcement officers for violations of the Fourth Amendment—such as claims alleging excessive use of force.

Nonetheless, even if a federal court allows a plaintiff to pursue a *Bivens* remedy for an alleged constitutional violation by a federal official, qualified immunity—discussed more in depth in this Sidebar—may nevertheless shield that federal official from liability.

The FTCA

The FTCA also provides a remedy for the wrongful acts of federal officials, including federal law enforcement. Subject to various exceptions, limitations, and prerequisites, the FTCA—enacted in 1946— allows plaintiffs to sue the United States for money damages for certain types of state law torts committed by its employees. The FTCAacts as a waiver of federal sovereign immunity in limited cases involving tortious acts—such as negligence—committed by United States employees within the scope of their employment. Unlike a *Bivens* claim, an action brought pursuant to the FTCA is one *against the United States* and not the individual employee. And a plaintiff may not sue the United States in federal court under the FTCA until he or she first exhausts administrative remedies in the relevant federal agency.

Generally, plaintiffs may not recover for intentional conduct committed by federal employees. However, in 1974—in response to a series of no-knock drug enforcement raids on private homes performed by federal law enforcement agents—Congress amended the FTCA to allow for claims of intentional torts of assault, battery, false imprisonment, false arrest, abuse of process, and malicious prosecution committed by certain federal law enforcement officers. The amendment applies to "investigative or law enforcement officer[s]" defined as "any officer of the United States who is empowered by law to (1) execute searches, (2) seize evidence, or (3) make arrests for violations of Federal law."

Congress enacted the 1974 FTCA amendment nearly three years after the Supreme Court's *Bivens* decision. In 1980, the Court clarified that the 1974 amendment to the FTCA did not preempt a *Bivens* claim, meaning that the judicially created *Bivens* remedies were still available to plaintiffs who could also bring an FTCA claim. In reaching its decision, the Court emphasized that Congress had expressed its intent that the FTCA and *Bivens* actions be "parallel, complementary causes of action." The Court also highlighted four factors that suggested the *Bivens* remedy is more "effective" than the FTCA, and therefore a *Bivens* claim should coexist with claims brought under the FTCA: (1) the *Bivens* remedy, because it seeks damages against individual officers, serves a "deterrent purpose," (2) a court may award punitive damages in a *Bivens* suit, while 28 U.S.C. § 2674 generally prohibits courts from awarding punitive damages against the United States in FTCA cases, (3) a plaintiff cannot opt for a jury in an FTCA action, and (4) an action under FTCA exists only if the state in which the alleged misconduct occurred has a law prohibiting the conduct.

In 1988, Congress passed the Westfall Act to substitute the United States as the defendant in FTCA claims to "protect Federal employees from personal liability for common law torts committed within the scope of their employment." Congress, however, did not extend the Westfall Act's protections for individual federal employees who commit *constitutional violations*, thus effectively preserving the *Bivens* remedy. Therefore, FTCA claims against the United States for certain intentional torts committed by federal law enforcement may remain available alongside the limited *Bivens* actions available against individual federal law enforcement officials. Some courts, however, have interpreted provisions of the FTCA to preclude recovery under both the FTCAand a *Bivens* action; thus in some jurisdictions, plaintiffs must choose whether to proceed under the FTCA or *Bivens*.

Considerations for Congress

As Congress continues to explore police reform proposals, one issue of consideration has been whether existing law adequately regulates federal law enforcement. Recently announced police reform bills in the House and the Senate include several proposed reforms that specifically aim to regulate how federal officers operate in the field. The Just and Unifying Solutions to Invigorate Communities Everywhere Act of 2020 (JUSTICE Act), for example, includes a provision that would direct the Attorney General to develop a policy banning the use of chokeholds by federal law enforcement agents except in situations involving deadly force. And the Justice in Policing Act of 2020 (JIPA), for example, would ban no-knock warrants in drug cases at the federal level, and would require federal law enforcement officers to use deadly force only as a last resort when necessary to prevent death or bodily injury. (A more detailed overview of the provisions in each bill can be found in this Sidebar.) serious These and other recent proposals aim to more broadly restructure existing criminal and administrative remedies regulating federal law enforcement officers. For instance, provisions in both the JUSTICE Act and the JIPA seek to create or amend existing criminal liability for police, including federal law enforcement officers. For example, Section 106 of the JUSTICE Act would create a new criminal offense for "knowingly and willfully falsify[ing] a report" that involved a law enforcement officer's violation of an individual's constitutional rights. And Section 101 of the JIPA would amend the mental state required for a conviction under Section 242 from "willfully" to "knowingly or recklessly." Other bills have been introduced to impose additional *administrative* oversight of federal law enforcement agencies. Current proposed legislation, such as H.R. 2203 and S. 2691, would establish a position within the Department of Homeland Security that would address complaints related to the CBP and Immigration and Customs Enforcement (ICE) and conduct training on the use of force and civil rights violations.

While recent legislation has addressed *civil* reforms, many of these efforts have focused on Section 1983 and would have no effect on federal law enforcement officers. For example, H.R. 7085—the Ending Qualified Immunity Act—and the Reforming Qualified Immunity Act would abolish or curtail qualified immunity for all officials who may be liable under Section 1983 and would therefore not apply to federal law enforcement agents in *Bivens* actions. The JIPA, however, would not only amend Section 1983 by effectively abolishing the qualified immunity defense for certain state and local police officers, but would also abrogate the defense in "any action under any source of law against" federal investigative or law enforcement officers, as defined in 28 U.S.C. § 2680(h). This provision would appear to eliminate the availability of qualified immunity in *Bivens* actions.

And with regard to *Bivens* actions generally, although the Supreme Court has recognized an implied cause of action for Fourth Amendment violations committed by federal law enforcement, as discussed above, the Court has expressed its disfavor with extending the *Bivens* doctrine in new contexts. According to some commentators, this judicial restraint in extending *Bivens* leaves individuals without a civil damages remedy against many federal actors who may have violated their constitutional rights. And there may be room for legislation with respect to *Bivens* and the FTCA as they relate to federal law enforcement. The Supreme Court has continued to emphasize that it is Congress's role to create a cause of action for monetary damages against federal government officials. Congress, therefore, could choose to codify a similar Section 1983-type action for claims against federal officials. In creating a new statutory cause of action, Congress could establish its parameters, including which federal officials would be liable, what federal rights would be protected, or whether officials are entitled to qualified immunity. For example, Congress could make all federal officials liable for violations of all constitutional rights—much like how Section 1983 regulates state and local officials—or could limit the remedy to cases involving federal law enforcement officials who commit certain Fourth Amendment violations—such as excessive use of force.

And if Congress chose to create a cause of action specifically for money damages against federal officials, it could also decide whether to make the individual actor liable, or whether the action would be—similar to claims brought under the FTCA—against the United States. Members of Congress have in the past proposed legislation to allow recovery against the United States for constitutional violations committed by its employees. Exposing the United States or federal employees to liability may present other policy considerations such as increased costs to the federal government in paying for judgments and additional burdens on the federal agencies in defending such lawsuits.

In: Police Reform …
Editor: Robert B. Smith
ISBN: 978-1-53618-504-1

Chapter 11

WHAT ROLE MIGHT THE FEDERAL GOVERNMENT PLAY IN LAW ENFORCEMENT REFORM?*

Nathan James and Ben Harrington

INTRODUCTION

Over the past few years, several high-profile police- involved shootings and alleged instances of excessive force have generated congressional interest in state and local policing. Congressional interest in policing reform revolves primarily around the public's confidence in the police and accountability for excessive use of force. What role should Congress play in facilitating efforts to bolster confidence in the police? Should Congress seek to improve law enforcement's accountability regarding the excessive use of force? These questions are bounded by limits of congressional authority.

---

* This is an edited, reformatted and augmented version of Congressional Research Service Publication No. IF10572, updated June 1, 2020.

LIMITS OF CONGRESSIONAL AUTHORITY

The federalized system of government in the United States limits the influence Congress can have over state and local law enforcement policies.

The U.S. Constitution established a federal government of limited powers. A general police power is not among them. That authority is largely reserved for the states. The Constitution, however, does vest Congress with legislative powers under the Spending, Commerce, Territorial, and Necessary and Proper Clauses, as well as under the enforcement sections of the Civil War Amendments.

Congress has exercised this authority in the past to enact legislation that relates to law enforcement matters. Yet even here, its authority is not boundless.

Congress may spend for the general welfare and thereby encourage states to take or refrain from various activities. In doing so, however, the encouraged state action must relate to the purpose for which federal funds are spent. Moreover, state action may be encouraged, not commandeered or compelled. Commandeering and compulsion are also beyond the scope of the Commerce Clause, which otherwise empowers Congress to regulate the flow, instrumentalities, and substantial impacts of interstate and foreign commerce. Congress may enact model legislation for federal enclaves, but its reach there is geographically limited. The Necessary and Proper Clause permits implementing legislation, but only to the extent this legislation reasonably relates to powers that the Constitution elsewhere grants to the federal government. Finally, each of the Civil War Amendments—the Thirteenth, Fourteenth, and Fifteenth Amendments— conveys the power to enforce its provisions by appropriate legislation, but that power is cabined by the terms of the amendment and by judicial interpretation of its breadth.

TOOLS AVAILABLE TO THE FEDERAL GOVERNMENT TO PROMOTE LAW ENFORCEMENT REFORM

If Congress wants to influence local policing, it can hone at least three items in the federal criminal justice toolkit: policing-related data collection by the U.S. government, federal processes to investigate local police misconduct, and the relationship between the Department of Justice (DOJ) and police throughout the United States.

Federal Data Collection Efforts on Police Use of Force The federal government collects and disseminates limited data on the use of force by state and local police. Several programs gather this kind of information, but none collects data on every use of force incident in the United States.

- On January 1, 2019, the Federal Bureau of Investigation (FBI) launched its use of force data collection system. The FBI program collects data on incidents that result in the death or serious bodily injury of a person, or when a law enforcement officer discharges a firearm at or in the direction of a person. Law enforcement agencies are encouraged, but not required, to participate. The FBI has yet to release any publications using these data.
- Every three years, in its Police Public Contact Survey (PPCS), the Bureau of Justice Statistics collects data on citizens' interactions with police, including police use of force. While the PPCS produces reliable national estimates of police use of force, it is a survey, not a census of all such incidents. The most recent data available are from 2015.
- The National Violent Death Reporting System (NVDRS), administered by the Centers for Disease Controland Prevention, operates in all states, the District of Columbia, and Puerto Rico. Researchers in these states gather and link records from law enforcement, coroners and medical examiners, vital statistics, and crime laboratories. The NVDRS can provide data on deaths resulting from "legal interventions."

Congress passed the Death in Custody Reporting Act of 2013 (DCRA, P.L. 113-242), which reauthorized the Death in Custody Reporting program. This act requires states to submit data to DOJ regarding the death of any person who is detained, under arrest, in the process of being arrested, en route to be incarcerated, or incarcerated at a municipal or county jail, a state prison, a state-run boot camp prison, a boot camp prison that is contracted out by the state, any local or state contract facility, or any other local or state correctional facility (including juvenile facilities). States face up to a 10% reduction in their funding under the Edward Byrne Memorial Justice Assistance Grant (JAG) program if they do not provide the data. Starting with FY2019, states have been required to submit data required by DCRA as a condition of receiving JAG funding.

Investigating Law Enforcement Misconduct

The federal government has several ways to ensure that state and local law enforcement practices and procedures adhere to constitutional norms. The first is *criminal* enforcement brought directly against an offending officer under federal civil rights statutes. Section 242 of Title 18 makes it a federal crime to willfully deprive a person of his or her constitutional rights while acting under color of law. Similarly, Section 241 of Title 18 outlaws conspiracies to deprive someone of his or her constitutional rights.

More broadly, a key federal statute focuses on the *civil* liability of law enforcement agencies as a whole, rather than the wrongdoing of individual officers. Section 12601 of Title 34 prohibits government authorities or their agents from engaging in a "pattern or practice of conduct by law enforcement officers ... that deprives persons of rights ...secured or protected by the Constitution or laws of the United States." It authorizes the Attorney General to sue for equitable or declaratory relief when he or she has "reasonable cause to believe" that such a pattern of constitutional violations has occurred.

The Influence of DOJ on Policing

DOJ and its component agencies, such as the FBI, can help shape policing in the United States. Such influence can be seen in at least four roles that DOJ and its components play on this stage:

- Enforcer—DOJ can investigate and prosecute federal laws related to police abuse of power. For example, the FBI can initiate cases involving official misconduct, which DOJ can prosecute. In addition, DOJ's Civil Rights Division can review the patterns or practices "of law enforcement agencies that may be violating people's federal rights" and seek civil remedies when "law enforcement agencies have policies or practices that foster a pattern of misconduct by employees."
- Policy leader—DOJ can serve as a model for state and local law enforcement. For example, it issues guidance for law enforcement agencies; sets policies for its own agencies that resonate broadly in federal, state, and local law enforcement; and provides training.
- Convener—DOJ brings together representatives from law enforcement agencies and local communities to discuss policing issues. For example, its Community Relations Service facilitates discussions among police, government officials, community residents, and various community groups. This component of DOJ does not investigate or prosecute crimes, take sides in a dispute, impose solutions, assign blame, or assess fault.
- Funder—DOJ awards grants to state and local police, as well as researchers probing important policing questions.

Law Enforcement Reform Efforts in the Current Congress

Despite limits on congressional power to shore up trust and accountability within local policing contexts, legislation introduced in the116th Congresses seeks to influence police practices. Such legislation would attempt to (1) better understand and track use of force by law enforcement; (2) reform how investigations of police-involved deaths are conducted; (3) require law enforcement agencies to provide more training on issues such as implicit bias or racial profiling to their officers; (4) promote diversity in police hiring; and (5) expand the use of body-worn cameras. Much of the legislation introduced in this Congress focuses on altering existing federal tools historically used to shape local policing.

Policy Options

There are several options policymakers might examine should they choose to play a role in facilitating better police-community relations and accountability for excessive use of force, including the following:

- placing conditions on federal funding to encourage law enforcement to adopt policy changes to promote better community relations by, for example, expanding training or reforming how use of force investigations are conducted;
- requiring DOJ to develop model policies or best practices regarding the use of force, training standards, or accreditation;
- expanding efforts to collect more comprehensive data on the use of force by law enforcement officers;
- providing grants to law enforcement agencies for the purchase of body-worn cameras for their officers;
- taking steps to facilitate investigations and prosecutions of excessive force by amending 18 U.S.C. Section 242 to reduce the

mens rea standard in federal prosecutions, or place conditions on federal funds to promote the use of special prosecutors at the state level; or

- using the influence of congressional authority to affect the direction of national criminal justice policy.

In: Police Reform ...
Editor: Robert B. Smith
ISBN: 978-1-53618-504-1

Chapter 12

OVERVIEW OF RECENT ANTI-LYNCHING PROPOSALS*

Peter G. Berris

INTRODUCTION

Following the death of George Floyd in police custody in May and the fatal February shooting of Ahmaud Arbery, interest has heightened in legislation that would criminalize lynching—often described as death or bodily injury caused by two or more individuals acting without legal authority. A number of states have enacted anti-lynching laws, as localized crimes like murder tend to be a subject of state, rather than federal law. Although the conduct criminalized under those state laws can implicate various federal laws, there is no federal law expressly governing lynching notwithstanding decades of legislative proposals on that front. In June, Members introduced two police reform bills—the George Floyd Justice in Policing Act of 2020 (Justice in Policing Act) and the Just and Unifying

* This is an edited, reformatted and augmented version of Congressional Research Service Publication No. LSB10504, dated June 29, 2020.

Solutions To Invigorate Communities Everywhere Act of 2020 (JUSTICE Act)—both of which include "substantively identical" sections that are described as anti-lynching provisions.

These sections build on earlier legislation from this and other Congresses. Indeed, the anti-lynching provisions contained in the JUSTICE Act and the Justice in Policing Act are largely identical to the proscribed conduct in two bills that had already gained significant traction in the 116th Congress. One, the Justice for Victims of Lynching Act of 2019 (H.R. 3536, S. 488), passed the Senate on February 14, 2019. A nearly identical anti-lynching bill titled the Emmett Till Anti-Lynching Act (H.R. 35) passed the House on February 26, 2020. Similar attempts to enact federal anti-lynching laws did not achieve bicameral approval in the 115th Congress—a fate for approximately 200 anti-lynching proposals in the last century. For example, in 1918 Representative Leonidas Dyer of Missouri introduced an anti-lynching bill to remedy the refusal of states to prosecute "the perpetrators of . . . lynchings" under their own laws.

Although Dyer's bill eventually "passed the House of Representatives in 1922 . . . it was ultimately blocked by filibuster in the Senate."

Title IV of the Justice in Policing Act and Title IV of the JUSTICE Act would each "create a new section of the federal criminal code entitled 'Lynching.'" Both bills would make it a federal crime to "conspire[] with another person to violate" one of the following four federal hate crimes statutes:

- 18 U.S.C. § 245, which, among other things, prohibits interference with an individual's participation in certain protected activity because of race, color, religion, or national origin;
- 18 U.S.C. § 247, which prohibits conduct including certain destruction of religious real property because of the religious character of the property, or because of the race, color, or ethnic characteristics of the people associated with that property;
- 18 U.S.C. § 249, which, among other things, prohibits causing bodily injury to another because of that person's actual or perceived race, color, religion, or national origin, or because of that

person's actual or perceived religion, national origin, gender, sexual orientation, gender identity, or disability where there is a sufficient interstatenexus;
- 42 U.S.C. § 3631, which, among other things, prohibits interference through threatened or actual force with housing rights because of race, color, religion, sex, handicap, familial status, or national origin.

Proponents of the legislation point to both its substantive and symbolic effects. Conspiring to violate the statutes listed above is already a crime under 18 U.S.C. § 371, a federal statute that broadly prohibits conspiracies to "commit any offense against the United States" when at least one person "do[es] any act to effect the object of the conspiracy" Ordinarily, to prove a § 371 conspiracy the government must demonstrate "(1) an agreement between two or more persons to pursue an unlawful objective; (2) the defendant's knowledge of the unlawful objective and voluntary agreement to join the conspiracy; and (3) an overt act by one or more of the members of the conspiracy in furtherance of the objective of the conspiracy." Federal prosecutors have used § 371 to prosecute hate crime conspiracies. Akey distinction between § 371 and the anti-lynching provisions in the Justice in Policing Act and the JUSTICE Act, however, is that the anti-lynching proposals would increase the maximum applicable prison term from five years under § 371 to ten years—or longer when authorized by the underlying statute. Moreover, the findings of the Justice in Policing Act and the JUSTICE Act note the symbolic value of creating a distinct anti-lynching statute that "recognizes the history of lynching in the United States" and thereby facilitates "reconciliation and a new understanding, on which improved racial relations can be forged."

One criticism of the legislation has been that it could impose significant penalties for relatively minor offenses. Earlier this month, Senate consideration of a stand-alone House-passed anti-lynching proposal stalled following objection by Senator Rand Paul of Kentucky, who expressed concern that the bill would impose up to ten years of imprisonment for "any bodily injury, including a cut, an abrasion, or a bruise, physical pain, illness, or any other injury to the body no matter how temporary." And, in fact, many of the hate crimes laws above cover non-violent actions, and hate crimes conspiracies may be established with a showing of just an agreement, intent, and an overt act. However, conspiracies to violate hate crimes statutes are already subject to a five year penalty under an existing federal statute. In addition, the scope of the anti-lynching proposals contained in H.R. 35, S. 488, the JUSTICE Act, and the Justice in Policing Act depends in part on the underlying hate crimes statutes—which apply to offenses motivated by a specific bias when there is sufficient federal jurisdiction. Practically speaking, the scope of the hate crimes statutes is also limited by prosecutorial discretion, which involves a "policy judgment" regarding whether "the fundamental interests of society require the application of federal criminal law to a particular set of circumstances." In certain instances federal prosecutors have pursued hate crimes prosecutions of shootings, arsons, assaults, and murders committed because of racial, religious, and other biases. Nevertheless, states "generally prosecute most hate crimes."

In: Police Reform …
Editor: Robert B. Smith
ISBN: 978-1-53618-504-1

Chapter 13

PROPOSALS FOR SYSTEMS OF RECORDS ON "WANDERING OFFICERS"*

Nathan James and Kristin Finklea

INTRODUCTION

Two major policing reform bills before Congress would attempt to reform law enforcement practices, especially practices that are considered to be biased against people of color. The two bills, H.R. 7120 and S. 3985, would, among other things, require state and local governments to report data on the use of force, promote the use of body-worn cameras, expand de-escalation training, and reduce racial profiling. Both pieces of legislation would also attempt to curb so-called "wandering officers" (i.e., law enforcement officers who are fired or resign under threat of termination but are later hired by another law enforcement agency, often in another state).

* This is an edited, reformatted and augmented version of Congressional Research Service Publication No. IF11585, dated June 25, 2020.

There are a litany of stories about law enforcement officers who are alleged or found to have engaged in misconduct, including the use of excessive force, being hired at law other enforcement agencies, and it is only discovered later that the officers had similar records at previous agencies. There is disagreement over how common the wandering officer phenomenon is and to what extent these officers may be a threat to the public. A 2020 study of law enforcement officers in Florida found the following:

- There are almost 1,100 wandering officers in any given year in Florida, and they constitute about 3% of all officers in the state.
- Fired officers tend to take longer to find new work than officers who separate from their agency voluntarily. Fired officers also tend to move to smaller agencies with fewer resources in communities with slightly higher proportions of residents of color.
- Wandering officers are more likely to be fired from their next job or to receive a complaint for a “moral character violation” than both officers hired as rookies and those hired as veterans who have never been fired.

RECOMMENDATION OF THE 21ST CENTURY POLICING TASK FORCE

In 2015, President Obama’s Task Force on 21st Century Policing recommended expanding the National Decertification Index (NDI) so it could serve as a national registry of decertified officers. The Task Force noted, “currently the criteria for reporting an action on an officer is determined by each POST [Peace Officer Standards and Training Commission] independently, as is the granting of read-only access to hiring departments to use as part of their pre-hire screening process. Expanding this system to ensure national and standardized reporting would assist in ensuring that officers who have lost their certification for misconduct are not easily hired in other jurisdictions."

NATIONAL DECERTIFICATION INDEX

NDI, a database operated by the International Association of Directors of Law Enforcement Standards and Training (IADLEST), contains information on police officers who have had their certifications revoked. Forty-six states have laws that allow for a law enforcement officer's license or certification to be revoked if he or she engaged in serious misconduct. In these states, a decertified officer is no longer allowed to work as law enforcement officer in the state where his or her license or certification was revoked.

NDI data are submitted by a state's POST Commission or a similar body. NDI is a "pointer system" and does not contain information about a specific officer or the actions leading to decertification. NDI only refers the querying agency to the agency holding the appropriate record. POST Commissions can query NDI, as may law enforcement agencies that have been granted access by the state's POST Commission. Some 375 law enforcement agencies have been granted direct access. All other agencies must rely on the state's POST Commission, and these commissions do not always query NDI.

Officer decertification standards vary by state. In some states, officers can only be decertified if they are convicted of a felony, whereas in others, officers can be decertified for misconduct that does not constitute a crime (e.g., using alcohol while on duty). Five states (California, Hawaii, Massachusetts, New Jersey, and Rhode Island) and the District of Columbia have not established the authority to decertify officers; for states that do have this authority, reporting data to NDI is voluntary in most cases.

Legislative Proposals

Both H.R. 7120 and S. 3985 would expand law enforcement's access to records related to officer misconduct so potential hires could be better screened, but neither bill would accomplish this by expanding NDI.

H.R. 7120, the George Floyd Justice in Policing Act, would require the Department of Justice (DOJ) to establish a public National Police Misconduct Registry. The registry would contain records of substantiated, pending, and unfounded complaints filed against law enforcement officers, disciplinary records, and termination records. Records would have to indicate whether the complaint involved the use of force or racial profiling. The registry would include records of lawsuits and settlements against law enforcement officers. Law enforcement agencies would also be required to submit records demonstrating that their officers have completed all certification requirements for law enforcement officers in that state. Federal law enforcement agencies would be required to submit records to the registry as well. For state and local governments, submitting records to the registry would be a condition for receiving funding under the Edward Byrne Memorial Justice Assistance Grant (JAG) program. To receive this funding, they must also establish that they have a certification and decertification program in place for the purpose of law enforcement officer employment.

S. 3985, the JUSTICE Act, would require each state and local government that receives JAG funding to maintain a system for sharing disciplinary records of law enforcement officers. Each state and local government would be required to maintain in its system, records on disciplinary actions, internal investigations, and commendations prepared by a law enforcement agency of that government. These records would have to be available for 30 years and would be available to other law enforcement agencies for the purpose of conducting pre-employment screenings. State and local governments would be required to query the record systems of all law enforcement agencies that have employed a job candidate in the past. State and local governments not meeting the records requirements would be ineligible for JAG funding.

Both bills would address some limitations of NDI. Currently, NDI only contains information on officers who have been decertified; state laws vary on when officers can be decertified, if at all; states exercise this authority to varying degrees; and states might not submit decertification records to NDI. These two bills would make a wider variety of disciplinary records available to hiring agencies and would provide incentives for law enforcement agencies to submit specified records. H.R. 7120 would establish a centralized system; S. 3985 would incentivize the establishment of independent state and local systems.

WANDERING OFFICERS FIND NEW JOBS

A 2020 article in the Yale Law Journal on wandering officers discussed how law enforcement officers who are fired from their jobs are able to find work in other agencies. The issues highlighted suggest that making more information available about officers' disciplinary histories might not prevent wandering officers from finding new policing jobs.

In some cases, law enforcement agencies do not complete thorough background checks for new hires; and even if they do, past employers might not be forthcoming with the reason for an officer's separation. In addition, law enforcement agencies might not report terminations or officer misconduct to their POST Commission because reporting to it is voluntary in most states and there are different standards for what conduct is considered to be reportable to a POST Commission.

In addition, state-by-state certification of officers can create problems for hiring agencies because an officer can be fired in one state, get certified in another, and then find employment with a new agency. Small law enforcement agencies that are understaffed and have limited budgets might not have the resources to conduct thorough background investigations and might be more likely to hire willing to settle for more modest salaries, limited opportunities for advancement, or assignments other officers do not want. These officers may also be able to start right away, compared to new recruits who must complete the training academy (and the agency might have to cover this cost) and must spend some time being trained in the field by other officers. Some law enforcement agencies might also be willing to hire officers who were fired from their last job because they assume these officers may be more conscientious when offered a second chance.

Legislative Issues

Policymakers may debate a number of questions about databases or systems of law enforcement officer disciplinary information.

Access

Congress may debate who should have access to information on such systems. Would these data be available to the public or would access would be limited to a particular subset, such as members of the law enforcement community?

Database Changes

Congress may debate whether officers with information contained in such databases or systems should be able to access them or submit additional information on their own behalf. In addition, they may question how or under what circumstances information is updated or removed.

Privacy Risks

Congress may question the utility of having certain personal information about law enforcement officers in databases that may be available in whole or in part to the public. Policymakers may look to other national databases, such as the National Sex Offenders Registry, for examples of federal involvement in the collection of sensitive data. They may also question whether there should be technology requirements to help keep the systems safe from cyber intrusion and data breach.

In addition to questions about the content of systems of disciplinary information, if policymakers want to address issues about wandering officers they might face the question of providing incentives to change the way officers are hired. Providing access to disciplinary records and requiring law enforcement agencies to search these records could address the issue of a lack of information about an officer's past misconduct. Yet, this requirement does not address the issue of law enforcement agencies hiring fired officers anyway, either out of a sense of brotherhood or to give the officers a chance to redeem themselves. It also does not address the issue of agencies that hire wandering officers because they have no better options (e.g., they have problems recruiting because they cannot offer competitive salaries or they are in an undesirable location). Congress might consider whether there is a need to provide incentives for states to enact laws that prevent agencies from hiring previously fired officers, or if it should provide assistance to agencies with limited resources so they can cover expenses related to hiring new recruits or expand the hiring pool by offering higher salaries, a wandering officer. Wandering officers might also be more appealing hires for these agencies because they may be willing to settle for more modest salaries, limited opportunities for advancement, or assignments other officers do not want. These officers may also be able to start right away, compared to new recruits who must complete the training academy (and the agency might have to cover this cost) and must spend some time being trained in the field by other officers. Some law enforcement agencies might also be willing to hire officers who were fired from their last job because they assume these officers may be more conscientious when offered a second chance.

Legislative Issues

Policymakers may debate a number of questions about databases or systems of law enforcement officer disciplinary information.

Access

Congress may debate who should have access to information on such systems. Would these data be available to the public or would access would be limited to a particular subset, such as members of the law enforcement community?

Database Changes

Congress may debate whether officers with information contained in such databases or systems should be able to access them or submit additional information on their own behalf. In addition, they may question how or under what circumstances information is updated or removed.

Privacy Risks

Congress may question the utility of having certain personal information about law enforcement officers in databases that may be available in whole or in part to the public. Policymakers may look to other national databases, such as the National Sex Offenders Registry, for examples of federal involvement in the collection of sensitive data. They may also question whether there should be technology requirements to help keep the systems safe from cyber intrusion and data breach.

In addition to questions about the content of systems of disciplinary information, if policymakers want to address issues about wandering officers they might face the question of providing incentives to change the way officers are hired. Providing access to disciplinary records and requiring law enforcement agencies to search these records could address the issue of a lack of information about an officer's past misconduct. Yet, this requirement does not address the issue of law enforcement agencies hiring fired officers anyway, either out of a sense of brotherhood or to give the officers a chance to redeem themselves. It also does not address the issue of agencies that hire wandering officers because they have no better options (e.g., they have problems recruiting because they cannot offer competitive salaries or they are in an undesirable location). Congress might consider whether there is a need to provide incentives for states to enact laws that prevent agencies from hiring previously fired officers, or if it should provide assistance to agencies with limited resources so they can cover expenses related to hiring new recruits or expand the hiring pool by offering higher salaries.

In: Police Reform …
Editor: Robert B. Smith
ISBN: 978-1-53618-504-1

Chapter 14

REFORMING PATTERNS OF UNCONSTITUTIONAL POLICING: ENFORCEMENT OF 34 U.S.C. § 12601*

April J. Anderson

INTRODUCTION

In the early 1990s, bystander video footage of Los Angeles police beating, clubbing, and stomping on black motorist Rodney King sparked national outrage, protests, and rioting. In response, Congress passed the Violent Crime Control and Law Enforcement Act of 1994, which contained a notable provision originally codified as 42 U.S.C. § 14141 and now found at 34 U.S.C. § 12601 (Section 12601). Specifically, Section 12601 serves as the primary federal law aiming to ensure that law enforcement agencies comply with the Constitution. More recently, bystander footage of Minneapolis police pinning George Floyd in a

* This is an edited, reformatted and augmented version of a Congressional Research Service publication LSB10494, prepared for Members and Committees of Congress dated June 15, 2020.

neckhold ignited protests, anger, and violence throughout the nation, prompting renewed interest among lawmakers in the role of the federal government in ensuring constitutional policing. Indeed, Floyd's death is only one in a series of similar incidents arousing public concern and protest. Some of these events, including the death of Freddie Gray in Baltimore police custody and the fatal shooting of Michael Brown by Ferguson, Missouri, police, spurred not only public outcry but also legal action by the Department of Justice (DOJ) under Section 12601. This Sidebar discusses the Section's requirements, DOJ's enforcement actions in recent years, and considerations for Congress.

Section 12601's Requirements and Procedures

Section 12601 authorizes the Attorney General to sue local law enforcement agencies for "engag[ing] in a pattern or practice of conduct" that "deprives persons of rights, privileges, or immunities secured or protected by the Constitution or laws of the United States." The statute provides no private right of action, meaning that individuals cannot sue to enforce it. Private parties may pursue other civil remedies for unconstitutional behavior, and separate, criminal statutes empower DOJ to prosecute individual officers for unconstitutional behavior. Section 12601, however, aims at institutional reform. These cases, as DOJ explains, are "geared toward changing polices, practices, and culture across a law enforcement agency." The term "pattern or practice," used in other statutes authorizing the Attorney General's enforcement, requires "more than an isolated, sporadic incident," and wrongdoing must be "repeated, routine, or of a generalized nature."

CONSTITUTIONAL VIOLATIONS AND SECTION 12601

Once they become a pattern or practice of police misconduct, violations of any constitutional right can support Section 12601 enforcement. DOJ's cases typically address multiple constitutional harms. Perhaps the most frequent focus of Section 12601 cases is a potential pattern of Fourth Amendment violations (including improper searches, seizures, detentions, and use of force). For example, investigation of the Warren Police Department in Ohio revealed a pattern of improper strip and body cavity searches, while in Newark, New Jersey, and Maricopa County, Arizona, investigators discovered widespread theft of property by police officers. Maricopa County deputies routinely seized small items as "trophies." In Baltimore and New Orleans DOJ identified patterns of unlawful stops. DOJ also brought to light excessive use of force in the Yonkers Police Department, the Seattle Police Department, the Puerto Rico Police Department, and others.

Nonetheless, any constitutional protection can justify a Section 12601 case. Other constitutional violations uncovered in Section 12601 investigations have included alleged Fifth Amendment and due process violations, such as coerced confessions in the Ville Platte Police Department and Evangeline Parrish Sherriff's Office of Louisiana. In settlements with the Puerto Rico Police Department and the Baltimore Police Department, DOJ imposed measures to curb patterns of First Amendment violations— officers' retaliation for perceived insulting remarks and attempts to stop bystanders from filming police with cell phone cameras. In another instance, DOJ charged Colorado City, Arizona, and Hildale, Utah, police with a pattern of violating the Establishment Clause for carrying out orders of fundamentalist Mormon leader Warren Jeffs.

Often DOJ's cases aim to remedy racial discrimination, in violation of the Equal Protection Clause of the Fourteenth Amendment. (Title VI of the Civil Rights Act of 1964 also authorizes these suits for departments with federal funding.) In Maricopa County, DOJ found that the sheriff department targeted Hispanics—responding to complaints that alleged no criminal activity, but reported people with "dark skin" congregating in an area, or employees speaking Spanish at a local business. In Suffolk County, New York, DOJ concluded police discouraged Latinos from filing complaints and failed to investigate anti- Latino hate crimes. In Baltimore, Maryland; Newark, New Jersey; and East Haven, Connecticut, DOJ imposed remedies for patterns of racially targeted traffic and pedestrian stops.

But DOJ's Section 12601 enforcement has exposed other forms of unconstitutional discrimination, as well. For example, in investigating the New Orleans Police Department, DOJ discovered it provided virtually no translation services. If a citizen of New Orleans asked for police assistance in a language other than English, according to DOJ findings, police routinely failed to respond to the call. DOJ has also found discrimination because of sex in Section 12601 investigations. For instance, DOJ determined that New Orleans police consistently declined to investigate domestic violence and rape because of stereotyped assumptions about female victims. In Puerto Rico, similarly, DOJ found police disregarded sex-related crimes and domestic violence.

INVESTIGATION TARGETS AND INVESTIGATION CHALLENGES

Attorneys in the Special Litigation Section at DOJ's Civil Rights Division in Washington, DC, take charge of Section 12601 cases, with occasional support from local United States Attorneys' offices. Some have noted that it can be difficult for local United States Attorneys' offices to take on cases against police, given their everyday work with local law enforcement.

DOJ relies on media reports, complaints, private litigation, and advocacy groups for leads on potential Section 12601 cases. Some have criticized the agency for opaque or unsystematic methods of choosing investigative targets. The Civil Rights Division takes complaints directly from community members, judges, police officers, and advocacy groups, but has explained that it is "not a complaint-driven agency." In addition to these sources, DOJ monitors academic investigative reports, leads from federal agencies, and private litigation. At times, jurisdictions invite DOJ to investigate. Sometimes these invitations amount to whistleblower complaints. But DOJ does not always investigate upon invitation. And critics note that such arrangements may not identify departments in greatest need of reform.

Investigations have sometimes trailed press coverage—as in Ferguson, where a civil investigation followed a decision not to criminally charge officers after a publicized shooting and nationwide protests. The agency has explained that a "high-profile incident—such as a shooting death, a use of excessive force, or a false arrest—standing alone never warrants opening a pattern-or-practice investigation" unless it turns out to be evidence of systematic failure. All in all, given finite resources, DOJ's Special Litigation Section explains that it "identifies far more jurisdictions that meet the basic criteria for opening an investigation than it is able to investigate."

Beyond resource questions, other factors may influence DOJ's decision to initiate a Section 12601 investigation. For instance, some have suggested that evidentiary limitations, such as unreliable data, may prevent DOJ from appropriately targeting its enforcement and initiating Section 12601 investigations. While federal law requires DOJ to compile data on arrest-related deaths and officers' use of excessive force, the Department's Bureau of Justice Statistics must rely on self-reporting from the approximately 18,000 police agencies nationwide. Experts examining the Bureau of Justice Statistics' 2003-2009 and 2011 data concluded that the reports had probably captured only half of relevant deaths. Furthermore, current law limits the Bureau's ability to share data traceable to a specific person or entity and may restrict DOJ's ability to use it for targeted enforcement. Currently, the DOJ's Federal Bureau of Investigation (FBI) collects data on use of force through an initiative started in 2019. FBI plans on releasing the first tranche of data this summer. Because local law enforcement agencies voluntarily report numbers, incidents are undercounted.

Besides data collection, some have suggested that other informational barriers hamper DOJ's efforts to enforce Section 12601. Many police department policies and some state laws limit public access to police disciplinary records based on privacy concerns, reducing the chance that misconduct will come to DOJ's attention and that the agency can identify patterns. Some departments require records to be destroyed periodically; in Cleveland, for example, a 2013 collective bargaining agreement required the removal of all disciplinary actions and penalties more than two years old from police personnel files.

Local laws and regulations governing police misconduct investigations may also limit DOJ's ability to establish a pattern of misconduct. Police departments routinely adopt rules such as imposing delays, sometimes of several days, before supervisors can question officers after an incident. Rules may also require police departments to give officers any available evidence before questioning them. Some departments bar investigation of anonymous complaints. These policies are sometimes enshrined in state-law "law enforcement officers' bill of rights" statutes, which afford police due process protections unavailable to other public employees. In other instances, state civil service laws or collective bargaining agreements grant similar privileges. Such restrictions on investigation and documentation of potential wrongdoing can make it harder for DOJ to determine whether a pattern of constitutional violations exists. Indeed, even with well-maintained records or access to witnesses, investigators may find it hard to assess misconduct incidents. Because of "the highly unstructured nature of police work" they must often weigh an officer's account against a civilian's.

Given these challenges, investigations and reform measures can be wide ranging and expensive—engaging attorneys, paralegals, investigators, consultants, and experts, sometimes for several years.

In a formal investigation, DOJ investigators review records and policies, interview police, contact concerned community members, consult political leaders, meet with unions, and seek out civilian witnesses to alleged misconduct. They may engage statistical experts and employ regression analysis of traffic stops or use of force. If DOJ concludes that it has uncovered a pattern or practice of unconstitutional behavior, it usually issues a public findings report.

SECTION 12601 REMEDIES AND CONSENT DECREES

Where there is a pattern or practice of unconstitutional policing, Section 12601 authorizes "appropriate equitable and declaratory relief to eliminate the pattern or practice." Thus, unlike a civil suit for monetary damages, Section 12601 requires a court to set rules to correct illegal behavior going forward. The Section aims "to identify, remedy and even prevent substantive violations." Typically, DOJ and the target jurisdiction negotiate a court-approved settlement—a consent decree—outlining steps for reform. If the parties cannot agree on appropriate measures, a court may try the case and impose reforms, but Section 12601 cases rarely go to trial. Most consent decrees set up an independent monitoring team, appointed by the court, to review progress and issue reports. For agencies with only minor problems, however, DOJ may issue only a court-enforceable "memorandum of agreement" or a "technical assistance" letter of voluntary recommendations.

In designing its settlement orders, DOJ relies on local leaders, experts, and nationally recognized best practices. Typical provisions include enhanced training, peer intervention initiatives, improved officer-to-supervisor ratios, hiring programs, increased use of equipment such as video cameras, and revisions to agency handbooks and policies.

As a police department implements changes, the monitoring team may track metrics like racial patterns in stops, documented grounds for suspicion supporting searches, and ratios of arrests to charged offenses. The monitoring process can last years—two years is a common goal—ending only with court approval. If a jurisdiction fails to comply, the court may intervene and even find officials in contempt.

Some have criticized DOJ's consent decrees in Section 12601 cases, and consent decrees generally, as expensive examples of federal overreach that sometimes distort separation of powers. In Baltimore and New Orleans, for example, the police departments' reform measures and monitoring may have cost the cities $10 million or more. Some complain unlitigated consent decrees can induce local and federal leaders to collude in a costly solution. Even in litigated cases of institutional reform, some contend that "[n]ominal defendants are sometimes happy to be sued and happier still to lose," escaping political accountability for the results. Court-ordered consent decrees may circumvent voter approval or typical budgetary processes, sometimes for years.

Perhaps in response to such criticisms, in 2017, then-Attorney General Jeff Sessions announced a "course correction" in police work toward providing "technical assistance and support" and away from "expensive wide-ranging investigative assessments." Citing the importance of local control and officer morale, Sessions stated that "[i]t is not the responsibility of the federal government to manage non-federal law enforcement agencies." Sessions ordered an immediate review of pending police matters.

PROSECUTORIAL DISCRETION AND DOJ'S ENFORCEMENT HISTORY

As with other law enforcement matters, DOJ may use its discretion in whether to pursue litigation, even if facts would support a case. Since 2017, DOJ has reported no new Section 12601 matters. Commenters vary in how they quantify Section 12601 enforcement in prior Administrations, employing different ways of assessing DOJ's activity and dating a case's beginning. By one observer's count, DOJ opened 22 investigations during the Clinton Administration and 21 during the George W. Bush Administration. Another, more recent commentator cites 20 new investigations during the Obama Administration, with 10 during the

George W. Bush Administration. DOJ's website lists some 23 matters between 2009 and 2016.

While the Trump Administration broke with prior Administrations' enforcement priorities in forgoing formal investigations, Section 12601 cases were never frequent. As of 2017, DOJ reported that it had opened 69 formal investigations in the statute's history. Historically, the DOJ has initiated about three pattern-or-practice investigations a year, with one such investigation leading to significant structural reform through a detailed consent decree and monitoring. To help put this number in perspective, there are about 18,000 law enforcement agencies in the nation.

CONSIDERATIONS FOR CONGRESS

Academics, advocates, and legislators have proposed many changes to Section 12601, and have identified other reforms that may indirectly enhance Section 12601 enforcement. To the extent that lack of resources hinders investigation, Congress could consider targeted appropriations. Other suggestions for increasing prosecutorial capacity propose giving state attorneys general or even private litigants authority to bring pattern-or-practice cases. To address potential concerns about federal overreach, that right could be limited to those cases when state law also authorizes suit although such a limitation may not be constitutionally required.

Because information, too, is a barrier to reform, some proposals—most recently the Justice in Policing Act of 2020, H.R. 7120, would enhance data collection for police use of force, accredit law enforcement agencies, and register police misconduct to reveal patterns. H.R. 7120 would give the Department of Justice administrative subpoena power in Section 12601 investigations. Mandatory record-keeping and retention procedures are among provisions in the legislation.

Other CRS products further describe issues relevant to Congress's consideration of Section 12601 and its enforcement, including limits on congressional power to regulate state and local law enforcement; additional statutes and recent proposals; and general policy considerations.

INDEX

B

C

D

E

G

H

I

J

L

M

N

O

P

R

S

T

U

V

W